PENGUIN C

THE ENGLISH

Jeremy Paxman was born in Yorkshire and educated at Cambridge. He is an award-winning journalist who spent ten years reporting from overseas, notably for *Panorama*. He is the author of five books, all of which are published by Penguin: *Friends in High Places: Who Runs Britain?*, *Fish, Fishing and the Meaning of Life*, *The English*, *The Political Animal* and *On Royalty*. He is currently the presenter of *Newsnight* and *University Challenge*.

THE ENGLISH

A Portrait of a People

JEREMY PAXMAN

PENGUIN BOOKS

PENGUIN BOOKS

Published by the Penguin Group

Penguin Books Ltd, 80 Strand, London WC2R 0RL, England

Penguin Group (USA) Inc., 375 Hudson Street, New York, New York 10014, USA

Penguin Group (Canada), 90 Eglinton Avenue East, Suite 700, Toronto, Ontario, Canada M4P 2Y3
(a division of Pearson Penguin Canada Inc.)

Penguin Ireland, 25 St Stephen's Green, Dublin 2, Ireland
(a division of Penguin Books Ltd)

Penguin Group (Australia), 250 Camberwell Road, Camberwell, Victoria 3124, Australia
(a division of Pearson Australia Group Pty Ltd)

Penguin Books India Pvt Ltd, 11 Community Centre, Panchsheel Park, New Delhi – 110 017, India

Penguin Group (NZ), 67 Apollo Drive, Rosedale, North Shore 0632, New Zealand
(a division of Pearson New Zealand Ltd)

Penguin Books (South Africa) (Pty) Ltd, 24 Sturdee Avenue, Rosebank, Johannesburg 2196, South Africa

Penguin Books Ltd, Registered Offices: 80 Strand, London WC2R 0RL, England

www.penguin.com

First published by Michael Joseph 1998
Published with minor revisions in Penguin Books 1999
Reissued in this edition 2007

1

Copyright © Jeremy Paxman, 1998, 1999
All rights reserved

The moral right of the author has been asserted

Printed in England by Clays Ltd, St Ives plc

ISBN: 978-0-141-03514-7

CONTENTS

For Jessica, Jack
and Victoria

PREFACE

Being English used to be so easy. They were one of the most easily identified peoples on earth, recognized by their language, their manners, their clothes and the fact that they drank tea by the bucketload.

It is all so much more complicated now. When, occasionally, we come across someone whose stiff upper lip, sensible shoes or tweedy manner identifies them as English, we react in amusement: the conventions that defined the English are dead and the country's ambassadors are more likely to be singers or writers than diplomats or politicians.

The imperial English may have carried British passports – as did the Scots, Welsh, and some of the Irish – but they really didn't need to think too hard about whether being 'English' was the same as being 'British': the terms were virtually interchangeable. Nowadays, nothing will so infuriate a Scot as to confuse the terms English and British, for England's Celtic neighbours are increasingly for striking out on their own. Elections in May 1999 to the new Scottish parliament and Welsh Assembly were, predictably, trumpeted by the Labour party (which had invented the whole idea of devolved governments) as strengthening the Union. Perhaps so. But it is unquestionably changed. Scotland, at least, has always been a nation, with its own legal and educational system, and civic and intellectual tradition. Now it has its own government and it is hard to think of political institutions which, once given power, have not sought more of it. The language has begun to reflect this changed relationship. Where a year or two ago events in Scotland were talked of as regional, they are increasingly spoken about as 'national'. The BBC has even issued instructions to its staff on the unacceptability of any longer talking of Wales as a 'Principality'.

Then there is the problem of Europe. Who knows how the collective ambition or delusion that has gripped the European political élite will end up? If it is successful, a United States of Europe will make the United Kingdom redundant.

And then there is the corrosive awareness that neither Britain, nor any other nation, can singlehandedly control the tides of capital that determine whether individual citizens will eat or starve. Increasingly, the main business of national governments is the culture of their citizens.

These four elements – the end of empire, the cracks opening in the so-called United Kingdom, the pressures for the English to plunge into Europe, and the uncontrollability of international business – set me wondering. What did it mean to be English?

Although these are political questions, this is not a political book in the narrow sense of the word. I set out to try to discover the roots of the present English anxiety about themselves by travelling back into the past, to the things that created that instantly recognizable ideal Englishman and Englishwoman who carried the flag across the world. And then I tried to find out what had become of them.

Some of these influences were relatively easy to spot. Obviously the fact that they were born on an island rather than living on a continental landmass had had an effect. They came from a country where Protestant reformation had put the church firmly in its place. They had inherited a deep belief in individual liberty.

Others were more opaque. Why, for example, do the English

seem to enjoy feeling so persecuted? What is behind the English obsession with games? How did they acquire their odd attitudes to sex and food? Where did they get their extraordinary capacity for hypocrisy?

I sought answers to the questions through travelling, talking and reading. Several years later, I am a bit the wiser and have a different set of questions.

And now I have just noticed that I am writing of the English as 'they', when I have always thought myself one of them. They remain elusive to the last.

CHAPTER ONE

THE LAND
OF LOST CONTENT

*Ask any man what nationality he would prefer to be, and ninety nine out
of a hundred will tell you that they would prefer to be Englishmen.*

CECIL RHODES

Once upon a time the English knew who they were. There was such
a ready list of adjectives to hand. They were polite, unexcitable,
reserved and had hot-water bottles instead of a sex life: how they
reproduced was one of the mysteries of the western world. They
were doers rather than thinkers, writers rather than painters, gardeners rather than cooks. They were class-bound, hidebound and
incapable of expressing their emotions. They did their duty. Fortitude
bordering on the incomprehensible was a byword: 'I have lost my
leg, by God!' exclaimed Lord Uxbridge, as shells exploded all over the
battlefield. 'By God, and have you!' replied the Duke of Wellington. A
soldier lying mortally wounded in a flooded trench on the Somme
was, so the myth went, likely to say only that he 'mustn't grumble'.
Their most prized possession was a sense of honour. They were
steadfast and trustworthy. The word of an English gentleman was
as good as a bond sealed in blood.

It is 1945. At last, the apparently endless war which has governed
every waking moment of the British population is ended and they
can relax. Everywhere in the industrial cities are gap-toothed me-
mentoes of the Luftwaffe. In the towns that had survived relatively

unscathed, the High Street is a jigsaw of different shop fronts, most of them little individual businesses, for this is, in Napoleon's famously scathing condemnation, 'une nation de boutiquiers', a nation of shopkeepers. The vast retail chains which will within a few decades have driven the small tradesmen out of business are there, but if you dropped into the chain of Boots chemists, it might as easily have been to change your books at the library. In the evening, maybe a visit to the cinema.

There is a strong case for agreeing with Churchill that the Second World War had been his country's 'finest hour'. He was talking about Britain and the British Empire, but the values of that empire were the values which the English liked to think were something which they had invented. Certainly, the war and its immediate aftermath are the last time in living memory when the English had a clear and positive sense of themselves. They saw it reflected back in films like *In Which We Serve*, Noël Coward's fictionalized account of the sinking of HMS *Kelly*. As the survivors of the destroyer, sunk by German dive-bombers, lie in their life-raft they recall the ship's history. What they are really calling up is a picture of the strength of England. The captain and the ratings may be divided by their accents, but they share the same essential beliefs about what their country represents. It is an ordered, hierarchical sort of place in which the war is an inconvenience to be put up with, like rain at a village fête. It is a chaste, self-denying country in which women know their place and children go dutifully and quietly to bed when told. 'Don't make a fuss,' say the wives to one another during an air raid, 'we'll have a cup of tea in a minute.' As the Chief Petty Officer leaves home his mother-in-law asks him when he'll be ashore again.

'All depends on Hitler,' he says.

'Well, who *does* he think he is?' asks the mother-in-law.

'That's the spirit.'

In Which We Serve was unashamed propaganda for a people facing the possible extinction of their culture, which is the reason it is so illuminating. It shows us how the English liked to think of themselves. The picture that emerges from this and many similar movies is of a stoical, homely, quiet, disciplined, self-denying, kindly, honourable and dignified people who would infinitely rather be tending their gardens than defending the world against a fascist tyranny.

I have lived all my life in the England which emerged from the shadow of Hitler, and have to confess an admiration for the place as it seemed to be then, despite its small-mindedness, hypocrisy and prejudice. It fell into a war that it had repeatedly been promised it could avoid, and in so doing advanced its fall from world eminence by decades. The revisionists tell us that so much of the British achievement in that war was not what it seemed at the time. Certainly, the English have clung fiercely to heroic illusions about the war, the favourite ones being the Little Ships at Dunkirk, the victory of the Few in the Battle of Britain and the courage of Londoners and other city-dwellers in the Blitz. All right, the role of the Little Ships has been exaggerated, the Battle of Britain was won as much by Hitler's misjudgement as by the heroism of the fighter pilots, and the Blitz by the courage and ruthlessness of Bomber Command's retaliatory raids on Germany. It may be demonstrably false that the English won the war alone, as any reading of Churchill's desperate attempts to secure American intervention will attest. But the fact remains that the country *did* stand alone in the summer of 1940 and had it not done so the rest of Europe would have fallen to the Nazis. Had it not had the great benefit of geography, perhaps, like the rest of Europe, from France to the Baltic, the country would have found willing executioners to do the Nazi bidding. But geography matters; it makes people who they are.

How many attempts have there been to explain what the Second World War did to Britain? One thousand? Ten thousand? What none of them can undermine is that in that titanic struggle the English had the clearest idea of what they stood for and, therefore, the sort of people they were. It was nothing to do with Hitler's pride in his Fatherland, it was something smaller, more personal, and I think, more quietly powerful. Take David Lean's 1945 tale of forbidden love, *Brief Encounter*. The couple meet in the tearoom of a railway station, where she is waiting for the steam train home after a day's shopping. A speck of coal dirt gets caught in her eye and, without a word of introduction, the gallant local doctor steps forward and removes it. The following eighty minutes of this beautifully written movie depict their deepening love and the guilt each feels about it. Trevor Howard's tall, spare frame, strong nose and jaw, Celia Johnson's *retroussé* nose and clear eyes seem to embody the ideal Englishman and Englishwoman. They belong to the infinitely respectable middle class, in which strangulated scheme of things 'levly gels' wish only to be 'relly heppy'.

The doctor begins his seduction with the classic English gambit of commenting on the weather. A few moments later he mentions music. 'My husband's not musical,' she says. 'Good for him,' says the doctor. Good for him? Why is it good for him? It makes it sound as if he has managed to fight off a killer disease. It is good for him, of course, because it recognizes a God-ordained right to philistinism and the rectitude of individuals who please themselves in their own homes. As Rachmaninov's Second Piano Concerto comes and goes in the background, their affair unfolds, measured out in cups of tea in the waiting room of Milford station. Celia Johnson's husband is the sort of man who calls his wife 'old girl' and to whom sympathy is the suggestion that they do the newspaper crossword together. 'I believe we'd all be different if we lived in a warm and sunny climate,' she thinks to herself at one point. 'Then we shouldn't be so withdrawn and shy and difficult.' Being English, she feels no animosity towards her husband, whom she considers 'kindly and unemotional'. Trevor Howard, equally trapped in a dry marriage, also expresses no hostility towards his wife and children. But the two of them are in the force of a passion they can hardly control. 'We must be sensible,' is the constant refrain. 'If we control ourselves, there's still time.'

In the end, despite all the protestations of undying devotion, the romance remains unconsummated. He does the decent thing and takes a job at a hospital in South Africa and she returns to her decent but dull husband. The end.

What does this most popular of English films tell us about the English? Firstly that, in the immortal words, 'we are not put on earth to enjoy ourselves'. Secondly, the importance of a sense of duty: wearing uniform had been a fact of life for most of the adult population. (Trevor Howard had been a lieutenant with the Royal Corps of Signals, with a number of entirely imaginary acts of heroism credited to him by the film studios' publicity machines. Celia Johnson had been an auxiliary policewoman: they knew all about sacrificing their pleasures for a greater good.) Most of all, the message is that the emotions are there to be controlled. It was 1945. But it could as easily have been 1955 or even 1965; the fashions might have changed, but the weather would still be damp and the policemen still avuncular. It would, despite the post-war Welfare State, be a country where everyone knew their place. Delivery carts, driven by men in uniform, still brought milk and bread to the front door. There were things which were done and things which were not done.

One could assume about these people that they were decent, and as industrious as was necessary to meet comparatively modest ambitions. They had become accustomed to seeing themselves as aggressed against, steady under fire, defiant against the enemy. The image is of the British troops at Waterloo withstanding all-out assault by the French, or the dome of St Paul's emerging from the smoke and flames of German bombs. They had a deeply held sense of their own rights, yet would proudly say they were 'not much bothered' about politics. The abject failure of both left- and right-wing extremists to get themselves elected to Parliament testified to their profound scepticism when anyone offered the promised land. They were, it is true, reserved and prone to melancholy. But they were not in any meaningful sense religious, the Church of England being a political invention which had elevated being 'a good chap' to something akin to canonization. On the occasions when bureaucracy demanded they admit an allegiance, they could write 'C of E' in the box and know that they wouldn't be bothered by demands that they attend church or give all they had to the poor.

In 1951, the *People* newspaper organized a survey of its readers. For three years, Geoffrey Gorer pored over the 11,000 responses. At the end of which he concluded that the national character had not really changed much in the previous 150 years. The superficial changes had been vast: a lawless population had been turned into a law-abiding one; a country which enjoyed dog-fights, bear-baiting and public hangings had become humanitarian and squeamish; general corruption in public life had been replaced by a high level of honesty. But

what seems to have remained constant is a great resentment at being overlooked or controlled, a love of freedom; fortitude; a low interest in sexual activity, compared with most neighbouring societies; a strong belief in the value of education for the formation of character; consideration and delicacy for the feelings of other people; and a very strong attachment to marriage and the institution of the family ... The English are a truly unified people, more unified, I would hazard, than at any previous period in their history. When I was reading, with extreme care, the first batch of questionnaires which I received, I found I was constantly making the same notes: 'What dull lives most of these people appear to lead!' I remarked; and secondly, 'What good people!' I should still make the same judgements.[1]

The reasons for this unity are obvious enough – the country had just come though a terrible war, which had required shared sacrifice. The population of England was still relatively homogeneous, used to accepting the inconvenience of discipline and unaffected by mass immigration. It was still insular, not merely in a physical sense but because the mass media had yet to create the global village.

It is the world of today's grandparents. It is the world of Queen Elizabeth and her husband, the Duke of Edinburgh. The young Princess Elizabeth married the naval lieutenant, Philip Mountbatten, in 1947. In an age of austerity (potatoes rationed to 3 lb per person per week and bacon to one ounce) the wedding brought a breath of spectacle and magic to a drab country. Philip wore his naval uniform for the occasion, Elizabeth had abandoned the forage cap she had been seen in during the war for a satin dress embroidered with 10,000 seed pearls. In the spirit of Trevor Howard and Celia Johnson, they might have expected to share a long life together. And they did. But they were the last generation to live by that code. Like one quarter of the couples who married in 1947, the royal couple reached their Golden Wedding anniversary in 1997, but by then, the predicament of Celia Johnson and Trevor Howard had become little more than an anthropological curiosity: less than one tenth of the couples who married fifty years on were expected to complete the same marathon. By then, women made up almost half the workforce, an astonishing change in light of the meekness fifty years earlier with which most had surrendered their wartime jobs when demobilized men demanded employment. The best part of 200,000 marriages now ended in divorce every year, with proceedings more often than not initiated by women, unprepared any longer to think 'we must be sensible'.[2] By the time of Prince Philip and Queen Elizabeth's celebrations, their four children had contracted three marriages, every single one of which had failed. The heir to the throne had divorced the woman intended to be the next queen, and she had met her death in a Paris underpass, alongside her playboy lover, Dodi Fayed, whose father, Mohammed, owned the most famous shop in the nation of shopkeepers, and made a habit of handing money in brown paper envelopes to Conservative MPs, who claimed to belong to a party based on English traditions of probity and honour. Diana's funeral had brought forth scenes of public mourning so bizarrely 'un-English' – the lighting of candles in the park, the throwing of flowers on to her passing coffin – that the wartime generation could only look on as baffled travellers in their own land.

The flower-throwers had learned their behaviour from watching television, for it is a Latin custom: the potency of the mass media can hardly be exaggerated. Fashions in food, clothing, music and entertainment are no longer home-grown. Even those customs which remain authentically indigenous are the fruit of a greatly changed 'English' population. Within fifty years of the docking of the *Empire Windrush* at Tilbury, disembarking 492 Jamaican immigrants, the racial complexion of the country had changed utterly. Mass immigration to Britain had been concentrated on England and most cities of any size contained areas where white people had become a rarity. In those places, talking about immigrants as 'ethnic minorities' was beginning to sound decidedly perverse. By 1998, it was white children who had become a minority at local-authority secondary schools in inner London and even in the suburbs they made up only 60 per cent of the secondary-school population. Over a third of inner London's children did not even have English as their first language.[3]

If the English people had changed, so too had the towns in which most of them lived. In his wartime celebration of Englishness, *The Lion and the Unicorn*, George Orwell managed to escape the dreamy right-wing pastiche about England being all hedgerows and gardens. Seeking to define a country that corresponded more closely to the reality of the lives of most of its citizens, he described a place of red pillar boxes, Lancashire clogs, smoky towns, crude language and lines outside labour exchanges. The picture is as recognizable as an L. S. Lowry painting, and like a Lowry, it is a period piece. The smoky mills have closed down as the textile trade has collapsed, the lines outside labour exchanges replaced by benefit offices in which clerks sit behind anger-proof glass screens. The red pillar boxes are still there, but the other red feature of the pavement, Sir George

Gilbert Scott's telephone kiosk, has been torn down, to be replaced by a functional steel and glass cubicle. If one survives, it is there as ornament to a 'heritage site', as one shop after another is colonized by burger bars and pizzerias. In these places, the world the English live in is emphatically not Made in England. The High Streets are either jammed with cars or pedestrianized, the newly laid cobbles, wrought-iron lampposts and litterbins a self-conscious imagination of how the place might have looked in Victorian days, had the Victorians had the questionable pleasures of the Big Mac. In those cities most self-conscious about their claim to be part of English history, like Oxford or Bath, the shops where you could have bought a dozen nails, home-made cakes or had a suit run up, have shut down and been replaced with places selling teddy bears, T-shirts and gimcrack souvenirs. Elsewhere, the small traders have vanished, replaced by branches of retail chains specializing in anything from kitchen utensils to babywear: a nation of shopkeepers become a nation of checkout operators. The police cruise the streets in cars or sit in vans waiting for trouble.

In another essay, George Orwell described the perfect city pub, a place called The Moon under Water.[4] It was down a side-street, busy enough to be welcoming, but quiet enough to have a conversation. It was unmodernized Victorian in style, had friendly barmaids who called everyone 'dear', served soft, creamy stout on draught, and good lunches in a room upstairs. Liver-sausage sandwiches, mussels and cheese and pickles were always available on the snack counter. At the back was a large garden, where children played on swings and a slide. At the end of his piece, Orwell came clean with what most of his readers must have suspected: The Moon under Water did not exist. It does now. There are fourteen Moons Under Water, all owned by a vast brewing conglomerate with headquarters in Watford. Its Manchester Moon Under Water claims to be the biggest pub in Britain, with 8,500 square feet of drinking space spread over three bars on two floors. There are sixty-five staff and an effigy of the *Coronation Street* character Ena Sharples, brooding over the place like some fertility goddess. It is noisy, in-your-face and on a Saturday evening packed with hundreds of young men and women getting aggressively drunk on frothy, imported American beer.

To outward appearances, England is changed utterly from the place it was. There is no shared endeavour or suffering, service in the armed forces has become a rarity, and austerity is a distant memory. Only a small minority subscribe to the old pieties about not spending money on personal enjoyment or adornment.

And yet this elusive, oblique identity is all the English have. The sheer embarrassment of it struck me in the early nineties when I had to attend the funeral in South Africa of a friend and colleague killed when his car ran off the road as he was trying to make a deadline. The church was in a prosperous white suburb, where the roads were lined with BMWs and every house had a sign hanging on the razor-wire warning of 'Instant Armed Response'. The service was conducted by a liberal Afrikaner minister who had not, I imagined, known John particularly well. The choir was made up of cleaning-ladies from the building where John had his office. They were poor, shoeless people (some literally), but when they sang 'Nkosi Sikeleli Afrika', the black anthem, the cavernous mock-gothic church rang with sweet passion. It wasn't just that they enjoyed singing. *They were singing something they believed in.* Then the minister spoke a simple tribute and, turning to a photocopied sheet, announced the next hymn. It was to be 'Jerusalem', Blake's strange British Israelite poem beginning, 'And did those feet in ancient time walk upon England's mountains green?'

'Sing, you English,' he boomed from the pulpit, 'sing!'

We did our best, in a self-conscious kind of way. But our music had none of the sweetness, or ardour, of the cleaning-ladies'. 'Jerusalem' is the closest thing the English have to an anthem, with a stirring tune and enigmatic words. But we couldn't manage it with any conviction. I guess we were embarrassed, but the truth is, the English have no national song, as they have no national dress: when national costume was a requirement of the Miss World pageant, 'Miss England' appeared ludicrously decked out as a Beefeater.

England's national day, 23 April, passes mostly unnoticed, while invented *British* ceremonial events like 'the Queen's official birthday' (her what?) are marked by artillery salutes, flag-flying and parties at British embassies around the world. The closest thing the English have to a national dance, Morris-dancing, is a clumsy pub-sport practised by men in beards and shiny-bottomed trousers. When the English play Wales or Scotland at soccer or rugby, the Scots have 'Flower of Scotland' to sing, the Welsh, 'Hen Wlad fy Nhadau', or 'Land of My Fathers'. The English team must mouth along with the *British* national anthem, that dirge-like glorification of the monarchy whose job it is to unite the disparate parts of an increasingly tattered political union. At the Commonwealth Games the organizers have adopted 'Land of Hope and Glory' as the English anthem. (But in early 1998 when Gillingham football club, languishing in the Second Division after failing to win thirteen consecutive games, began playing 'Land of Hope and Glory' on the public address system before matches to try to boost morale, they received furious protest letters from fans, on the grounds that the only people likely to be motivated by the song would be fascists.) There are over 500 other distinctly Scottish songs, many of which are widely known: go into an English pub and ask for a verse of 'There'll always be an England', 'The Yeomen of England', or any other of the old national songs and you will be met with baffled silence. Or worse. The only song an English sports crowd can manage with any enthusiasm is the slave spiritual 'Swing Low, Sweet Chariot' at rugby matches, and a few superannuated pop songs, often with obscene lyrics, at soccer games.

What does this paucity of national symbols mean? You could argue that it demonstrates a certain self-confidence. No English person can look at the swearing of allegiance that takes place in

American schools every day without feeling bewilderment: that sort of public declaration of patriotism seems so, well, naïve. When an Irishman wears a bunch of shamrock on St Patrick's Day, the English look on with patronizing indulgence: scarcely anyone sports a rose on St George's Day. This worldly wisdom soon elides into a general view that *any* public display of national pride is not merely unsophisticated but somehow morally reprehensible. George Orwell noticed it as long ago as 1948 when he wrote that

In left-wing circles it is always felt that there is something slightly disgraceful in being an Englishman, and that it is a duty to snigger at every English institution, from horse-racing to suet puddings. It is a strange fact, but it is unquestionably true, that almost any English intellectual would feel more ashamed of standing to attention during 'God Save the King' than of stealing from a poor box.[5]

No one stands for 'God Save the Queen' any more, and any cinema manager who tried to revive the custom of playing the national anthem would find the place empty before he'd reached the end of the first verse. At the time of Orwell's irritation, left-wing intellectual disdain was cheap because the English didn't need to concern themselves with the symbols of their own identity: when you're top dog in the world's leading empire, you don't need to. And since 'Britain' was essentially a political invention, it was necessary to submerge the identities of the constituent parts of the United Kingdom within it. The beleaguered tribe of Protestant settlers transplanted to the north of Ireland clung to the British identity fiercely because they had nothing else, but in other places on the Celtic fringe, traditional identities could easily co-exist with being British, a fact the English were happy to acknowledge, since it rather proved the Union was what they said it was, a Union of distinct places. Hence, the nicknames: Scots are Jocks, Welshmen Taffies and Irishmen Paddies or Micks, but – another sign of their dominance – it is noticeable there is no similar designation for the English.

The comic history book *1066, And All That* decided 'the Norman Conquest was a Good Thing, as from this time onwards England stopped being conquered and thus was able to become top nation'.[6] The authors had recognized that the history of the United Kingdom is the story of the advance of England. Written in 1930, it finishes with the Treaty of Versailles ending the First World War, which decreed that 'England should be allowed to pay for the War', and that there should be many more countries – 'a Bad Thing as it was the cause of increased geography'. The final sentence reads, 'America was thus clearly top nation, and History came to a .'[7] The British have been trying to adjust to that full stop for three generations.

The problem is a lot less acute for the Scots or the Welsh because they never fully extinguished their identity within the idea of being British. The model Englishman and Englishwoman was available to anyone who chose to aspire to it, hence the success of Eton and her imitations in seducing the children of new money, and hence the proliferation of imitations of Eton from India to Malawi. But a successful Scot could always turn to (and the two were by no means mutually exclusive) an ancestral identity which was quite distinct. Scotland maintained its own legal and educational systems. As a compensation, perhaps, for the loss of independence, the Scots kept alive a vibrant feeling of their own history, 'a sense of identity with the dead even to the twentieth generation', as Robert Louis Stevenson puts it in *Weir of Hermiston*. A 'traditional' dress, the kilt, had been reinvented for them as a variant of the Highlanders' belted plaid (possibly by an Englishman, incidentally, the Quaker iron-foundry owner, Thomas Rawlinson, to clothe his workers). At the very time that the English were becoming most regimented to meet the demands of industry and empire, Sir Walter Scott was hymning the wild romanticism of the Highlander. Is it any wonder that when the Empire disintegrated, the Scots had plenty to fall back upon?

The English had no alternative identity to rescue them. It is hardly surprising that they have taken the collapse of British power harder than most, for the rest of the kingdom comforts itself with the chippy consolation that the English are the authors of their own nemesis. When the novelist A. S. Byatt was editing a collection of English short stories, she looked at a recent series of essays, *Studying British Cultures*, designed to promote an understanding of the different intellectual traditions of the islands. She found 55 page references to Scottishness, 20 pages on Caribbean cultures, 27 pages on the Welsh and 28 on the Irish. The three mentions of Englishness were all in the preface and only concerned with challenging 'the hegemony of England'. 'You get the feeling', she commented, 'that the English only exist to be discarded and challenged.'[8]

The English have, characteristically, taken this disdain to heart, because they have such a strong streak of natural gloominess. There's no need to exaggerate the personal significance of this – the country has one of the lower rates for suicide in Europe, only a small fraction of the rate in Hungary or even Switzerland. But, in the old saying, 'every Englishman is born a double Scotch below par', and the English find comfort in a belief that the place is doomed. The popular novelist E. M. Delafield gave it as her belief that the English Creed included four elements: firstly that 'God is an Englishman, probably educated at Eton, secondly that all good women are naturally frigid, thirdly that it is better to be dowdy than smart', and lastly that 'England is going to rack and ruin'. When Nirad Chaudhuri visited England in 1955, he told a politician how welcoming and civilized he found the country. 'You are seeing it at a very favourable time,' came the Eeyoreish reply. When Richard Ingrams, the former editor of *Private Eye*, tried to compile an anthology of writing about England he was so struck by the prevailing pessimism that he decided it would have been as easy to pull together a collection called *Going to the Dogs*.

This curiously retiring, unintrospective, pessimistic people cannot continue as they are for much longer. They find themselves governed by a party whose organizing principles come from across the Atlantic and whose leadership caucus comes from north of the border. They have seen Scotland and Wales given forms of self-government, and an overweening European Union which believes the future of the continent to lie not so much in nation states as in a complex of relationships between a federal heart and regional pulses. The disintegration of empire is at last hitting the British Isles: the first colonies will be the last to gain their independence. At the same time, the pressures from outside the British Isles are irresistible: 'We are now coming to the end of the British story', writes the left-wing author Stephen Haseler. 'A thousand years of separate development (in which the last 300 or so have seen a strong, self-conscious and highly successful nation-state) is finally drawing to its close – under the twin forces of globalisation and the dynamic of European unity.'[9]

Everyone is so damned apocalyptic. *Anyone for England?*, a 247-page philippic from Clive Aslet, the editor of *Country Life*,[10] sought explanations for the national identity crisis in predictable targets from the use of metric weights and measures and the replacement of the old hard-backed blue passport by the floppy burgundy European Union travel document, to feminism, the redesign of Harris tweed, fast-food restaurants and the rise of youth culture. 'Day and night the ogres of Brussels can be heard stamping about the corridors of the European Union, as their cry of "Fee, fie, fo, fum, I smell the traditional habits, tastes and foodstuffs of an Englishman" reverberates across the Channel',[11] runs a typical sentence. Can the author really believe the identity of a people is no more than its weights and measures, or the side of the road on which they drive their cars? Does either of these authors – Haseler from the left or Aslet from the right – believe that other countries in the European Union, from Portugal to Sweden, do not face the same pressures?

Everywhere I went while researching this book, I heard the same comparison. The English glance across the Channel at the traditional enemy and they're jealous. 'Look at the French,' said a Conservative MP. 'Their problems are as great as ours. But they know who they are, even if they don't know where they're going. Not only do we not know where we're going. We don't even know who we are any longer. Haven't a clue.' Evidence to support him came in a comparison of the attitudes of English and French primary school-children which appeared in the *Times Educational Supplement* under the banner 'English – and not very proud of it'.[12] This was the headline-writer's characteristically gloomy way of encapsulating the results of a study of 850 ten- and eleven-year-olds who had been asked how they felt about their countries. More precisely, they had been asked to say whether they endorsed statements like 'I feel very proud of being French'. Fifty-seven per cent of French children strongly agreed with the sentence, against a mere 35 per cent of English children posed a similar question about England. When required to amplify their feelings about their country, the English children cast around for reasons to be glad they were English and said things like 'It's not too hot or cold, we have clean food and water ... English people are good and healthy ... being an independent country ... Manchester United come from England' and so on. The French children, by contrast, talked about 'notre beau pays' (our beautiful country), 'parce qu'on est libre' (because one is free), or said things like 'nous sommes tous égaux' (we are all equal). One even wrote 'car la France est un pays magnifique et démocratique et accueillant' (because France is a magnificent, democratic and welcoming country). The difference is interesting, although not necessarily for the reasons the headline-writer supposed. By the age of eleven, the English children had developed the pragmatic, question-answering skills which characterize the English intellectual tradition, while their French counterparts were reciting a lot of hand-me-down slogans. A more sceptical person might ask why an absence of jingoism is held to be a bad thing, why the French authorities have found it necessary to brainwash their young children about the glory of France, and whether a country was more sure of itself because it needed to make that effort.

But it is typical of the English to ignore the silver lining and to grasp at the cloud. The belief that something has rotted in England is widely held: a people cannot spend decades being told their civilization is in decline and not be affected by it. One political party after another has made promises to restore the integrity and standing of the country, which have turned out to be outrageous lies. It would not matter in Italy, where they don't believe in the state anyway and where the institutions which do matter to them – family, village, and town – remain demonstrably alive. The English put their faith in institutions, and of these, the British Empire has evaporated, the Church of England has withered away and Parliament is increasingly irrelevant.

And it is not merely that the external sureties have gone, so, it seems, have internal certitudes. I once asked the author Simon Raven what he thought being English meant and he replied with a disconsolate caveat, 'I'd always *hoped* it meant gentle manners, cricket, civility between the classes, lack of malice towards others, fair dealing with women, and fair dealing with enemies. But now I wonder.' John Cleese, who looks increasingly like the crusty old colonels he once parodied, is also beginning to sound like them. 'We could have made all sorts of generalizations about England if we had been talking thirty years ago,' he told me. 'Nowadays, it seems to me that you can't assume anything.' The diarist, gadfly and gardener Roy Strong amplified the philippic: 'Families are falling apart, religion's discredited. So where does our sense of identity come from? What holds this country together? Not bloody much!'

When I started thinking about this book, I wrote to the playwright Alan Bennett. He was once introduced to a New York press conference as 'what we in England call a national treasure', as if he were the gardens of Sissinghurst or a pot of Women's Institute home-made raspberry jam. If anyone could understand Englishness, he surely would. What makes plays like *Forty Years On*, *The Old Country*, *An*

Englishman Abroad and *A Question of Attribution* so distinctively English – as well as being *about* England – are the layers of ambiguity with which they are constructed. (I had been particularly taken by a scene in *The Old Country* where Hilary, the spy who has defected to Moscow, muses about England: 'We're conceived in irony. We float in it from the womb. It's the amniotic fluid. It's the silver sea. It's the waters at their priest-like task, washing away guilt and purpose and responsibility. Joking but not joking. Caring but not caring. Serious but not serious.'[13] It captures one of the essentials of Englishness.

So I wrote to Alan Bennett, asking if he would like lunch or tea to talk over the subject. Back came a picture postcard of Peny-y-ghent.

Thank you for your letter. I'm hopeless at this kind of thing, though. If I could put into words what I mean by Englishness (and what I like and detest about it) I wouldn't write at all, as coming to terms with it is what gets me going. I really wouldn't be any help, but good luck with it. I used to stay in your village thirty years ago. I hope it hasn't changed.

Did he really believe he was 'hopeless' at 'this kind of thing'? What kind of thing? Was he just finding a polite way of telling me to get lost, blaming himself for not wanting to waste my time when he thought it would be a waste of his? Was he genuine in claiming he wouldn't write if he knew what Englishness was, when his life has been spent anatomizing it? And that final comment about the village and the hope that it hadn't changed: that too was essentially English, the prayer of a people marching backwards into the future, for whom change always means change for the worse.

Instead, I started from scratch and decided we might as well admit that the English are not an easy people to love. They have none of the charm of the Irish, the affability of the Welsh or the directness of the Scots. You have only to spend five minutes in a foreign bar where a group of English are gathered to feel at best indulgent of their monoglot cringe and at worst ashamed as they shout for food and drink which reminds them of home. Even the quieter

English possess that veneer of manners which conceals an infinite capacity for contempt: you can really only feel above your neighbours if you don't know them very well. The English resort to an entirely unjustified pretence at superiority at the drop of a hat, yet produce the vilest football hooligans in Europe. To be fair, they have a more attractive side to their character, as well. They tend not to proselytize aggressively about their way of life any longer. And does any other society put such a premium upon having a sense of humour?

If you want to find out about what makes the English who they are, you quickly make two discoveries. Firstly, that this offshore island has been sufficiently intriguing to attract quite awesome numbers of foreign visitors eager to share their impressions with the rest of the world: there are libraries filled with books of reminiscences and travellers' tales. Secondly, very little at all has been written on the subject of English nationalism. This is mainly because, while you can find nationalist movements aplenty in Estonia or Ethiopia, they scarcely exist in England. Some of the reasons you can guess at quickly – no foreign occupation, no attempt to extinguish indigenous culture. And there is the obvious point that, apart from at a few football and cricket matches, England scarcely exists as a country: nationalism was, and remains, a *British* thing.

So, as Britain declines, all sorts of nasty things are crawling out from under stones. Not long ago I received a brown manila envelope. The address was written in block capitals, a nondescript if not particularly educated handwriting. There was a postmark: 'Hull'. Mercifully, I opened the envelope with the point of a biro. It was just as well. The top edge of the single sheet of paper inside had been sewn with razor blades. On one side was a cartoon British soldier in World War Two tin helmet lying in a slit trench, rifle to his shoulder. Underneath, the same hand had scrawled, 'Don't move, nigger.' Overleaf was a gallows and a hangman's noose. My initials had been drawn inside the rope. At the bottom of the page was scratched in giant letters PROUD TO BE BRITISH. I forget quite what inspired this attack. A similar nasty smell used to hang over the anti-Semitic mail I received when another dunderhead got it into what passed for his mind that I was part of a worldwide Jewish conspiracy to destroy the British state. There is nothing uniquely British about these comparatively very anodyne experiences, as any victim of German, French or Swiss racism could attest. My point is only that this sort of prejudice is attached to the idea of Britain rather than England.

For a while after the Act of Union some people – and acts of Parliament – called Scotland 'North Britain' and England 'South Britain', self-consciously referring back to a time before England. The hugely ambitious took to calling Ireland 'West Britain'. All were making a political point and the terms are almost unheard-of now: the North British call themselves Scots, while the South British are as or more likely to say they are English or Welsh as British. The only place where this rule does not apply is the north of Ireland, where Catholics will tell you they're Irish and Protestants will claim to be British. But they too are making a political point. The Orange parades in Northern Ireland, those booming, swaggering marches every 12 July, are almost the only popular rituals to celebrate Britishness in the British Isles. (The others are official events like Trooping the Colour or semi-official, flag-waving sessions like the last night of the Proms.) But the sight of thin-lipped old men in bowler hats and orange sashes marching to their pipe-and-drum bands means nothing to the rest of Britain. The paradox is that this great proclamation of belonging, that the Ulster 'loyalists' are in some deep sense the same as the rest of us, merely serves to make them look utterly different.

English nationalism, when you can find it, tends to take other expressions. They are more confused, because the English are no longer quite sure what it is that makes them what they are: the self-confidence of the imperial years was the enemy of introspection.

It is elusive because it has no defining racial or religious boundaries. It is bloody-minded, quiet and often private and is, deep down, an elective identity. But something is stirring out there. In 1995 the greetings-card retailer, Clinton's, began producing the first cards to celebrate St George's Day. Within two years, the shops were selling over 50,000 every April. In the summer of 1996 there was a noticeable increase in the number of English football fans at the European championships, 'Euro '96', who had chosen to daub their faces with a red cross on a white background, instead of the more commonplace Union Jack. By April 1997, the *Sun* had leapt on the bandwagon, printing a half-page cross of St George in its English editions and asking readers to stick it in the window. It was an idea which did not catch on, but it was interesting that someone in Rupert Murdoch's empire – which has not grown rich by overtaxing the higher faculties of its customers – should have noticed the way the wind seemed to be blowing. The following year, the English Tourist Board was organizing a week of events across the country entitled 'St George Invades Britain' on the grounds, a spokesman explained, that 'People have been embarrassed to be English'. At the soccer World Cup that summer, the cross of St George seemed to outnumber the Union flags. When St George's Day came around in 1999, the *Sun* marked the occasion with a four-page pullout, '100 Reasons Why It's Great to be English'. They included the Weather (23), Pork Scratchings (28), Page Three Girls (45), Charles Dickens (55), the M25 motorway, 'the world's biggest circular traffic jam' (71), Agatha Christie (88) and 'Deidre' the newspaper's own agony aunt (95).

But what are the English supposed to be celebrating? The author of *The Magus* and *The French Lieutenant's Woman*, John Fowles, has thought deeply about the difference between being British and being English, and concludes that while the colours of Britain, to which the marching loyalists swear allegiance, are red, white and blue, the colour of England is green. 'What is the red-white-and-blue Britain?' he asks. It is the Britain of the Hanoverian dynasty and the Victorian and Edwardian ages; of the Empire; of the Wooden Walls and the Thin Red Line; of 'Rule Britannia' and Elgar's marches; of John Bull; of Poona and the Somme; of the old flog-and-fag public-school system; of Newbolt, Kipling and Rupert Brooke, of clubs, codes and conformity; of an unchangeable status quo; of jingoism at home and arrogance abroad; of the paterfamilias; of caste, cant and hypocrisy.[14]

He doesn't care for it, and apologists for the achievements of the Empire could doubtless recite as long a list of positive qualities – the rule of law, exploration, scientific advance, individual acts of courage, Burton and Speke, Livingstone, Florence Nightingale and Captain Scott – with which to fight back. But two things seem unanswerable. Firstly, that Britain (as opposed to England, Scotland and Wales) is a political idea. Secondly, that once it had been invented, it consistently sought to justify its existence by exerting influence elsewhere. The proof of the success of the red-white-and-blue flies on flagpoles from the Orkneys to Fiji. The green England is something quite different. John Fowles thought that the fact England was virtually an island had created a people who 'watch across water from the north', a people who were observers rather than experiencers. And their geography had given them the freedom to be pioneers in law and democracy.

But first we have to define what we are talking about. Some aspects of Englishness remain constant over the centuries, others are forever changing. Just as they can no longer be identified by their language, nor can the English be defined in racial terms: I consider myself English, but am a quarter Scottish, and who knows what else further back. But we could all make lists to challenge that of George Orwell. Off the top of my head, mine would include 'I know my rights', village cricket and Elgar, Do-It-Yourself, punk, street fashion, irony, vigorous politics, brass bands, Shakespeare, Cumberland sausages, double-decker buses, Vaughan Williams, Donne and Dickens, twitching net curtains, breast-obsession, quizzes and crosswords, country churches, dry-stone walls, gardening, Christopher Wren and Monty Python, easy-going Church of England vicars, the Beatles, bad hotels and good beer, church bells, Constable and Piper, finding foreigners funny, David Hare and William Cobbett, drinking to excess, Women's Institutes, fish and chips, curry, Christmas Eve at King's College, Cambridge, indifference to food, civility and crude language, fell-running, ugly caravan sites on beautiful clifftops, crumpets, Bentleys and Reliant Robins, and so on. They may not all be uniquely English, but the point about them is that unlike the touchstones of Britishness, which tend to be primped, planned and pompous, if you take any three or four of these things together, they point at once to a culture as evocatively as the smell of a bonfire in the October dusk.

So before the English submerge themselves in gloom again, it is worth noticing that there is something positive about the fact that the English have not devoted a lot of energy to discussing who they are. It is a mark of self-confidence: the English have not spent a great deal of time defining themselves because they haven't needed to. Is it necessary to do so now? I can only answer that it seems something the English can no longer avoid, for the reasons outlined earlier. Those countries which do best in the world – the ones that are safe and prosperous – have a coherent sense of their own culture.

CHAPTER TWO

FUNNY FOREIGNERS

The best thing I know between England and France is the sea.
DOUGLAS JERROLD, The Anglo-French Alliance

In 1836, Mrs Frances Trollope landed at Calais and overheard the conversation of a young man making his first visit to France. He was accompanied by a more experienced traveller, wise to the ways of the world beyond the white cliffs of Dover. She recalled the exchange. '"What a dreadful smell!" said the uninitiated stranger, enveloping his nose in his pocket handkerchief. "It is the smell of the continent, sir," replied the man of experience. And so it was.'[1]

The adage is that geography makes history. But if such a thing as a national psychology exists, it too may be made by geography. Would the French have such an abiding fear of Germany had they not had the German army march over their borders so often? Could Switzerland have maintained its amoral prosperity had it not been a land of mountains? The very absence of a geography for the Jews is what created Zionism, one of the most powerful ideologies of the twentieth century. The first profound influence upon the English is the fact that they live on an island.

This is how they have thought of their nearest continental neighbours. Obscene drawings were 'French postcards' or 'French prints'. Prostitutes were the 'French Consular Guard' (allegedly from the streetwalkers outside the French consulate in Buenos Aires). They could well be wearing wide-legged underwear – French knickers. If a man used their services, he would 'take French lessons'. If he caught syphilis as a result, he contracted 'the French disease', 'French gout', 'French pox', 'French marbles', 'French aches', or was said to have been paid a 'French compliment'. He might acquire 'a French crown', the symptomatic swellings of which would be 'French pigs'. If particularly badly 'Frenchified', he might lose his nose through the disease, in which case he ended up breathing through 'a French faggot-stick'. The way for a man to protect himself from these scourges was to wear a 'French letter' or 'French safe', or just a French (unless you *were* French, in which case, you used a *capote anglaise*).

And it didn't stop with sex. There was a general tendency to ascribe almost *any* irregular or bad behaviour to the French. When asked how he liked his beef, an Englishman might reply, referring to their untrustworthiness, 'Done like a Frenchman' – turned and turned again. Dr Johnson even claimed to have read a dissertation which attempted to prove that the weathercock – 'an artificial cock set on the top of a spire, which, by turning shows the point from which the wind blows' was designed after the French national symbol, the cockerel. 'Pedlar's French' was cant. Someone who shot an out-of-season pheasant was said to have 'killed a French pigeon'. In 1940s cricket, a 'French drive' was a lucky snick through the slips. Well into the 1950s, English people were still excusing their swearing by asking people to 'pardon my French' (John Major was said still to be using the phrase in the 1990s) and talking of unauthorized absences as 'French leave'. A tonsil-tickling embrace is still known as a French kiss, as if somehow it would never have occurred to an English person to stick their tongue into another person's mouth if the French hadn't invented it.

The French have had all these distinctions showered upon them because they are the ancestral enemy. Once upon a time, when England was at war with Spain, syphilis was 'the Spanish pox' and corruption was 'Spanish practices'. By the time the Dutch had become the main trading rivals, the English were inventing phrases like double Dutch for gibberish, or Dutch courage for the bravery of drunkenness. The pattern applies across Europe; syphilis was known as the German disease in Poland and Dutch pox in Portugal, reflecting local hostilities. But the Anglo–French rivalry is in a class of its own. The French have countered with expressions like *le vice anglais* for flagellation, *les Anglais ont débarqué* for menstruation, *filer à l'anglaise* for 'taking French leave' or *damné comme un Anglais*. Somehow, though, they don't seem to have quite the same instinctive vehemence: the French have had other, continental, neighbours to worry about. The animosity in the English terms reflects a bizarre schizophrenia about the French people.

Among the English middle class the French are worshipped for their food, their wine, their climate. Every year 9 million English tourists pack their bags and head for France. Many will be bearing with them votive offerings of baked beans, Marmite, marmalade and tea, before making for Provence, Dordogne or Brittany. Having eaten Englishly in their villas, they head home laden with cheeses, wines and pâtés, goodies they swear are unobtainable at home. They may despise the French fear of Germany, but they adore French *savoir-faire* – an expression for which their own language can only produce the lumpen and inadequate 'know-how'. The English might still affect occasional distaste at the French idea of *terrain*, which encourages them to wash less frequently and spend more on fragrances (when he knew he would be returning to France from his Egyptian campaign, Napoleon wrote to Josephine 'Ne te lave pas, j'arrive': 'Don't wash, I'm coming'), but secretly they are jealous that the society seems somehow 'closer to the natural order of things'. If they have views about the politics of France, they are infuriated by, yet secretly admire, the naked self-interest and blatant disregard for world opinion and public treaties which drives government policy. They torment themselves with worries about why England has no cafés full of intellectuals smoking, drinking coffee and developing impractical ways of reordering the universe. The France to which these aspirant lotus-eaters aspire is a place of impossibly stylish women and lavender-breezed sunshine.

It was ever thus. The Grand Tour, the forebear of modern tourism, was in some respects an inferiority complex with travel documents, its purpose to introduce wealthy English to the sophistications of European life: the English engagement with the continent was that of country cousins invited to a big city ball. The Grand Tour was wasted on many of those who made the journey, simply because they were too young to appreciate what they were experiencing. And many of those who were mature enough to take it in lost no chance to express their disgust at anything from continental food to lavatories. Horace Walpole described Paris as 'a dirty town with a dirtier ditch calling itself the Seine ... a filthy stream in which everything is washed without being cleaned, and dirty houses, ugly streets, worse shops and churches loaded with bad pictures'.[2] But even that great Englishman Dr Johnson felt that a man who had not visited the continent was 'always conscious of an inferiority, from his not having seen what it is expected a man should see'.[3] On arrival in Paris in 1775 at the age of sixty-six, he exchanged his customary brown coat, black stockings and plain shirt for white stockings, a new hat and an elaborate French wig. He was so determined not to be embarrassed by his poor French that he would speak only in Latin.

The effect of the Grand Tour was to make the English élite more tolerant of foreign ideas: it is always easier to lampoon and sneer from a distance. Indeed, by the late eighteenth century, the complaint was that becoming frenchified was a condition of advancement in England. Dramatists like Corneille and Racine became admired more than Shakespeare, while English poets like Pope and Addison aped French verse styles. But the experience of the rest of the English could not have been more different. Put shortly, vast numbers of them have always hated the French. And the feeling is mutual. There is scarcely a town of any size in England which is not 'twinned' with a French town, to foster better understanding between the two cultures. But it is an empty exercise: for all the reciprocal visits between councillors, the *vins d'honneur* and school trips, the two cultures remain profoundly divided and mutually suspicious. The French Minister for Cultural Affairs, Maurice Druon, got it pretty right when he said of the two countries in 1973 that 'the élites tend to admire one another and the peoples to despise one another'.

Centuries of hostility cannot be overcome by a few toasts and speeches from middle-aged worthies. We all need enemies, and the French are so wonderfully convenient – near to hand and yet apparently oblivious of the interests of anyone else. The two nations are now well matched economically and militarily, so provide ready foils for one another: each can patronize, but cannot dismiss, the other. And then the French keep giving the English reasons to despise them. Can anyone doubt that had Hitler successfully invaded Britain, a Vichy-style government would have emerged from somewhere? The point is that it didn't happen, so the English have still not exhausted the moral capital they accumulated during the last world war. As to the later ungrateful efforts of the French to exclude Britain from the European Economic Community, they just confirm the worth of the hostility.

Soldiers who fought on the Western Front in World War One and experienced the full capacity of the French peasants, for whom they were supposed to be fighting, to rob them of their pay in exchange for an egg, came to understand the shallowness of the *Entente Cordiale*. When Robert Graves went up to Oxford with other demobilized infantry officers at the end of the war he noticed that

Anti-French feeling among the ex-soldiers amounted almost to an obsession. Edmund, shaking with nerves, used to say at this time: 'No more wars for me at any price! Except against the French. If there's ever a war with them, I'll go like a shot' . . . Some undergraduates even insisted that we had been fighting on the wrong side: our natural enemies were the French.[4]

George Orwell saw something similar. 'During the war of 1914–18', he wrote, 'the English working class were in contact with foreigners to an extent that is rarely possible. The sole result was that they brought back a hatred of all Europeans, except the Germans, whose courage they admired. In four years on French soil they did not even acquire a liking for wine.'[5]*

The great-grandsons and -daughters of the First World War veterans have scarcely more moderate views. England remains the only European country in which apparently intelligent people can use expressions like 'joining Europe was a mistake', or 'we should leave Europe', as if the place can be hitched to the back of the car like a holiday caravan. An analysis of the British market for the French Tourist Office in 1996 advises, in measured disdain, that 'even though they have a well-developed sense of humour and can laugh at themselves, they remain conservative and chauvinistic. The British are profoundly independent and insular, constantly torn between America and Europe'.[6] They are right: one of the consequences of living on an island is that everywhere is overseas.

There is a legendary English newspaper headline which tells everything you need to know about the country's relations with the rest of Europe.

FOG IN CHANNEL – CONTINENT CUT OFF

How unfortunate for continental Europeans to be so at the mercy of the weather.

---

* It is interesting that for all the abuse the English can throw at the French, the English have never developed similar terms involving the Germans: German measles hardly counts. The Germans have only *die englische Krankheit* – rickets.

It would be hard to exaggerate the importance of the fact that they are islanders to the mentality of the English. The elderly John of Gaunt says it all in Shakespeare's *Richard II* when he speaks of

> This fortress built by Nature for herself
> Against infection and the hand of war,
> This happy breed of men, this little world;
> This precious stone set in the silver sea,
> Which serves it in the office of a wall,
> Or as a moat defensive to a house.[7]

In this understanding of England, its first privilege is to be isolated from the rest of Europe. There were obvious practical benefits. Living on an island gives you defined borders; lines on maps are arbitrary, beaches and cliffs are not. England has many quite distinct regional identities; but the Mancunian and the Cockney, the Somerset farmer and the Burton-on-Trent brewer, are yoked together by the cordon of the sea. And since character does not change suddenly from one side of a land border to another, people who live on a continental landmass are both more aware of other cultures and of the chance nature of what passport you carry. By the time of John of Gaunt's speech, the English had already absorbed Wales and were on the cusp of union with Scotland. They had neither the worries nor the benefits of having proper borders. As a consequence of the fact that the sea defined their perimeters, the English developed what, in 1960, Elias Canetti considered 'the most stable national feeling in the world'. The sea was there to be ruled: 'The Englishman sees himself as a captain on board a ship with a small group of people, the sea around and beneath him. He is almost alone; as captain he is in many ways isolated even from his crew.'[8]

Yet, before the sixteenth century, the English can hardly be called a nation of natural seafarers. All the great voyages of discovery up to then had been made by Continental mariners. The English were a land-loving people and the sea which surrounded them was, as John of Gaunt put it, more a moat than anything else: where are the sailor heroes in the works of Shakespeare? True, by the time he was writing, the English had begun the behaviour which would accumulate the world's greatest empire. But they took to the sea more as nautical gangsters than anything else – how else are we to think of a figure like Sir Francis Drake? It was only as their wealth and ambitions grew that the English realized that the sea which had always been their protection also gave them a unique opportunity. Virtually alone among the major countries of Europe, England had no need of a standing army as a precaution against possible invasion. And whereas countries with territorial borders could not march their army across them without either forming alliances or waging wars, the navy which defended the British islands could go where it pleased. Once they had committed themselves to the sea, the English were inclined to see the rest of Europe as nothing but trouble, thus beginning the tension between maritime and Continental strategies which has run through British defence policy for centuries. As Churchill once told the House of Commons:

Whereas any European power has to support a vast army first of all, we in this fortunate, happy island, relieved by our insular position of a double burden, may turn our undivided efforts and attention to the Fleet. Why should we sacrifice a game in which we are sure to win to play a game in which we are bound to lose?[9]

And what spectacular winning it was! To those who thought like Churchill, the English Channel was almost wider than the Atlantic. When you are surrounded by the sea you are as cut off from your nearest neighbour as your farthest trading partner, and the sea which separates you from your nearest neighbour also links you with your remotest. Any planned invasion of England would be a matter of vast organization, the provision of ships, and calm weather: there was no border just to be marched across. Isolation also gave the opportunity to enter wars, alliances and intrigues, selectively. Once they had begun to accumulate an empire, all of which was accessible only by sea, entanglements on the European landmass were an irrelevance. In 1866, ten days after the battle of Sadowa, at which Bismarck's Prussian army routed the Austrians, thus laying foundations for the German Empire, Disraeli delivered himself of the view that 'England has outgrown the continent of Europe'. He felt that 'The abstention of England from any unnecessary interference in the affairs of Europe is the consequence, not of her decline of power, but of her increased strength. England is no longer a mere European power; she is the metropolis of a great maritime Empire . . . she is really more an Asiatic power than a European'.[10]

It is because the island neurosis is so deeply ingrained in the English mind that the Dunkirk evacuation of May 1940 has such a powerful hold on English memories of World War Two. The escape of 220,000 British and 110,000 allied French soldiers from the encircling Nazi army was a remarkable achievement and is, with the Battle of Britain and the Blitz, for the English one of the three most venerated events of World War Two. As the last soldiers were plucked from the beaches, the *New York Times* roared that 'So long as the English tongue survives, the word Dunkerque will be spoken with reverence . . . It is the great tradition of democracy. It is the future. It is victory'.[11] It was, in fact, the consequence of catastrophe. The lasting impression of that 'victorious' retreat, celebrated in speeches, paintings and poems, is of an armada of boats – fishing-smacks, pleasure steamers, sailing-yachts and little dinghies – snatching British soldiers from the jaws of death while, in the skies above, Allied pilots fight off the Nazi air attack. Elements of the myth are embellished: the role of the 'little ships' was exaggerated for one thing. But that does not matter. There are three reasons the story appeals so strongly to the English. Firstly, it speaks to their sense of separateness: it was the moment when Britain was, finally, alone against the Nazis. King George VI even told his mother that

'Personally I feel happier now that we have no more allies to be polite to and pamper'. Secondly, it is a story of the success of the Few against the odds. Thirdly, it demonstrates to the English what they have known for centuries, that the European continent is a place of nothing but trouble and that their greatest security is behind the thousands of miles of irregular coastline around their island home.*

This island idea has a special place in the English imagination. It begins in childhood with Enid Blyton's *Famous Five* adventures on Kirin Island, continues through *Treasure Island*, by Robert Louis Stevenson (a Scots author admittedly, but the plot to discover the hidden treasure is hatched by English West Country folk) and goes on. Jonathan Swift's *Gulliver's Travels* works because of the belief that there may, somewhere out there, be other islands stranger than any yet discovered by English seamen. (Swift was born and raised within the English Pale in Ireland as a son of the colonial class, so he probably had an acute sense of the island mentality.)

The extraordinary story of Alexander Selkirk, a ne'er-do-well sailor cast ashore on an uninhabited island off the Pacific coast of South America, was another tale which seized the English imagination. After a row with the master of his ship Selkirk had opted to be abandoned off the coast of Chile, on the island of Juan Fernandez, and was not retrieved until 31 January 1709, when another English privateer anchored off the island to make repairs and tend the sick after rounding Cape Horn. To their astonishment, the crew discovered a man dressed in goatskins and speaking English, albeit with some difficulty. He had been alone for over four years. The

---

* It is interesting that both Napoleon and Adolf Hitler recognized this English perspective: each imagined a post-war world in which they would run the continent of Europe, while the British maintained an overseas empire. The way Hitler saw it, as he told Field Marshal von Rundstedt, 'Germany will dominate Europe, and England the world outside.'

captain's description of Selkirk's rescue in his *A Cruising Voyage Around the World* struck an immediate chord with the English public. An account appeared in the essayist Sir Richard Steele's *The Englishman* (Selkirk was, incidentally, another Scot) in 1713. Six years later, Daniel Defoe took the story of Selkirk's exploits hunting wild goats, first making knives for himself and then goatskin clothes, as the basis for *Robinson Crusoe*, one of the first and certainly one of the most enduringly successful novels of all time.

Seabound security gave the English an early self-confidence and their relative isolation promoted the growth of an idiosyncratic intellectual tradition. It produced some very odd geniuses, like Blake or Shakespeare. It probably has something to do with the fact that England has produced so many very good travel writers. Freedom from the fear of sudden invasion also promoted individual freedoms: more vulnerable countries justified strong, top-down systems of government which could summon an army at days' notice. The fact of being an island even dictated the shape of English cities: when there was a natural defence in the sea, there was no need for towns to be contained within walls; the consequence was that they grew higgledy-piggledy. There was no organizing plan for a city like London, it just grew as villages joined up. On the other hand, because there was no need for encircling walls, when they chose to do so, the city fathers could incorporate large open spaces near its heart.

Nor did the creation of an empire dampen the essential insularity of the English. In 1882, the idea was canvassed of driving a railway tunnel under the Channel. It was, you might think, just the sort of engineering challenge which the land of Isambard Kingdom Brunel (another adopted Englishman – his father was French) might have seized upon. Instead, *Nineteenth Century* magazine organized a petition opposing the idea, on the grounds that 'such a Railroad would involve this country in military dangers and liabilities from which, as an island, it has hitherto been happily free'. This was no voice crying from the rural backwoods: the letter rapidly gained signatures from the Archbishop of Canterbury, the poets Tennyson and Browning, the biologist T. H. Huxley, the philosopher Herbert Spencer, 5 dukes, 10 earls, 26 MPs, 17 admirals, 59 generals, 200 clergymen and 600 other worthies.[12]

This insularity gave the English a great self-confidence, but it did nothing for their sophistication. It is hard to escape the conclusion that, deep down, the English don't really care for foreigners. Before it was necessary for foreign visitors to reverence the British Empire, one visitor after another commented on the remarkable vanity of the English. In 1497, a Venetian noticed that 'the English are great lovers of themselves, and of everything belonging to them; they think that there are no other men than themselves and no other world but England; and whenever they see a handsome foreigner they say "he looks like an Englishman" and that "it is a great pity that he should not be an Englishman"'.[13] In describing a visit to England by Frederick, Duke of Württemberg in 1592, a German author commented upon the fact that 'the inhabitants . . . are extremely proud and overbearing . . . they care little for foreigners, but scoff and laugh at them'.[14] Another visitor, the Dutch merchant Emmanuel van Meteren, noticed the same arrogance when he listed the qualities of the English character. 'The people are bold, courageous, ardent and cruel in war, but very inconstant, rash, vainglorious, light and deceiving, and very suspicious, especially of foreigners, whom they despise.'[15] An Italian physician who toured the island in 1552 decided that the arrogance of the people was such that they considered the average alien to be 'a wretched being, but half a man (semihominem)'.[16] Milton boasted, 'Let not England forget her precedence of teaching nations how to live.'[17]

The picture had hardly changed by the middle of this century. In 1940, George Orwell, who had noticed how little ordinary soldiers were affected by their exposure to foreign cultures in World War One, turned his attention to the boys' magazines the *Gem* and the *Magnet*. He hated almost everything about them, from their conservative politics to their absurdly dated *mise-en-scène*.

As a rule [he wrote] it is assumed that foreigners of any race are all alike and will conform more or less exactly to the following patterns:

FRENCHMAN: Wears beard, gesticulates wildly.

SPANIARD, MEXICAN, etc: Sinister, treacherous.

ARAB, AFGHAN, etc: Sinister, treacherous.

CHINESE: Sinister, treacherous. Wears pigtail.

ITALIAN: Excitable. Grinds barrel-organ or carries stiletto.

SWEDE, DANE, etc: Kind-hearted, stupid.

NEGRO: Comic, very faithful.[18]*

Note that the Americans do not appear in this list of hilarious stereotypes. But then, speaking English, they weren't really foreigners. It would have been impossible for 'Frank Richards', the author of these hugely successful stories, to have got away with the simple-minded caricatures Orwell despised had the English not had a profound ignorance of foreigners.

As he had been turning them out for thirty years, Orwell assumed the name to be a *nom de plume* for a team of writers. He underestimated the man: Richards once wrote 18,000 words in a single day, and his lifetime output was estimated at the equivalent of a thousand ordinary novels. To his astonishment, after the article appeared Frank Richards (real name Charles Harold St John Hamilton and still only sixty-four) demanded the right of reply. On the question of stereotypes he wrote, 'As for foreigners being funny, I must shock Mr Orwell by telling him that foreigners *are* funny. They lack the sense of humour which is the special gift to our own chosen nation: and people without a sense of humour are always unconsciously funny.'

The English isolation created a curious ambivalence about foreigners, who walked a knife-edge; their unusualness could inspire either awe or disdain. In the eighteenth century, English nationalism

* *Horizon*, May 1940.

drew much of its strength from the fact that polite English society was inclined to fawn on what was seen as foreign sophistication. When Voltaire came to London 'he was treated almost like a visiting potentate'.[19] In painting and music, native artists suffocated under the reign of foreign-born geniuses like Sir Godfrey Kneller (born Gottfried Kniller) and George Handel (Georg Friedrich Haendel). It is interesting how durable this self-pitying belief that the English will only applaud foreign ability has proved. Sir Roy Strong, who takes four inches in *Who's Who* to list his achievements, from running the Victoria and Albert Museum to publishing books about the garden trellis, wailed to me once that 'I'd have been taken a lot more seriously and got a great deal further had I been called Strongski'.

On the other hand, hatred of foreigners, particularly the foreigners most readily to hand, the French, could be taken in almost with a mother's milk. Nelson once called a midshipman to his cabin to instruct him in the three essentials to survival in the Royal Navy. 'First, you must implicitly obey orders, without attempting to form any opinion of your own respecting their propriety; secondly, you must consider every man as your enemy who speaks ill of your King; and, thirdly, you must hate a Frenchman as you do the devil.' Nor does it seem that this was merely the sort of jingoistic remark the great man threw into quarter-deck pep-talks. His letters are littered with outbursts against the French. '*Down, down* with the French villains,' Nelson wrote in one of them. 'Excuse my warmth; but my blood boils at the name of a Frenchman ... You may safely rely that I never trust a Frenchman... I hate the French most damnably.'[20]

Picking on the French had obvious political benefits: they were, after all, the main imperial rivals, which meant that ordinary citizens of each country stood as much chance of meeting on the battlefield as anywhere else. Their foreignness meant they could be ascribed bizarre physical characteristics. Napoleon was an obvious target. There were the famous 'defects of the Consular constitution', the cause of Josephine's repeated nocturnal disappointments, which belong to the 'Hitler has only got one ball' school of propaganda. It became so common for English cartoonists to depict Napoleon as a yellow-skinned pygmy with an enormous nose that when the chaplain to the British Embassy arrived in Paris he was astonished to find him 'well-proportioned and handsome' and not at all what the *Morning Post* had described on 1 February 1803 as 'an unclassifiable being, half-African, half-European, a Mediterranean mulatto'.

What is so striking is that unflattering delusions about French people seemed to have reached the very soul of the average Englishman. Even in peacetime, in the most peaceful of places, they could harbour the oddest of beliefs about the French. A good example comes from Captain Henry Byam Martin, the master of the *Grampus*. His job in the 1840s was to drift through Polynesia, where the French were laying the foundations of an empire, doing whatever he could to spread British influence. In his personal diary, discovered and published only relatively recently, he wrote that 'The French find themselves thwarted by the predilections of the people in favour of the English. They know that they are universally detested by the Tahitians – by the men for overbearing insolence – by the women for their dirt and incorrigible ugliness'.[21]

There is something splendid about that 'incorrigible ugliness'. It demonstrates the visceral quality of the prejudice against the French. The English have a similar blindness about themselves, unable to recognize the 'perfidious Albion', the country of whom Napoleon said: 'The English don't respect treaties. In future they must be covered with black crêpe.' English sea-captains like Byam Martin considered themselves straightforward and dependable, and they were altogether happier dealing with exotic islanders, whom they bluffly thought they could understand; unlike the French, who were untrustworthy and wholly incomprehensible.

The difficulty in persuading the English that they needed to engage more closely with their European neighbours was that they had an alternative friendship so readily to hand in the shape of the United States. It is not, and has not been for generations, a relationship of equals, but the English ruling class, endowed at school with all the benefits of a classical education, have comforted themselves with a classical allusion. During World War Two, Harold Macmillan explained how the relationship worked to Richard Crossman, then Director of Psychological Warfare in Algiers.

We, my dear Crossman [he began], are Greeks in this American empire. You will find the Americans much as the Greeks found the Romans – great big, vulgar, bustling people, more vigorous than we are and also more idle, with more unspoiled virtues but also more corrupt. We must run Allied Force Headquarters as the Greek slaves ran the operations of the Emperor Claudius.[22]

It was one of Macmillan's most treasured prejudices, comforting in being ineffably patronizing, and self-deluding at all levels from the political to the personal: for all his appearance as the quintessential Edwardian gent, Macmillan was the son of an Indianapolis doctor's daughter.

The friendship with America saved the British at a time when the country stood alone. Reading Churchill's own account of his attempts to cajole the United States into joining the war against Hitler, you are struck by how profoundly he believed that because the two nations shared so many beliefs that they *must* share a common destiny. Churchill's description of the meeting with President Roosevelt on the British battleship *Prince of Wales* in Placentia Bay, Newfoundland, in August 1941, the meeting at which the Atlantic Charter was agreed, conveys the feelings. They held a joint religious service, for which Churchill had chosen the hymns, including 'Onward, Christian soldiers' and 'O God, our help in ages past'.

This service was felt by us all to be a moving expression of the unity of faith of our two peoples, and none who took part in it will forget the spectacle presented that sunlit morning on the crowded quarterdeck – the symbolism of the Union Jack and the Stars and Stripes draped side by side on the pulpit, the British and American chaplains sharing in the reading of the prayers; the highest naval, military and air officers of Britain and the United States grouped in one body behind the President and the close-packed ranks of British and American sailors, completely inter-mingled, sharing the same books and joining fervently together in the prayers and hymns familiar to both ... Every word seemed to stir the heart. It was a great hour to live. Nearly half those who sang were soon to die[23] [the *Prince of Wales* was sunk that December by a force of eighty-four Japanese torpedo-carrying aircraft].

There is no denying the force of the scene, nor the ties of history, culture and language which pressed in so powerfully on Churchill. In military terms, the relationship between the two countries bore great fruit, first in the liberation of Europe, then through collab-oration on the atomic bomb and, in the Cold War decades, with the sharing of intelligence, particularly signals intelligence from electronic eavesdropping. Whatever the economic imbalance, the British con-vinced themselves that they brought something special to the party. A note circulated among the British delegation sent to Washington to discuss arrangements for repaying the American war loan ran as follows:

> In Washington Lord Halifax
> Whispered to Lord Keynes
> 'It's true they've all the money bags.
> But we've got all the brains.'

Certainly, without the relationship with the United States, there was no guarantee of any successful outcome to the war. But in the longer term, the alliance enabled the British to delude themselves that they remained an independent power in the world. Characteristically, what the British had seen as 'independence' was merely independence from the rest of Europe. The relationship with the United States was merely one of being free to do as they pleased, as long as

Washington did not object, as the British discovered in 1956 when they tried to invade Egypt to secure the Suez Canal, without American approval. But by then, the die was cast; Britain had thrown in her lot with what was seen as a kindred Anglo-Saxon culture across the Atlantic. In the context of British history it was understandable: Europe meant war, America the aid which ended war. But the price of British overdependence on the United States was that the country closed its eyes to much else happening in Europe and aggravated its estrangement from the European Community to which, belatedly, it sought admission. It has never caught up since. By the 1990s, with the continent of Europe no longer divided between communism and democracy, when the 'Special Relationship' with Britain mattered a great deal less to the United States, it was left blowing in the wind.

The relationship with the United States is still 'special'. It shows in the curious personal friendships which can develop between political leaders who literally as well as metaphorically speak the same language – Thatcher and Reagan, or Blair and Clinton. While Harold Wilson successfully kept Britain out of the Vietnam débâcle, in other post-war conflicts, from Korea to Kosovo, British governments pride themselves on their readiness to send forces to fight alongside (for) America. It shows in the vast British investment in the United States (greater than that of any other European country); in the fact that there is more American investment in Britain than in any other European country; in the interpenetration of British and American cinema, where a certain kind of villain always has an English accent; in the English-Speaking Union, the Atlantic Council and dozens of other clubs; and in the fact that more than twice as many people travel between Britain and North America as cross the Atlantic to or from any other European state. Indeed, you need to add together all the travellers from Germany, France and the Netherlands to North America, to exceed the British people travelling.[24]

The comparison with ancient Greece and Rome is made less

frequently now, as it becomes clearer than ever to the English that the world is Made in America. How do you explain to a country dressed in jeans, T-shirts and baseball caps that they belong to a culture which gave the world that universal item of clothes, the tailored man's suit? You don't. It doesn't matter any more.

CHAPTER THREE

THE ENGLISH EMPIRE

When people say England, they sometimes mean Great Britain, sometimes the United Kingdom, sometimes the British Isles – but never England.
GEORGE MIKES, How to be an Alien

One of the characteristics of the English which has most enraged the other races who occupy their island is their thoughtless readiness to muddle up 'England' with 'Britain'. It is, to listen to some English people talk, as if the Scots and Welsh either did not exist, or were just aspiring to join some master race which has always been in control of its God-ordained destiny. The English would do well to mind their language.

Unlike England, which was totally or partially subjugated by Romans, Vikings, Anglo-Saxons and Normans, Scotland was never fully conquered by *any* foreign invader until after it had become part of the 'United Kingdom'. A nationalist reading of Scottish history shows the Act of Union, which united the country with England, to have been signed by bribed Scottish aristocrats. In the Highlands there is *still*, nearly two centuries after the Clearances, outrage at 'the Scottish holocaust', when families were driven from the land to make way for wide-scale sheep-farming. As one Scots nationalist put it to me, this was 'the most efficient ethnic cleansing in Europe, perpetrated by Anglicised homosexual clan chiefs and landlords, assisted by police, army, the Church of Scotland and MPs, to create the biggest desert in Europe'. He went on to claim that the reward of the Scottish islanders for their disproportionately great sacrifice in the Second World War was to have the highest unemployment and emigration rate in the Union. 'They would have been better off if Hitler had won the war: at least there would still be people living in the now derelict villages,' he concluded furiously.[1]

It is also true that the British Empire was in large part the creation of Scots: once dreams of their own empire had died in the disastrous attempt to establish a colony on the isthmus of Panama in 1698, Scots served with huge distinction in the British army, built roads and bridges, became great traders and built vast fortunes. The famous signal at the Battle of Trafalgar, 'England expects that every man will do his duty,' is said to have been hoisted by John Robertson, a sailor from Stornoway on the Isle of Lewis. 'In British settlements from Dunedin to Bombay, for every Englishman who has worked himself up to wealth from small beginnings, you find ten Scotchmen,' wrote Sir Charles Dilke in 1869, adding mischievously, 'It is strange indeed that Scotland has not become the popular name for the United Kingdom.'[2] The last words of Lieutenant General Sir John Moore – a Glasgow-born Scot – say it all. As he lay mortally wounded by a blast of grapeshot at the battle of Corunna in 1809, he certainly had no doubts about whom he was serving. He died saying, 'I hope the people of England will be satisfied. I hope my country will do me justice.'

The foundations for what the medieval historian John Gillingham calls the *true* Thousand Year Reich – the one within Britain – were based upon English assumptions of their moral incomparability, often held to date from their conversion to Christianity. But William of Malmesbury, in his *Deeds of the Kings of the English*, gives another reason for their self-proclaimed superiority, the sixth century marriage of King Ethelbert to Bertha, daughter of the *rex Francorum*. It 'was by this connexion with the French that a once barbarous people began to divest themselves of their wild frame of mind and incline towards a gentler way of life'.[3]

In this interpretation, it was the French influence which began to civilize the English. Certainly, although the Norman conquerors five centuries later may have been uninvited, once they had taken control, the English showed a tremendous willingness to embrace mainland European ideas. Laws of marriage, property, war and sexual behaviour all changed. Intermarriage between the natives and their new rulers was commonplace, and by the 1140s the English élite were writing (in Latin) and talking (in French) about their land as the 'seat of justice, the abode of peace, the apex of piety, the mirror of religion', whereas Wales was 'a country of woodland and pasture . . . abounding in deer and fish, milk and herds, but breeding a bestial type of man'.[4] William of Newburgh described the Scots as 'a horde of barbarians . . . It is a delight to that inhuman nation, more savage than wild beasts, to cut the throats of old men, to slaughter little children, to rip open the bowels of women'.[5] Gerald de Barri thought the Irish 'so barbarous that they cannot be said to have any culture . . . they are a wild people, living like beasts, who have not progressed at all from primitive habits of pastoral farming'.[6] Richard of Hexham was horrified by the barbaric way the Scots waged war:

[They] slaughtered husbands in the sight of their wives, then they carried off the women together with their spoil. The women, both widows and maidens, were stripped, bound and then roped together by cords and thongs, and were driven off at arrow point, goaded by spears . . . Those bestial men who think nothing of adultery, incest and other crimes, when they were tired of abusing their victims, either kept them as slaves or sold them to other barbarians in exchange for cattle.[7]

It wasn't just their habits of agriculture and war which made the English feel superior, it was their sex lives too. John of Salisbury – one of the clergy who was with St Thomas Becket when he was stabbed to death in Canterbury Cathedral – described the Welsh as living like 'beasts': 'they keep concubines as well as wives'.[8]

These comments at least demonstrate that 'taking up the white man's burden' was no nineteenth-century invention. In the twentieth century, the English have learned to shy away from generalizing about West Indians or Asians, yet still feel free to make sweeping assertions about their immediate neighbours. The nursery rhyme,

> Taffy was a Welshman, Taffy was a thief;
> Taffy came to my house and stole a piece of beef:
> I went to Taffy's house, Taffy was not at home,
> Taffy came to my house and stole a marrow-bone.

has been expunged from most children's anthologies, although you can still find it in second-hand bookshops. Presumably it was originally a reference to the raiding parties that came across the English border from Wales. But even in these more touchy times, the English caricature of the Welsh continues to be that they are wheedling, duplicitous windbags, full of bogus sentimentality. In an attack on the stereotypes which dominate English television soap opera, the *Sunday Times* television critic (one of the many Scots who had taken the high road to London) asserted in 1997 that 'Wales enjoys a panoramic range of prejudice. We all know that the Welsh are loquacious dissemblers, immoral liars, stunted, bigoted, dark, ugly, pugnacious little trolls',[9] on the assumption that it was just the small-change of the union. He discovered that a lot of Welsh have got sick of the stereotype; they referred the article to the Wales Commissioner for Racial Equality, a Mr Ray Singh.[10]

English prejudices about Scotland are less abusive. The Scots are mocked for their meanness and their gloom: it is, as P. G. Wodehouse said, 'never difficult to distinguish between a Scotsman with a grievance and a ray of sunshine'. The Welsh, when they are praised at all, are celebrated for 'Celtic' qualities – as poets and singers – whereas the Scots, especially the Lowland Scots, are respected as doctors, lawyers, engineers and businessmen. To continue the generalizing, the English regard the Scots as tough, cantankerous and upstanding (except when drunk). Certainly, the two greatest public moralizers of twentieth-century England, Archbishop Cosmo Lang and the first boss of the BBC, John Reith, were both Scots.

It is, of course, quite possible that both sets of generalizations are as they are for the simple reason that they're true. But how they see their neighbours must also tell us something about the English. Both Scotland and Wales were effectively annexed by England. But the Scots joined the partnership as *apparently* balanced partners and saw their king, James VI of Scotland, become England's James I (although some of them do still get miffed at descriptions of the present Queen as Elizabeth the Second: the Scots had no Elizabeth the First). They maintained, and maintain, separate legal and educational systems and a distinct intellectual tradition. The relationship between England and Wales, by contrast, has never remotely looked a relationship of equals. Once Owen Glendower's rebellion against the colonizers had been extinguished, early in the fifteenth century, the principality became an adjunct of England. Henry VIII may have removed punitive laws banning the Welsh from owning land in England (they had been brought in following Glendower's uprising), but, despite the Welsh blood in his veins, he still required those who held public office there to use the English language.* Despite these inhibitions, the Welsh continued to use their own language between themselves, so that it is estimated that as late as the 1880s, three out of four Welsh people still spoke it by choice.[11] Perhaps this should have made them more, rather than less, their own masters. But, crucially, they had no capital city to match the pretensions of Edinburgh, nor separate legal, educational, or (until the arrival of non-conformism, by which time it was too late) religious institutions.

For the two centuries after King James united England and Scotland, the English seemed to have veered between hostility for

---

* It was a mark of the court's very different attitude to the Scots that Henry also made it an offence for an Englishman to sell a horse to a Scot.

the Scots – for their 'treachery' in the Civil War, and the Jacobite rebellions of 1715 and 1745 – and indifference. 'Scotland ... is certainly the sink of the earth', was how one grandee put it in a letter after the battle of Culloden. He received the reply from the Duke of Newcastle, the Prime Minister's brother, 'As to Scotland, I am as little partial to it as any man alive ... However, we must consider that they are within our island.'[12] It is hard to escape the feeling that both the animosity and the affected indifference were expressing the same feeling, that deep down the English rather respected the Scots. The most celebrated English contempt for the Scottish belonged to Dr Johnson, who thought 'seeing Scotland is only seeing a worse England'. Boswell records his reaction on being told that Scotland had 'a great many noble wild prospects': 'I believe, sir, you have a great many,' replied the great man. 'Norway, too, has wild noble prospects; and Lapland is remarkable for prodigious noble wild prospects. But, sir, let me tell you, the noblest prospect which a Scotchman ever sees, is the high road that leads him to England.'[13] Even Johnson himself was unable to explain his prejudice, but the Scots could console themselves with the thought that at least they had managed to get under his skin: the only thing he could find to tell Boswell about Wales was that it 'is so little different from England that it offers nothing to the speculation of the traveller'.

But by the eighteen hundreds, the picture of the Scots as blood-thirsty traitors was giving way to positive enthusiasm, as the English embraced the romance of the Highlanders, George IV arriving on a visit to Edinburgh dressed in full Highland rig. Scotland retains a social status through its connections with the monarchy and aristo-cracy, the enduring romantic folly of the Highland estates and the fact that half of Chelsea claims to belong to some clan or other. If you include Scots in disguise, like Andrew Bonar Law, Harold Macmillan and Tony Blair, the country has provided 11 of the 49 Prime Ministers since George III came to the throne, a contribution out of all proportion to its share of the population. The Welsh are another matter altogether. They have produced only one memorable Prime Minister, David Lloyd George, but at least he stands head-and-shoulders above many of the rest of the holders of that office this century. Figures like Aneurin Bevan have kept the radical Welsh tradition alive, but their advancement has been barred not only because so many of the English are, with rare exceptions in their history, inherently conservative, but because they just find it so difficult to trust the Welsh. When Neil Kinnock failed to lead the Labour party to victory in the 1992 election, the party sensed it was partly because of English distrust of the Welsh, and immediately replaced him with a Scot, John Smith. Smith possessed the subfusc Scottish virtues that the English appreciate. They are the qualities of Lowland Scots, listed by the historian Richard Faber as 'industry, economy, toughness, caution, pedantry, argumentativeness, lack of humour'.[14] The last is certainly unfair to Smith, who, had he not been struck down by a heart attack, would no doubt have become the first Scottish Labour Prime Minister since Ramsay MacDonald in the 1930s.

One consequence of the fact that so much Welsh and Scottish ambition was bound up in Britain and the British Empire is that in neither place has much of the nationalist cause advanced far beyond the 'We Hate the English' stage. For every Scots and Welsh nationalist leader working out a coherent relationship with the rest of Europe, there are a thousand who simply harbour a sullen resentment of the English. They are still at the stage which Douglas Hyde, later to become the first president of Eire, described a century ago as 'a dull, ever-abiding animosity' towards England which ensures that they 'grieve when she prospers and joy when she is hurt'.[15] One famous Scottish reporter has even dubbed foreign teams playing England at cricket – *cricket* for heaven's sake – honorary Scots. So the West Indies are the Black Jocks, India the Dark-brown Jocks, Australia the Upside-down Jocks and New Zealand the Upside-down, Closed-on-Sunday Jocks.[16] In this chippy view of the world it doesn't matter who wins, just as long as England loses. A Scottish friend who was trying to keep up with the Euro '96 football championship while on a sailing holiday called into a bar in the little port of Stranraer in south-west Scotland to watch the semi-final between England and Germany. After extra time, the scores were level at 1–1. At the end of the penalty shootout, the England central defender Gareth Southgate had his penalty saved by the German keeper, thereby ending England's European Championship dreams. 'The place erupted,' he remembered. 'There was an old man sitting in the corner. I'd never seen him before in my life. And we kissed each other. *That's* how bad we wanted the English to get beat.'

The only English neighbour to have outgrown this stage is the one to whom they have behaved worst: not Scotland or Wales, but Ireland. Here, perhaps because their involvement has brought them nothing but trouble, the English attitude can swing from indulgence to dislike in no time. Having a far stronger sense of being an oppressed people for most of their history, Irish folk memory keeps alive a chain of acts of cruelty by the English from the murder of prisoners during the twelfth century, through the appalling slaughter of Oliver Cromwell's campaigns and the official indifference to the famine of the 1840s, right up to the British army's shooting dead of unarmed civilians in Londonderry on 'Bloody Sunday' in 1972.

It is because English dominion in Ireland was always more precarious than anywhere else in the British Isles that they behaved with the greatest arrogance. (Although born in Ireland and registered in Dublin, when the Irish tried to claim the Duke of Wellington, he remarked that 'just because a man is born in a stable, it doesn't make him a horse'.) The relationship has always been deeply ambivalent, shot through with contradictions. Victorian England was eager to celebrate the importance of Celtic blood to the 'English race', while simultaneously quailing at the potential of the raw Ireland beyond the colonial Pale. Dr Johnson's teasing of the Scots is positively benign by comparison with the crude abuse the English have thrown at the Irish. A *Punch* piece of the 1860s claimed to have found the Missing Link in human evolution, 'the Irish yahoo', in parts of London and Liverpool:

When conversing with its kind it talks a sort of gibberish. It is, moreover, a climbing animal, and may sometimes be seen ascending a ladder with a hod of bricks. The Irish yahoo generally confines itself within the limits of its own colony, except when it goes out of them to get its living. Sometimes, however, it sallies forth in states of excitement, and attacks civilized human beings that have provoked its fury.[17]

The 'joke' belongs to the period: the English, as we shall see, were in the grip of a delusion that they belonged to a higher order of beings. It followed that those who rejected the embrace of the Empire were part of a lower order. But the fact of being a recognizable colony, with the English colonial class belonging to a different religious denomination, backed by its own army of occupation, eventually worked to Ireland's advantage. Once the colonists had packed their bags, Ireland was able to shape its own identity within the European Union, seizing the opportunities offered by membership of the European Union far more readily than other parts of the British Isles, which have had to stagger into the future dragging behind them the baggage of their involvement in an empire which is no more.

How were the English able to get away with their prejudices? Firstly, of course, they were unassailably the dominant power in the islands, so what others thought didn't matter much. Secondly, by the nineteenth century they were presiding over the most successful empire the world had ever seen, in which it was clear that what got results were the practical, self-disciplined qualities of the Anglo-Saxon: it followed that the best thing an emotional Celt could do was to acquire them, instead of messing about with sentimental excursions into the history of a marginalized people. And thirdly, so many of the Celts suffered from an inferiority complex about their own birthplaces. 'The land of my fathers,' said Dylan Thomas, 'my fathers can keep it.' The self-loathing lives on. In *Trainspotting*, one of Irving Welsh's smackheads says to another:

It's nae good blaming it oan the English fir colonizing us. Ah don't hate the English. They're just wankers. We can't even pick a decent, healthy culture to be colonized by. No. We're ruled by effete arseholes. What does that make us? The lowest of the fuckin' low, the scum of the earth. The most wretched, servile, miserable, pathetic trash that was ever shat intae creation.[18]

The cultural accomplishments the Celts had to set against the Anglo-Saxon empire were vestigial: the ancient civilization to which they claimed to belong was an oral culture which had taken whatever rhetorical heights it achieved to druidical graves. Scottish pride has still hardly properly recovered from the revelation that Ossian's *Fingal*, the Gaelic epic which James Macpherson claimed to have discovered while travelling around Scotland in 1760, and which Gibbon declared showed 'the untutored Caledonians glowing with warm virtues of nature', was an elaborate hoax. The Scots were left with the sort of effusion W. B. Yeats fell into in *The Celtic Twilight*, talking of 'the great Celtic phantasmagoria whose meaning no man has discovered, nor any angel revealed'.[19] Yet Yeats himself spoke, and wrote and read in English, and admitted that 'everything I love has come to me through English'.

For every pseudo-druidical Welsh eisteddfod (dating back to all of 1792), which celebrated native poetry and song, huge numbers were engaging with Anglo-Saxon reality. So great has been the intermarriage that it is virtually impossible to be sure how many pure-bred Celts still exist. Their history is one of relentless reverse – the last native Cornish speaker died in 1777, the last speaker of Manx in 1974, the last speaker of Deeside Gaelic in 1984. There are more native speakers of Chinese in Northern Ireland than there are native speakers of Irish. Whatever vigour remains in the languages survives as a consequence of political ideology and the subsidy of English taxpayers, as the Welsh-language television channel and the great number of Irish speakers among former IRA prisoners attest.

Against these ancient cultures, the English seemed to have developed a culture which had become world-beating. And it was because the English dominated the organization which dominated so much of the world that the words 'England' and 'Britain' were soon being used interchangeably. Walter Bagehot's monumental work on the relationship between Parliament, the crown and the courts of the United Kingdom – still the classic introduction to the subject, despite being over 100 years old – is called *The English Constitution*. In the 1920s Andrew Bonar Law, a Canadian of Scots-Ulster descent, and therefore, one might have thought, sensitive about these things, was happy to be called 'Prime Minister of England'. In the 1930s, the *Oxford History of England* began to appear: it deals with Scottish universities under the heading of English education, and the internal affairs of colonies as part of English history.

But the artificiality of any belief in Anglo-Saxon racial purity becomes clear the moment you start to examine the roots of the English people. The original inhabitants of the country do not seem to have been a particularly advanced civilization. Some amulets, toe-rings and bracelets that survive from Celtic Britain have a certain simple charm. But its priests encouraged human sacrifice and cannibalism. The most sophisticated tribe, the Belgae in Kent, grew wheat and flax, and while they could tend cattle, they were, apparently, incapable of making cheese and knew nothing about horticulture. That was the height of 'English' sophistication before the arrival of the Romans, and the further you travelled from the south coast, the more 'uncivilized' the tribes became. It is not necessary to make a long list of the benefits of Roman rule, for the evidence is there on any map of England. And in drawing a border from the Tyne to the

Solway, the Romans included 'England' inside the limits of the civilized world, and left Scotland outside. England owes its existence as a single entity to foreign invasion.

But the Romans do not, of course, qualify as 'English'. How many remained when, after 400 years, the decision was taken that the colony was no longer worth defending against the attacks of Saxons, Irish and Picts we do not know, but in strictly ethnic terms they cannot, surely, be considered to be part of the English race, whatever it is. According to eighth-century historians, the first 'English' English arrived in England in three small ships that bumped ashore on the pebbles of Pegwell Bay in Kent in the middle of the fifth century. They, too, were warriors. The two or three hundred soldiers who plashed up the beach had either (according to one account) been invited in by King Vortigern to repel Pictish raiders, or (according to another) been offered refuge as exiles. Either way, the first thing you discover about the English, is that they are not English – in the sense of coming from England – at all. They had arrived from Jutland, Anglen and Lower Saxony. The 'English race', if such a thing exists, is German.

These first English people certainly demonstrated characteristics which have reasserted themselves periodically through the English story. Firstly, they showed early symptoms of that urge to smash things which seizes the country from time to time, whether in the destruction of the monasteries or the levelling of town centres in the 1960s. In the case of the Angles, Saxons and Jutes, it was the demolition of the cities built during the Roman occupation, when they tore down stone dwellings and threw up wooden buildings organized around feudal clan structures. Their advances in agriculture – the development of ploughing and crop-rotation – must count as worthwhile achievements. But the fairy tale of Pope Gregory's appreciation of the handsomeness of the English when he saw captured slaveboys on sale in a Rome street-market ('They are not Angles but angels') does nothing to disguise the fact that Augustine and the fellow missionaries given the mission to convert these 'angels', thought they were travelling to the end of the civilized world.

The reputation of the invaders went before them as a result of their plundering raids along the coast. Vortigern's idea may have been to lure them in as allies with the promise of land and supplies, but within nine years, they had already displayed a second characteristic for which their enemies despise the English, and perfidiously revolted. Vortigern bought them off by offering Kent to their king, Hengist. With pickings so easy, more invaders followed and divided the country between them. The West Saxons held the area known as Wessex, the East Saxons had Essex, the South Saxons had Sussex and the Middle Saxons, what became known as Middlesex. To the north lay the Kingdom of Mercia, to the east were the Angles, and, further north, the kingdom of Northumbria.

The next wave of foreign invaders, from Norway and Denmark, fought their way across England and left their spoor in about 1,400 towns or villages with Scandinavian placenames. Over 400 of them remain in Yorkshire, where places like Wether*by* and Sel*by* incorporate *by*, the Danish word for village, 300 in Lincolnshire where Mable*thorpe* and Scun*thorpe* recall hamlets – *thorp*s in Danish – with more in Norfolk and Northamptonshire. So, by the time of the most celebrated invasion, that of the Normans in 1066, there was less an indigenous English people than a ragout, part Celtic Briton (part pre-Celtic, even), part Roman, partly Angles, Saxons and Jutes, partly Scandinavian. All the Norman Conquest could do was to add a little seasoning.

For almost 900 years after the Norman Conquest the population remained remarkably stable. Elsewhere in Europe borders were repeatedly redrawn. France, for example, only took formal sovereignty over Nice in 1860, while Alsace-Lorraine was under German rule from 1871 to 1918 and again from 1940 to 1945. England, centrally administered since the Conquest and with manageable borders in the comparatively small distances where they were not defined by the sea, was a much more stable entity. It was thus able to remain profoundly ignorant of other races. Civic leaders in Hartlepool are still trying to live down the story that when a live monkey was washed ashore from a shipwreck during the Napoleonic wars, local people hanged it from a gallows on the beach, on the grounds that since it had been unable to understand their questions, it must have been a French spy.

Had the monkey been a deaf-and-dumb Englishman, what might have saved him from hanging? Stripped naked, is there any English type? Long before the Saxons, Vikings, Normans and the rest had arrived, Tacitus remarked upon the physical diversity of the island the Romans had occupied: he thought it reflected the different genetic inheritances of their roots. Yet still we generalize that the Welsh are shorter and darker than the English, particularly the fairer English from the parts of the island heavily settled by the Saxons and Scandinavians, or that red hair is evidence of Celtic ancestry. Portraits of those English wealthy enough to have been immortalized in oils do seem to show some characteristics shining through, despite Oscar Wilde's disdain about the English face ('once seen, never remembered'). However plain, the women tend to be shown with long necks, while the men are more bothered about showing off their houses or horses. But it is the job of the artist to please his patron and we cannot be sure how far family portraits tell the truth, anyway. There is a constant refrain from foreign visitors about how the wet climate has given English women a stunningly rich complexion; the consistent defect noted is that so many of them seem to have such big feet.

Rushing in where angels fear to tread, in 1939 an American ethnologist felt confident enough to declare that 'although the British are quite variable in facial form, the features by which a foreigner would remember them would be a longness and narrowness of head and face, floridity, and a pinched prominence of nose'.[20] Apart from the flushed complexion, it does not really convey John Bull. In 1998, pathologists from Manchester University produced the first facial reconstruction of 'Cheddar Man', the skeleton of a Stone Age man who had died in the Cheddar Gorge, Somerset, some 9,000 years earlier. They concluded he had been almost six feet tall, with a 'slightly lopsided head, broad face, rounded forehead and a blobby nose'. The scientist leading the team commented that he 'probably looked pretty much like any modern inhabitant of a Somerset pub', which led to howls of anguished protest from Somerset publicans. After twenty years living in England and studying English portraiture, the German *émigré* Nikolaus Pevsner decided that you could confidently attribute physical characteristics to the 'English race':

To this day [he wrote], there are two distinct racial types recognizable in England, one tall with long head and long features, little display and little gesticulation, the other round-faced, more agile and more active. The proverbial Englishman of ruddy complexion and indomitable health, busy in house and garden and garage with his own hands in his spare time and devoted to outdoor sports, is of the second type. In popular mythology this type is John Bull.[21]

This is painting with a very broad brush: there are a dozen other archetypes, too. And if it really was possible fifty or a hundred years ago to discern something of an Englishman from his facial and body appearance, it was much more likely to be a deduction about social class than anything else. The wealthy ate well and prospered. The poor ate badly and it showed. That thin Old Etonian George Orwell remarked, with the sort of sweeping condescension of which only someone of his background was capable, that 'the prevailing physical type does not agree with the caricatures, for the tall, lanky physique which is traditionally English is almost confined to upper classes: the working people, as a rule, are rather small, with short limbs and brisk movements, and with a tendency among the women to grow dumpy in early middle life'.[22] (This is getting dangerously close to the John Glashan cartoon in which two well-dressed women pass a group of workmen digging a hole in the ground. 'I think working-class people are wonderful,' says the first. 'Yes, I love the sharp animal-like way their eyes dart about,' says the second.)

A eugenicist would have to conclude that in strictly racial terms, the English are a lost cause. Despite the long period of relative insulation, they remain an undistinguished-looking lot. Daniel Defoe had a much more accurate idea of the ethnic origins of the English three centuries ago. When he heard English people disdaining foreigners as having corrupted blood, he described 'the most scoundrel race that ever lived', the English.

> In between rapes and furious lust begot,
> Betwixt a painted *Briton* and a *Scot*:
> Whose gend'ring offspring quickly learnt to bow,
> And yoke their heifers to the *Roman* plough:
> From whence a mongrel half-bred race there came,
> With neither name nor nation, speech or fame
> In whose hot veins now mixtures quickly ran
> Infus'd betwixt a *Saxon* and a *Dane*.
> While their rank daughters, to their parents just,
> Receiv'd all nations with promiscuous lust.
> This nauseous brood directly did contain
> The well-extracted blood of Englishmen . . .
> . . . A True Born Englishman's a contradiction!
> In speech, an irony! In fact, a fiction![23]

There are plenty of other contributors one could add to Defoe's list of antecedents – immigrants from Flanders in the fourteenth and sixteenth centuries, Huguenots fleeing persecution in France in the seventeenth century or, later, Jewish refugees from eastern Europe. Any sensible reading of history would have to conclude that for the English to talk of racial purity is whistling in the wind; there is scarcely a family in the land which has no Celtic blood in it, to say nothing of Romans, Jutes, Normans, Huguenots, and all the others who have added their contribution to the national bloodstock. Defoe was right. The English are a mongrel race, and it has taken the development of communities living in England that are visibly different to demonstrate the point.

CHAPTER FOUR

'TRUE BORN ENGLISHMEN'
AND OTHER LIES

For he might have been a Roosian,
A French, or Turk, or Proosian,
Or perhaps Ital-ian!
But in spite of all temptations
To belong to other nations,
He remains an Englishman!

SIR WILLIAM SCHWENCK GILBERT (1836–1911),
HMS Pinafore

Bernie Grant, the most colourful of Britain's post-war black MPs, once found himself invited to a reception for Commonwealth parliamentarians. He had represented the tough inner-London seat of Tottenham for five years, during which time he had established a reputation for shooting from the hip which had made him one of the best-known backbenchers in Parliament. The Queen and the Duke of Edinburgh passed among the politicians, shaking hands. The Duke was the first to arrive in front of Grant.

'And who are you?' asked the Duke in his usual offhand manner.

'I'm Bernie Grant, MP,' he answered proudly.

To which the Duke responded, 'And in which country is that?'

Grant took the Duke of Edinburgh's ignorance in good part, but it was symptomatic. Even locked up in Buckingham Palace, the Queen's consort must have occasionally looked out of the window or read the papers, and been aware that about 6 per cent of the

English population isn't white and could not in any sense be said to belong to an English, Scots or Welsh 'race'. (Neither, of course, can he: on marrying Princess Elizabeth, Prince Philip had been required formally to renounce his claim to the Greek throne and to stop using his title from the House of Schleswig-Holstein-Sonderburg-Glucksburg.) But in a gathering of politicians from around the globe he was unable to imagine that his own adopted country could be represented by someone with a black skin. You can imagine the Duke, whose ability to make clumsy comments is legendary, telling the story against himself in the exclusively white circles of Buckingham Palace, doubtless proving that 'they all look the same'.

To her credit, the Queen did a lot better when she was introduced, immediately volunteering, in a splendid reversal of roles, 'You're Bernie Grant, aren't you? I've seen you on the telly.'

Grant, a one-time telephonist and trade union firebrand, had arrived in the House of Commons in 1987, through an apprenticeship in London councils and some deft behind-stairs intrigue that left a knife sticking out of the back of the man who was supposed to inherit the safe Labour seat of Tottenham. He was destined to become a hate figure for the right wing not so much because of the colour of his skin but for the fact that he *identified* with the black community. In the remark that will haunt him to the grave, when a group of predominantly black young men rioted on Broadwater Farm housing estate, he remarked that 'the police got a bloody good hiding'. One of the officers, PC Keith Blakelock, had died horrifically, stabbed and hacked to death by the frenzied crowd. The comment was enough to make Grant a pariah, and his hard-left political beliefs earned him the title Barmy Bernie from the *Sun*.

If anyone might be expected to encapsulate the meaning of being black and British, it is Bernard Alexander Montgomery Grant, his middle two names having been given him by wartime parents who wanted to honour two British field marshals. To his parents, he was always 'Monty'. Having become the first black council leader in

Britain, Grant was determined to celebrate his arrival in Parliament in suitable style. At one of his earliest State Openings of Parliament, when the British Establishment dress up in their traditional robes and funny hats, he had made a pact with the two other black MPs that they would all wear traditional African dress. When the day dawned, in Grant's words 'they chickened out', and he was left as the only male MP not wearing a suit and tie but resplendent in batakari, the brightly coloured cotton robes of West Africa. It was as explicit a statement as you could get that Britain was now a multiracial society. If some MPs looked sniffy, the Speaker, Bernard Weatherill, seemed to have no doubts. He scribbled a note and sent it down. It said, 'Congratulations! You look splendid.'

But his successor as Speaker, the Labour MP Betty Boothroyd, was less sure-footed. Introduced to him at another reception she chatted away, plainly unaware that he was a parliamentary colleague, even a member of the same political party. Later, when Sharon, Grant's white partner, went to the ladies' lavatory, she found Boothroyd having a quick cigarette. 'You didn't know who he was, did you?' she asked. 'Of course I did,' said the Speaker, 'he's the former High Commissioner from Sierra Leone.'

Bernie Grant's presence in England was the consequence of empire. But none of this English identity crisis would have happened had the British Empire not disappeared. This is not the place for another piece of imperial pathology; the British have grown accustomed to looking back at their former eminence as the traveller looked at the two vast legs in the desert that were all that remained of the statue of Ozymandias, king of kings. 'Look on my works, ye Mighty, and despair!' declaimed the words on the pedestal, while all around, 'the lone and level sands stretch far away'. Certainly, the decline in earthly power has been precipitous. In 1900, half the ships on the high seas were registered in Britain, and the country controlled about one third of world trade. By 1995, the share had dropped to under 5 per cent. Kings across the Continent tried to ape the British monarch by building an empire: the Belgians seized one of the few fetid corners of Africa that neither the British nor French had collared; Wilhelm II of Germany set about building a fleet to rival the Royal Navy. Even as late as 1935 Mussolini was raining bombs and poison gas down on a medieval army in Abyssinia in pursuit of an empire he thought would give Italy a moral authority equal to that of the British.

But British power and influence went beyond earthly dominion. They more or less invented much of the modern world. 'We were all born in a world made in England and the world in which our great-grandchildren will mellow into venerable old age will be as English as the Hellenistic world was Greek, or, better, Athenian', is the way one academic puts it.[1] They developed the current forms of soccer and rugby, tennis, boxing, golf, horse-racing, mountaineering and skiing. The English created modern tourism with the Grand Tour and Thomas Cook's first package tour. They developed the first modern luxury hotel (the Savoy with electric lights, six lifts and seventy bedrooms). Charles Babbage produced the world's first computer in the 1820s. A Scot, John Logie Baird, was one of the inventors of television, in an attic in Hastings. He held his first public demonstration in Soho, London. Sandwiches, Christmas cards, Boy Scouts, postage stamps, modern insurance and detective novels are all products 'Made in England'. When the Italian writer Luigi Barzini was searching for a way to demonstrate the dominance of British culture he merely noted that when, in the third decade of the nineteenth century, the rest of Europe adopted funereal black as the main colour of men's clothes, it was a form of homage.[2] It recognized not merely the political and military might of the Empire and the economic clout of British steam, coal and steel, it advertised the perceived British virtues – honesty, prudence, patriotism, self-control, fair play and courage – which had made the nation great.

In their gloomier moments, the English tend to think that all that remains of their contribution to the world is a little ullage – the names of a few grand hotels – the Bristol, Cambridge, Grande Bretagne – the international codifications of time and place, fathoms and uniforms, and the fact that English is the language of the third millennium. Now, *le style Anglais* exists only as fashion shorthand: the sort of people you see in tailor-made tweeds tend to be affluent Germans with a background in machine-tool manufacturing. Even the schools which tried to mass-produce English gentlemen, driven by the spirit of the amateur, now preach that the only way to survive is by professionalism in a meritocratic world.

By and large, the British have handled the end of Empire well, bowing to the inevitable, running down the flag and packing their bags with relatively little fuss. But the psychological consequences for themselves have taken much longer to deal with. It would have been a great deal easier for the English to cope with had the whole enterprise not been invested with such extraordinary moral purpose.

The Empire was created by initiative, greed, courage, mass production, powerful armed forces, political scheming and self-confidence. A technologically advanced country with few natural resources needed a big trading area. And the technology made the subjugation of 'primitive' peoples inevitable. The image engraved on the hearts of patriots was that of General Gordon making his last stand on the steps of a fort in Khartoum, as heathen savages overwhelmed the gallant British garrison. In fact, what made Britain rule the world was better displayed at the battle of Omdurman twelve years later. Although mainly hymned for the unsuccessful charge of the 21st Lancers – in which Winston Churchill was a young officer – what determined the outcome was the fact that the British happened to have six Maxim guns. As the Dervish forces rushed the lines, the gunners had only to get the range. The casualty figures tell it all: 28 British dead for *11,000* Dervish dead. 'It was not a battle but an execution,' wrote an eyewitness. 'The bodies were not in heaps – bodies hardly ever are; but they spread evenly over acres and acres.'[3]

I do not wish to deny the courage and verve of many of the empire-builders. It is just that the history of imperialism is the alliance of self-interest and technology. But what gave the British Empire its belief in itself was the delusion that it was driven by a moral purpose, that there was a God-ordained duty to go out and colonize those places unfortunate enough not to have been born under the flag. The assumption of superiority became an article of faith. When the United States looked as if it was beginning to amass an empire by annexing the Philippines in 1898, Kipling paid the compliment of including the country among those called by destiny to 'Take up the White Man's burden – Send forth the best ye breed' – to 'serve' peoples who were 'half-devil and half-child'.[4]

The Empire gave the English the chance to feel blessed. And the greater its success, the more blessed they felt. By the end of the nineteenth century the British (for which read English) way of doing things was a model for the rest of the world. Visitors to London were bowled over by the sheer affluence of the place and often made a connection between prosperity and moral purpose. 'As the heart is to the physical structure of man, so England is to the political and moral organization of Europe,' gushed a Polish exile to his enslaved countrymen. 'The wealth of England has passed into proverb; her monetary resources are unlimited; her capital in possession, invested, or floating upon the waters, is inconceivably enormous.'[5] All of which tended to make the English, who naturally assumed that what was actually being described was a list of specifically English characteristics, believe that somehow all other races were just aspirant Englishmen and Englishwomen.

Long before the English had begun accumulating worldwide possessions, foreign visitors had been commenting on their idiosyncrasies. The fact of being islanders had inevitably made them different, insulated from currents that swept over the rest of Europe: by the time an intellectual typhoon that had blown over the Continent crossed the Channel, it could be no more than a directionless zephyr. Self-containment gave the English the chance to change selectively. And now they found themselves masters of the greatest empire in the world. No wonder it went to their heads. To have been born English, said Cecil Rhodes, was to have won first prize in the lottery of life. They began to believe they had some divinely ordered mission to discharge. Even those, like John Ruskin, who entertained dreams of social reform at home (at one stage he tried to create an English utopia by enrolling supporters in a guild under the cross of St George) succumbed. As he put it in an Oxford lecture in 1870:

There is a destiny now possible to us, the highest ever set before a nation, to be accepted or refused. We are still undegenerate in race, a race mingled of the best northern blood. This is what England must either do or perish; she must found colonies as fast and as far as she is able, formed of her most energetic and worthiest men . . . their first aim must be to advance the power of England by land and sea.[6]

Cecil Rhodes went further, asserting as bald, indisputable fact that 'we happen to be the best people in the world, with the highest ideals of decency and justice and liberty and peace'. It therefore followed logically that, as Rosebery was to observe in 1884, the Empire was 'the greatest secular agency for good the world has seen'.[7] Grand statements like these blithely ignored one or two simple truths about the imperial project, notably the fact that it was built not to some messianic plan but accumulated as the result of individual acts by young men who saw it as a route to adventure and riches.

Furthermore, while the young men who built the Empire may have carried all sorts of misplaced ideas about their own superiority, they were prone to the same emotional and physical needs as young men anywhere. The belief – if they held it – that they were 'the best people in the world' did not stop them taking their trousers off. Men who went to work for the Hudson's Bay Company, for example, in

Canada, soon began to avail themselves of the local custom of offering sexual hospitality. Many acquired local Indian 'wives' with whom they might have families, and for whom they would provide when they returned to England at the end of their tour of duty.[8] Sir James Brooke, the man who almost singlehandedly brought Sarawak under British influence, simply by buying a boat, sailing there and getting himself made rajah, had a private secretary with a native mistress and openly declared his ambition 'to amalgamate races'. He actively discouraged white wives accompanying their husbands in their postings. The colonial community in East Africa quickly showed the loucheness which would distinguish it into the 1930s. When Richard Meinertzhagen arrived in 1902, he found that most of his brother officers were 'regimental rejects, heavily in debt; one drinks like a fish, one prefers boys to women and is not ashamed. On arrival here I was amazed and shocked to find that they all brought their native women into the mess'.[9]

Some soldiers posted to the Orient also soon decided that other rules applied once they were safely beyond the reach of English society. Posted to India in the 1830s, Captain Edward Sellon discovered that eastern courtesans

understand in perfection all the arts and wiles of love, are capable of gratifying any tastes, and in face and figure they are unsurpassed by any women in the world . . . It is impossible to describe the enjoyment I have experienced in the arms of these syrens. I have had English, French, German and Polish women of all grades of society since, but never, never did they bear a comparison with those salacious succulent houris.[10]

It is difficult, to say the least, to reconcile this account of the pleasures of imperial service with Sir Charles Dilke's conviction that there was a natural 'antipathy everywhere exhibited by the English to coloured races'.

What seems to have happened is that the more the British Empire became a responsibility of government instead of an adventure, the more conscious the governing bureaucracy became of the need to keep the English 'pure'. As possessions were accumulated abroad, morality was asserted at home. The evangelicalism of the early nineteenth century did much to purge English public life of the looseness of the eighteenth century, and the wave of puritanism which swept the country in the 1880s consigned the easy-going tolerance of earlier days to history. In January 1909, after a scandal in Kenya involving alleged abuse of power by a white official, Lord Crewe, Secretary of State for the Colonies, issued the circular that became known as 'The Morals Despatch' or 'The Concubine Circular'. 'Gravely improper conduct' was the term the memo used to describe the practice of colonial officers taking local mistresses, continuing that

it is not possible for any member of the administration to countenance such practices without lowering himself in the eyes of the natives, and diminishing his authority . . . it is his duty to set an honourable example to all with whom he comes into contact.[11]

The contrast with the attitude of the French could hardly be starker. The authorities in Paris concluded that the easiest and healthiest way to deal with the problem in their West African possessions was to encourage their officials to make temporary marriages with local women. In 1902, the French Colonial Office's Director of African Affairs (pun unintended) commended the advice of a Dr Barot to young men destined for service in the tropics. Unless capable of two years or more of celibacy, the safest thing was to marry a local woman. The arrangement protected the French officer from the 'alcoholism or sexual debauchery unfortunately so common in hot countries'. A native wife had the additional advantage of making the white man more popular: local men did not fear he would try to steal their own. There were also reasons of realpolitik: 'It should be remembered that most of the treaties signed with great Negro chiefs have been ratified by a white man's marriage with one of their daughters.' While there was no suggestion that the alliance was permanent ('On returning to France one sends the young lady back to her family, after making her a present which will immediately assure her of a husband'), there were predictable consequences of such marriages. The French government subsidized two schools especially to cater to the resultant mixed-race children, recognizing, said the wise doctor, that 'it is by creating mulatto races that we most easily Gallicise West Africa'.[12]

Lord Crewe, whose recreation was the selective breeding of shorthorn cattle, would doubtless have dismissed the advice as yet another example of the moral turpitude of the French. It was true that in India, the greatest British possession, a mixed-race Anglo-Indian class did develop, and came to be seen as a buffer between the rulers and the 'natives'. But in general, the British élite justified the Empire to itself as a sort of religious mission. In 1912 Lord Hugh Cecil summarized Britain's vocation in the world as 'to undertake the government of vast, uncivilised populations and to raise them gradually to a higher level of life'.[13] The obvious solution to the problem was for wives to accompany their husbands when they were posted to the outer reaches of empire: once the memsahibs were in place, the shutters went up. 'The white woman is perhaps the real ruin of empires' is the way one Australian put it after seeing what happened in New Guinea.[14]

By that stage, the English were mortally infected with the belief that they possessed some unique gift from God. As Ogden Nash wrote:

> Let us pause to consider the English.
> Who when they pause to consider themselves they get all reticently thrilled and tinglish,
> Because every Englishman is convinced of one thing, viz;
> That to be an Englishman is to belong to the most exclusive club there is.

The evidence of their superiority was all around. The British Empire was the greatest in the world. It was run from England. Ergo, Englishmen were superior to other races. Had the club not been so exclusive, had the English ideal not become so closely tied up with the need to empire-build, they might have found it easier to cope with the country's reduced status in the world. As it was, the end of the imperium seemed to suggest that there was no place for the Englishman or -woman in the world.

Michael Wharton, 'Peter Simple' of the *Daily Telegraph*, sits in the corner of the sitting room of his cottage, while outside the wind blows through the leaves of the Buckinghamshire beech trees. Forty years since he started his column, he still sends it in to the newspaper every week, not-so-secretly suspecting that it is kept on as a sort of period piece, a reassurance to the dwindling band of elderly readers who remember the paper when England was a different place. It appears, with its curious mix of news, comment and fantasy, buried away in increasingly obscure corners of the paper, like a dotty old relative given house-room by the young couple who've inherited the mansion. He has little sense these days of who, if anyone, reads his column. Occasional letters are forwarded from a secretary in the obelisk in London's Docklands where the paper is now exiled. 'They're mainly from lunatics. They imagine I want to bring back hanging and flogging. And they hate the Irish.'

The bigots who write to him sense a kindred spirit in Peter Simple. His idea of England is the authentic whine of a lost people. A typical lamentation reads as follows:

In the past 50 years they [the people of England] have seen everything that is distinctively English suppressed and derided. They have seen all the evils that flow from the gutters of America – vile entertainment, degenerate pop music, feminism, 'political correctness' – infect their country.

They have seen their decent manners and customs corrupted. They have seen sexual deviance elevated in official esteem and even officially commended. They have seen parts of their country colonised by immigrants and been forbidden by law to speak freely of the consequences.

All of this they have suffered and have not spoken yet. If they are going to speak now, they have left it very late. Unlikelier things have happened in the past; but not many.[15]

In the flesh, this horseman of the apocalypse turns out to be more baffled than furious, with gentle and courteous manners. When we met, I asked him what he thought about multiculturalism.

'Multiculturalism? The English people are always being told about it by politicians and bishops and the like, but it means absolutely nothing to most of them. It's a nonsense, an idea we've been force-fed but no one has accepted. The English are docile and easy-going, which I suppose is why it's happened.'

At this point, his blind old labrador walked into the room and collided with the television, which was covered by a large brown antimacassar.

The Peter Simple idea of England is, in essence, the England of Sir Arthur Bryant, the most popular of twentieth-century nationalist historians. (His lifetime output included over forty books, selling over 2 million copies.) It is only a small leap from Bryant's idea of an England of squires, parsons, yeomen and quaint, cider-drinking yokels – all of them off-white in complexion – to the conviction that all immigration by other colours is inevitably wrong. Arthur Byrant himself acknowledged the contribution that European refugees had made to English culture. But they, of course, were off-white in colour, too. Mass immigration from other cultures was something else. In March 1963, Bryant told readers of the *Illustrated London News* that 'an influx . . . of men and women of alien race, accentuated by strongly marked differences of pigmentation and mould of feature, as well as of habits and beliefs' would be very undesirable.[16]

Few influential people paid Bryant any heed. Every autumn, the Conservative party conference would be lapped by a swell of motions from the shires demanding Something Be Done to stop immigration. And every year, the hierarchy huddled together and then ignored them. In both 1963 and 1968 the hierarchs were obliged to make concessions and to promise curbs on immigration. In 1968, the spur had been the inflammatory speech by Enoch Powell, in which he had foreseen an apocalypse: 'As I look ahead, I am filled with foreboding. Like the Roman, I seem to see "the river Tiber foaming with much blood".'[17] The reference to the Aeneid may have been lost on most of his listeners, but what became known as 'the rivers of blood' speech caused outrage, and consigned Powell to the political wilderness, an example, said his followers, of the woolly-minded liberal conspiracy by the Establishment to ignore reality.

Only a fool would claim that there is not a significant section of the English population who still share Enoch Powell's belief that the influx of large numbers of members of alien cultures has been a mistake. In their mind, the issue of immigration is the explanation for the fact that the country has gone to the dogs. Yet, by and large, race relations in Britain are not bad. Despite their country's independence from Britain, 2 million Irish citizens living in the United Kingdom retained the right to vote, a privilege not reciprocated by the Irish government for seventy years. Many Irish citizens fought with British forces during the Second World War, a cataclysm quaintly referred to by the studiedly 'neutral' Irish government merely as 'The Emergency'. But it is not, of course, the Irish that people are talking about when they refer to race relations. The Irish are white, and what bothered Bryant and Powell and the rest was the arrival of people with a different-coloured skin.

They were certainly right about its suddenness. In 1951 the total population of Caribbean and South Asian people in Britain was 80,000, most of them living in a handful of cities and ports. Twenty years later, it had reached one and a half million. Forty years on, the 1991 census put the ethnic minority population at just over *3 million*. It is quite an explosion. Furthermore, rather than being spread across the United Kingdom, immigrants are concentrated in England – where ethnic minorities represent over 6 per cent of the population – and comparatively absent from Scotland and Wales. Over two thirds of the entire ethnic minority population of Britain is concentrated in the south-east of England and the West Midlands. Parts of cities like London, Leicester or Birmingham now appear to have no connection whatsoever with the England of Arthur Bryant. In these places, multiculturalism is much more than a pious utterance from bishops and politicians. It is a fact of life, in which the Church of England has been replaced by mosques or temples and the old corner grocers by halal butchers and sari shops. In Spitalfields, east London, where in the late seventeenth and early eighteenth century Huguenot refugees had set up a silk-weaving, 60 per cent of the population is now Bangladeshi. In parts of Bradford, over half the population comes from Pakistan. Yet these city districts are almost never entirely taken over by Asians, Africans or West Indians. There are only three local-government wards in the whole of England where fewer than one in five of the population is white (Northcote ward in Ealing, west London, has the highest concentration of non-white people, at 90 per cent).[18] Nowhere in England has reached the levels of the United States, where entire tracts of cities are exclusively black.

The laws of citizenship are also relatively liberal: anyone born in Britain to legally resident parents can become a British citizen. The contrast is with Germany. By early 1997 there were 7.2 million immigrants living in Germany – 9 per cent of the population. But those who tried to formalize their status found that it took them up to fifteen years' residence before they could even begin to apply for citizenship, and years more to obtain it. The reason is that long after Hitler brought the idea into opprobrium, German officialdom still clings to the belief that it acts on behalf of a '*Volk*', whose nationality is a question of blood. Your family may have been living in Kazakhstan for generations, but if you have the name Schmidt or Müller, you can acquire a German passport at once:[19] citizenship is genetically determined.

Generally the English can be proud of their achievements in the field of race relations. Sudden, large-scale immigration was not something that was thought through, and, without wanting to minimize the real problems that can still face members of ethnic-minority communities, the tensions could have been a great deal worse. All sorts of things have helped. The vigour of English regional accents and identities means that in one generation it is impossible to tell on the telephone the colour of a Mancunian, Liverpudlian or Brummie's skin. The country's exuberant youth culture is largely colour-blind. A rather English sensitivity helped: Robert Taylor, now a successful photographer, vividly remembers as an excited young chorister being invited to sing with his choir at Hereford Cathedral. As the choir was passing through the cathedral cloisters, the bishop's wife appeared, chasing a small black dog. 'Come here, Sambo,' she shouted, looked up and saw a single black child in the choir. 'Oh, I'm sorry,' she blurted out apologetically.

But it is still noticeable that while you will often meet a person who describes themselves as 'black British' or 'Bengali British', you rarely come across someone who says they are 'Black English'. Bernie Grant calls himself British, because 'it includes other oppressed peoples, like the Welsh or the Scots. It would stick in my throat to call myself English.' Others will tell you that as immigrants they can feel British, but that to believe yourself English, you need to have been born in the country, an attitude which applies as much to white immigrants as to black or Asian ones. British seems an inclusive term: just as you can be both Scottish or Welsh and still be British, so you can be Somali British or Bangladeshi British.

Of course, racial prejudice still exists. But what is striking about so many of these immigrants is their exuberant optimism about their adopted home. It is not merely that so few plan to return to the land they left, but that so many seem so much to appreciate what they have found in England. When, in January 1998, the *Daily Telegraph* decided to find out how immigrants had settled in, they heard an astonishingly positive response. Dr Zaki Badawi, chairman of the Council of Imams and Mosques, felt there was no better place in the world to be a Moslem: what he loved about the country was the fact that it could laugh at itself. Surinder Gill, an Oxfordshire grocer, appreciated the fact that he found the police unbribable. Abi Rosenthal, a musicologist who fled Germany, believed that qualities of fairness and discretion made England 'a far more civilized country than the one I'd come from'. Omnia Mazouk, a consultant paediatrician in Liverpool, thought it 'wonderful to be in a country where merit is rewarded and there are no jobs for the boys'. Hari Shukla, a Hindu teacher who left Kenya in 1973, said that while most of Europe was now multicultural, no other European country had achieved the same degree of integration.[20]

It is a long way from the world of Peter Simple, many of whose readers, I suspect, have probably never met an Asian or a West Indian, apart from the proprietor of the corner shop or an occasional bus conductor. They were prepared to see black or Asian people coming to England to do the jobs that English people did not wish to do. But they didn't expect they would come in such numbers, nor that they would bring their culture with them: what they seem to have expected were people who would have been English had they not happened not to have been born in England.

Their attitude, did they but know it, is not so far from Bernie Grant's belief in his 'Britishness'. The conviction lodged deep in their minds is that the Englishman or -woman is 'free-born' in a free society. The adopted citizen may be 'British', but that is something quite different. What they resent most of all is that some things have become unsayable and doubt about multiculturalism is one of them, left to be muttered in corners or grunted by thugs in tattoos and big leather boots. The tolerant beliefs of the ruling élite, who have worked to make discrimination illegal, have, by and large, triumphed. Over a Calvados in central London, the author Simon Raven was splenetic on the subject:

It's just thoroughly unEnglish to say you can't say some things. Free expression is part of the intellectual life of this country. We had two or three black people when I was at Cambridge, princes, that sort of thing. But they were gentlemen. In general, the English were happy to see black people, and happy to see the back of them, too.

That last sentence could have come straight from Peter Simple's column. Yet there is something odd about Michael Wharton's quizzical disdain for the new England that has evolved in the half-century he has been writing his column. For the dark secret about this apparently thoroughbred Englishman is that Wharton himself is half German, the descendant of Jews who did well in the Bradford wool trade. It is the same with so many who most loudly proclaim their Englishness. The journalist Peregrine Worsthorne, whose *Sunday Telegraph* columns thundered throughout the 1980s about the dangers to the integrity of England, had a father who rejoiced in the name of Colonel Koch de Gooreynd. Stephen Fry, who made his acting career playing the quintessential English butler, Jeeves, is half Hungarian-Jewish. The surname of that 'most English' of popular poets, John Betjeman, was German Dutch; the 'quintessentially English' architect Lutyens was descended from a Schleswig-Holstein family. Many of those Conservatives who shouted most loudly about protecting England from takeover by the European Union, like Michael Howard and Michael Portillo, came from immigrant families. Those lines about 'remaining an Englishman' were set to music by Sir Arthur Sullivan, whose mother came from an old Italian family.

It is a roundabout way of saying that the sentiments in W. S. Gilbert's song were right when they talked about resisting the temptation to belong to other nations. Being English *is* a matter of choice.

CHAPTER FIVE

WE HAPPY FEW

*The people of England are never so happy as when you tell
them they are ruined.*
ARTHUR MURRAY, The Upholsterer, 1758

If being English is a state of mind, the question to ask is what they
think makes them who they are. I started trying to find out by taking
a trip to Cheltenham and the offices of the most unfashionable
quarterly magazine in the country.

When *This England* was founded in 1967 under the slogan AS
REFRESHING AS A CUP OF TEA!, it proclaimed its ambition to
'capture the true spirit of England in every edition'. Drawing its title
from the dying John of Gaunt's lyrical speech in *Richard II* ('This
blessed plot, this earth, this realm, This England, this nurse, this
teeming womb of royal kings'), the magazine's softly stated ambition
was to be 'wholesome, straightforward and gentle'.[1] Inside, there
was much use of the classic opening threnody 'a century ago . . . but
now', plentiful illustrations in a sub-Norman Rockwell style, and the
promise, 'I hope you like our choice for a book serial . . . a pre-First
World War story of a cheeky Cockney called Edwards who reveals
his confessions as a jobbing gardener!'

This astonishingly flaccid pitch turned the magazine into a remarkable commercial success, with each quarterly issue selling up to a
quarter of a million copies. Thirty years on, each edition was still
selling more than the combined sales of each edition of the *Spectator*,

New Statesman, *Country Life* and *Tatler* added together. The editor, whose inspired hunch had invented the thing, described his readers as 'not just dukes, but wonderful dustmen as well, and pensioners from the East End, and judges and ferry boatmen, and vicars' wives in remote missionary stations, and royalty and shopgirls, and lads and lassies from Lancashire and all over the globe . . . decent, God-fearing, plain-speaking crusaders whether they wear mitres or mini-skirts'.[2] The metropolitan response to this studiedly provincial blast came from the *Sunday Times*'s Atticus column: 'it's alright for the wonderful dustmen. They have a wonderful place to put it.'

The magazine has learned to shrug off this sort of sneering, comforted by the steady sales graphs, the lucrative sidelines of St George ties, tieclips and lapel badges and the sacks of unsolicited mail which arrive every week. To a casual reader, it can look as if the thing is written by its readers, none of whom is burdened by a training in journalism. There are many wartime memories and much patriotic enthusiasm for royalty, folk-customs and village life. But its quiet, chocolate-box style and banner, 'Britain's loveliest magazine', belie an astounding editorial robustness. The promise of sentiment-ality cloaks a torrent of outrage. Ploughing through the whimsy you make a remarkable discovery – if this really is England speaking to itself, not only does the country keep looking backwards, it *enjoys* feeling persecuted. The photographs are designed to reassure – lots of sheep grazing in front of country churches, streams babbling through southern villages, beefeaters in scarlet and gold tunics. But the copy speaks a much more apocalyptic message: England is about to vanish for ever.

We are in the middle of a carefully-crafted plot going back many years which is designed to create an easily manageable, European super-state to be run like a socialist republic. That means one overall (but unelected) government, one puppet parliament, one federal army, navy and air force, one central bank, a single currency and one supreme court of law. Our precious Monarchy will be replaced by a President on the Continent, the

Union Jack will be banned in favour of that horrid blue rag with those 12 nasty yellow stars and we shall all have to sing the new Euro anthem to the tune of Beethoven's *Ode to Joy* . . . except that its title will really mean 'Goodbye Britain'.[3]

The people who will bring this catastrophe about are our 'quisling' national politicians. But the sense of embattled persecution doesn't stop there. A regular feature, 'Our English Heroes', tells the stories of people like the lone boy sailor awarded a posthumous VC. There is alarming news that the European Commission is trying to make the English bulldog an illegal breed, because they 'prefer the fluffy little French poodle which always does as it's told'. The magazine has its own 'Silver Cross of St George', awarded to heroes nominated by readers, like the retailer who defies regulations by continuing to sell paraffin by the gallon, instead of in litres. It worries about the fact that the BBC fails to mark St George's Day. Even 'The Battle for the Real Counties of Britain', a campaign to restore ancient county names, is written in the language of the jackboot, with enemies all around and all-powerful – 'officialdom, the Post Office, politicians, journalists, teachers, television newsreaders' – who have succumbed to the mistaken belief that local government has been reorganized. 'Schoolchildren, defenceless against such an onslaught, were taken by the hand and led by their teachers into "Cleveland", "Merseyside", the "West Midlands".'[4] It sounds as if they were being led into the gas chambers.

The enemy, of course, is really the march of time – not a single article looks forward to the future. The magazine has a profitable sideline in tapes by Eric Coates ('England's Master of Light Music'), the Forces' Sweetheart, Vera Lynn, Billy 'Wakey Wakey' Cotton, Victor Sylvester, Henry Hall and dozens of others, advertised alongside its bestselling cassette, *This Was Our Finest Hour*, 'a unique triple album of memories and melodies that inspired the British people to Victory in the Second World War'. Apart from a handful of services ('LOST YOUR MEDALS? WE CAN REPLACE THEM NOW!',

'HAVE YOU WRITTEN YOUR MEMOIRS? WE CAN ARRANGE PUBLICATION'), the limited number of advertisements are mainly appeals from military benevolent funds and animal sanctuaries to be remembered in readers' wills.

Roy Faiers, who invented this strange but curiously successful formula, was sitting at his desk in a Victorian mansion in Cheltenham eating a slice of Women's Institute fruit cake when I arrived. It had been easy to find the house because it was the only one in the street flying the British flag from the roof. I don't know what I'd expected, some mixture of G. K. Chesterton and Genghis Khan, I suppose. I remembered a letter in one of the back-issues in which a satisfied reader had said he would like to see a copy of the magazine available in every school, library and hospital in the land, on the grounds that he saw *This England* as 'the British equivalent of Hitler's *Mein Kampf*, but, of course, based on Christian Principles'. But instead of Adolf Hitler, he turned out to be silver-haired, affable and easy-going. Apart from sudden protestations like 'Oh, the Queen Mother! We all love her . . .', he was quiet, thoughtful and likeable.

There were three union flags and a Cross of St George on his bookshelves, a photograph of the Queen on the wall, and plenty of books about dance bands. When he told me that at one time he had been fishing correspondent for the *Grimsby Telegraph* it did not seem surprising.

Roy Faiers had also concluded that Englishness was not a matter of race. His magazine, which sells nearly 20,000 copies in Australia, and many thousands more in other parts of the old Empire, obviously appeals to expats, by keeping alive a memory of the quieter, slower country they left behind. But Faiers had decided that you didn't have to be English to be 'English'. 'The actor James Stewart, for example, he was American, but he had Englishness. He didn't brag about himself. He wasn't pushy. He had one wife all his life. You could trust him with your wallet. That's English.' This is certainly how the English like to think of themselves – gallant, upstanding, modest, absolutely trustworthy and with impeccable manners. It is the ideal of the English gentleman. But, by itself, it does not quite answer the question of what Englishness is. Plainly, it cannot simply be a question of class.

'For years, George Formby was the most successful performer in Britain. He was diffident about his fame and he didn't like to show off his wealth. But his wife did – no diffidence at all. He was English. She wasn't.' I could see what he was getting at, although it struck me as hard on the woman. After all, while George Formby had been awarded the Order of Lenin for popularity with the Russian proletariat, she had the authentically English distinction of being World Clog Dancing Champion. So what, I asked him, was Englishness?

'Englishness is very deep. It's a spirit, the spirit of St George. The idea of St George is a fight against evil.'

Whether it's true or not, this is interesting. Quite why St George became the patron saint of England is a mystery. Edward Gibbon's description of him as a corrupt bacon supplier to the Roman army who later became Archbishop of Alexandria, subsequently murdered by a mob, is nowadays discredited. A history of the Catholic calendar portrays him in a more favourable light – horribly tortured and martyred for protesting the murder of fellow Christians by the Roman emperor Diocletian. In England, he seems to have been venerated for his courage, long before the Norman Conquest. But it was knights returning from the Crusades who popularized the George and the Dragon myth, which was perhaps a Christian version of the legend of Perseus' rescue of Andromeda from a sea monster. There does seem to have been some genuine enthusiasm for him – Edward III made George patron saint of the Order of the Garter and built St George's Chapel at Windsor in the middle of the fourteenth century. As late as 1614 blue coats were still being worn in the saint's honour on 23 April. But George never set foot in England and also does duty as the patron saint of Portugal, as well as being at one time or another the guardian of Malta, Sicily, Genoa, Venice, Aragon, Valencia and Barcelona. He is a vague, workaday figure, of little spiritual or theological importance.

But when you look back at how the English like to portray themselves, you can see why St George was a convenient sort of patron saint. In identifying with their adopted hero they could assume for themselves a mantle of valiant integrity. It is striking how many of the crucial battles of English history, from the Spanish Armada in 1588 to the Blitz in 1940, have been presented as a struggle of David against Goliath. Angus Calder makes the following list of opposites to show how the English saw themselves and the Germans during the Second World War:

ENGLAND	GERMANY
Freedom	Tyranny
Improvisation	Calculation
Volunteer spirit	Drilling
Friendliness	Brutality
Tolerance	Persecution
Timeless landscape	Mechanisation
Patience	Aggression
Calm	Frenzy
A thousand years of peace	The Thousand Year Reich[5]

Whether it accorded with reality or not, it seems to have been important to the English to believe that, like St George, they had been roused from their bucolic idyll to fight monsters.

In one of the most celebrated summons to battle in the English language, Shakespeare has Henry V urge his men on to attack Harfleur with the words, 'God for Harry! England and St George!' It is the most economical patriotic quadrivium possible – God, homeland, monarch and sense of moral purpose. But Harfleur, which the English had besieged during their invasion of France in September 1415, really fell when it was starved into surrender. Henry then marched his troops towards the English garrison at Calais, when they found the way barred by a vastly greater force of French troops between the villages of Agincourt and Tramecourt. English propaganda, with which Shakespeare was familiar, probably exaggerated the scale of the French numerical superiority, but modern estimates suggest that the English army of some 6,000 men was set against a force of between 40,000 and 50,000. On the eve of the battle of Agincourt, Shakespeare tackles the idea of bravery-against-the-odds. Walking in on a meeting of his senior officers, Henry hears them talking anxiously about the French superiority in numbers. Not only are the English outnumbered, the French troops are all fresh, while the English are battle-weary. Westmoreland sighs for reinforcements:

> O! that we now had here
> But one ten thousand of those men in England
> That do no work today.

Henry cuts in by saying he doesn't want a single additional soldier, because the more soldiers there are, the more the honour will have to be shared. Rather, 'he which hath no stomach to this fight' may leave at once, all expenses paid, and return to England; he would prefer not to risk his life in that man's company. Those who remain will acquire a shared dignity: anyone shedding his blood with the king will become the king's brother. In the hierarchical context of the late sixteenth century, it is an astonishing proclamation. The call to arms, 'We few, we happy few, we band of brothers', has become the rallying cry of the English idea of heroism.

Agincourt turned out a famous victory. Although pinned between two hills, the English mounted attacks from either wing, their archers rained down a ceaseless torrent of arrows, and the French forces were uncoordinated and ill-disciplined. In less than three hours' fighting it was all over. The French dead included three dukes, nearly a dozen counts, 1,500 knights and up to 5,000 men-at-arms. English accounts of the battle talk of their casualties being fewer than forty, although more modern estimates put the total at more like two or three hundred. Whether because he feared the arrival of French reinforcements or for other reasons, Henry ordered that most of the French prisoners be killed. Bishop Beaufort told Parliament the French defeat was punishment from God.

The most celebrated modern reinvention of the Few was made on 20 August 1940, when Winston Churchill praised the Battle of Britain fighter pilots. The Germans had taken the Channel Islands at the end of June that year, and Hitler's order to prepare an invasion of England (Operation Sea Lion) came soon afterwards. The Luftwaffe's first task was to neutralize the RAF and take over forward airfields from which the British might mount a counter-attack. Goering thought it could be done in four days. With almost 3,000 aircraft at his command and those on the French coast within twenty-five minutes' striking distance of England, it did not look an extravagant boast.

On the first day, the Germans met much stronger opposition than they had expected, losing 75 aircraft to the RAF's 34. Yet still the waves of attackers roared in. Churchill's preferred vantage point was the Operations Room of No. 11 Group, Fighter Command. His staff officer, General Ismay, recalled a visit on 16 August, when

at one moment every single squadron in the group was engaged; there was nothing in reserve, and the map table showed new waves of attackers crossing the coast. I felt sick with fear. As the evening closed in, the fighting died down, and we left by car for Chequers. Churchill's first words were 'Don't speak to me; I have never been so moved.' After about five minutes he leaned forward and said, 'Never in the field of human conflict was so much owed by so many to so few.' The words burned into my brain.[6]

Well they might, for they make up the most resonant sentence to have emerged from the Second World War. Churchill's speechwriting involved perhaps weeks of what his secretary, John Colville, called 'fertilising a phrase'. But although he spent days polishing the rest of the speech he delivered to Parliament on 20 August 1940, that sentence appeared unchanged. It needed no work, for it said it all, recognizing the courage of the pilots in their flimsy fighters and at the same time speaking to a profound sense of a small island surrounded by menace, but unbowed. In fact, in purely numerical terms, under the direction of the Minister of Aircraft Production, Lord Beaverbrook, Hurricanes and Spitfires were being turned out in Britain at over three times the rate of the Messerschmitts coming off the production lines in Germany. As the historian John Keegan remarks, 'despite Churchill's magnificent rhetoric, Fighter Command fought the Battle of Britain on something like equal terms. It would manage throughout to keep 600 Spitfires and Hurricanes serviceable daily; the Luftwaffe would never succeed in concentrating more than 800 Messerschmitt 109s against them'.[7]

But it was still to be a close-run thing. On 30 August, the electricity supply was cut along 130 kilometres of coast, thus taking seven radar stations off the air, and leaving the only early warning of enemy approach in the eyes and ears of the Observer Corps. Airfield hangars and ops rooms were hit, planes destroyed on the ground, aircraft factories damaged. In the air, the real British problem was a shortage of pilots, not aircraft. Privately, Hitler had told his generals that he would not invade unless he was sure of victory. But instead of continuing with the attacks on airfields, famously, Hitler changed tactics and we see another characteristic of the English imagination of themselves.

On the night of 24–25 August, London was bombed. Berlin was then hit in retaliation. Instead of continuing to try to destroy the British military machine, the Nazi objective now became to flatten the capital and thus sap the national will to continue the war. The Blitz started on 7 September and went on for fifty nights, but the bombing had quite the reverse effect to the one Goering expected:

rather than weakening the people's resolve, it strengthened it. Children had already been evacuated to the countryside, 2 million Anderson shelters were distributed to be put up in back gardens, and every employer with more than thirty staff was required to supply a night fire watcher: the bombing became a trial of wills. A leaflet dropped by German planes, *A Last Appeal to Reason, by Adolf Hitler*, the translation of a Hitler speech to the Reichstag on 19 July, simply caused amusement. *The Times* reported one woman had found a use for the enemy propaganda: she was selling the leaflets as souvenirs to raise money for the Red Cross.[8]

As the Blitz hit London, another much-loved caricature emerged to stand alongside the tweedy, sensible, Women's Institute fundraiser: the unconquerable capital and its indomitable people. The *Evening News* pointed out that 'Every morning, no matter how many bombs have been dropped in the night, London's transport runs, letters are delivered, milk and bread comes to the door, confectioners get their supplies, and the fruiterers' windows are filled.' The *Daily Telegraph* despatched a reporter to give this marvel of logistics a human face. One Londoner responded to his questions about the bombing with a quote worthy of the Ministry of Information:

I tell you, mister – and I'm not just kidding you because you're a newspaper chap – the people round 'ere is A1, and no mistake. Not a bleedin' moan out of one of 'em. There was one chap – very badly 'urt 'e was – and all 'e wanted to know was if 'is wife was OK. And there was the old lady at No. 51 – the 'ouse came down on 'er and they dragged 'er out of the basement and sent 'er to 'ospital. She didn't want to go. Would 'ave it she was quite all right. Not bloody bad for over seventy![9]

The cheeky Cockney and the tweedy countrywoman were united in the belief that there was a right and wrong way of doing things. Extraordinarily, even the men dropping bombs on them seemed to have got the point about a certain basic civility. A German fighter pilot shot down over southern England walked up to a farm worker

with his hands up and said: 'A cigarette and a cup of tea, please.'
The *Daily Express* reported that another Messerschmitt pilot lying
on the ground some distance from his machine was approached by
Mrs Betty Tylee and Miss Jean Smithson. He had an Iron Cross on
his chest. His first question was: 'Are you going to shoot me now?'
'No,' said Mrs Tylee, 'we don't do that in England. Would you like
a cup of tea?'[10]

It is worth dwelling on the Second World War for two reasons.
Firstly, because wartime tends to exaggerate those things which draw
a nation together. And secondly, because World War Two and its
aftermath was the most recent occasion on which the English had
a clear sense of common purpose. By their own accounts, the picture
that emerges is of a quiet people who would rather not have had
the inconvenience of war. They certainly only seem to have woken
up to its reality at the last possible moment. They saw themselves
as law-abiding and civilized. They were certainly sure enough of
themselves not to hate, but to laugh at Nazism. And, for all their
fear, they took pride in being outnumbered.

The idea of the Few occurs time and again through popular
accounts of English history. Military victories are what officialdom
chooses to memorialize, and they provide the opportunity for sport
at the expense of old enemies. (The late Woodrow Wyatt, Labour
MP and author of the *News of the World*'s ironically titled 'Voice of
Reason' column, was once asked by a French hotel receptionist
to spell out his surname. 'Waterloo, Ypres, Agincourt, Trafalgar,
Trafalgar,' he replied.) But those military events which have the
greatest imaginative resonance in the English mind are not necessarily
triumphs at all. Almost the only military event in the British occupation of India which remains in the popular imagination is the siege
of Lucknow. It is not the victories at the Alma or Sebastopol that
are recalled from the Crimean War, but the doomed charge of the
Light Brigade. Few could name an event of the Zulu wars apart
from the battle at Rorke's Drift, when 139 British soldiers held off

4,000. What is known about the campaign to take French Canada beyond the death of General Wolfe in the attack on Quebec, of the battle for Corunna apart from the death of Sir John Moore, of the British Sudan campaigns apart from the image of General Gordon dying as the Mahdi's followers stormed Khartoum, of the Boer War but the siege of Mafeking, of the First World War but the disasters of the Somme and the 41,000 lost at Gallipoli? World War Two is memorialized less for the drive on Berlin than for the British retreat from Dunkirk, a moment when British soldiers were plucked from the Continent and ferried back to the security of their island.

There is a certain element of myth-making in all these scenes, but their durability tells us something about the way the British see themselves. The common thread is sacrifice in an against-the-odds adventure. The realpolitik, the self-interest that had often put the armies there are forgotten. The impression is always of a small, nobly embattled people. As long ago as the Hundred Years War, the English victories when outnumbered three to one by the French at the Battle of Crécy or perhaps five to one at Poitiers (1356), came to be presented as the result of some special favour from God. Six hundred years later, the belief was still alive. The 1944 film version of *Henry V*, starring Laurence Olivier, was given financial backing by the British government not merely because it would provide worthwhile overseas propaganda, but because it propagandized within Britain, by playing on the sense of embattled persecution. The best-known news photograph of the Blitz, the picture that told the British people they would never be beaten, was the image of the dome of St Paul's cathedral, 'the parish church of the Empire', emerging graceful and unscathed from the smoke and destruction of an incendiary bomb raid. Taken by a *Daily Mail* staff photographer, Herbert Mason, it was printed in the newspaper with the caption 'The Firmness of Right against Wrong'. 'What better image could there be of a Protestant citadel being safeguarded amidst Armageddon by the watchful eye of Providence?"[11] asks the historian Linda Colley.

This sense of being uniquely persecuted and uniquely guarded must, obviously, be connected with religious belief. But the relevant text is not in the Bible. It is John Foxe's *Book of Martyrs*, a lurid piece of propaganda detailing the suffering and death of Protestants executed during Queen Mary's attempt to turn England back to Rome. It ought to be taken as the third Testament of the English Church. The book first appeared in 1563. It had expanded by 1570, the year of Elizabeth's excommunication, to 2,300 pages of often gory descriptions of the oppression of English Protestants at the hands of the Roman Catholic Church. Anglican authorities ordered it to be displayed in churches across the country, and the illiterate had it read to them. It stayed on show in many churches for centuries, a ready reference for anyone who doubted the willingness of Englishmen and -women to die for their beliefs. By the end of the seventeenth century, perhaps 10,000 copies were in circulation. Throughout much of the following hundred years, new editions were produced, often in the form of serializations: after the Bible, it was the most widely available book in the land.

John Foxe's purpose in describing the executions of the victims of persecution was to demonstrate the Church of England as 'the renewing of the ancient church of Christ': it was the church in Rome that was deviant. Christianity, Foxe suggested, had arrived in England in the reign of King Lucius of Colchester, and only later with missionaries from Rome. (Another fable, the Glastonbury Legend, tells, of course, that Joseph of Arimathea brought Christianity – and the Holy Grail – to England soon after the crucifixion.) The accession of Mary to the throne, and the reign of terror that followed as she tried to restore the supremacy of the Roman Catholic Church, was, therefore, some mad aberration. In the description of the execution of Ridley and Latimer, bishops of London and Worcester, there occurs the phrase that echoed down the centuries of English history.

Condemned to be burned at the stake for their refusal to recant and acknowledge the authority of Rome, on 16 October 1555 the two men were brought to a ditch outside Balliol College, Oxford. There they were made to listen to a humbug called Dr Richard Smith preach a sermon on the cruel text 'If I give my body to be burnt and have no charity, it profiteth me nothing'. Then their outer clothes were stripped from them and given to the crowd. They were shackled to a stake by a chain round their waists, and faggots of wood piled up around their feet. Ridley's brother is said to have appeared with a bag of gunpowder, which he tied round the bishop's neck, to shorten the agony. Ridley asked him to do the same for the elderly Latimer, after which the wood at their feet was set alight. As the flames licked around them, Latimer is said to have cried out to his fellow bishop, 'Be of good comfort, Master Ridley. We shall this day light such a candle by God's grace in England, as I trust shall never be put out.' Latimer died quickly, Ridley only after revolting agonies.

As propaganda, Foxe's book was a skilful piece of work. It had a veneer of historical respectability, it dealt with real events, it played upon real fears. And it could be terrifically gruesome. The story of Katherine Cawches, burned at the stake with her two daughters in St Peter Port, Guernsey in 1556, contains an account of how the pregnant belly of one of her daughters exploded. Out popped a newborn baby, carried clear of the flames by the force of the explosion, only to be taken from the crowd of onlookers and thrown back into the fire by a bailiff. Foxe adds that the child therefore 'was both born and died a martyr, leaving behind to the world, which it never saw, a spectacle wherein the whole world may see the Herodian cruelty of this graceless generation of popish tormentors, to their perpetual shame and infamy'.[12]

The influence of this great tract must have been profound. At a religious level, the historian Owen Chadwick believes that the steadfastness of the victims, from Ridley and Latimer downwards, baptized the English Reformation in blood and drove into English minds the fatal association of ecclesiastical tyranny with the See of Rome ... Five years before, the Protestant cause was identified with church robbery, destruction, irreverence, religious anarchy. It was now beginning to be identified with virtue, honesty, and loyal English resistance to a half-foreign government.[13]

Not only did *The Book of Martyrs* identify the Roman Catholic Church with tyranny, it associated the English with valour. Any citizen could enter almost any church and discover for themselves the ruthlessness of foreign powers. They learned at the same time of the unbending courage of the English casualties. The effect of the book was not merely to dignify English Protestantism and demonize Roman Catholicism, but to hammer home the idea of themselves as a people alone. Being embattled had a moral purpose.

It sometimes seems that the English *need* to think of themselves like this. At the bathetic level of *This England*, the enemy 'doing their damnedest to destroy a way of life it took the English a thousand years to perfect' is an unholy alliance of metric measurements, town planners, unelected bureaucrats, squatters, vandals, abortionists, adulterers, offensive advertising, political correctness, modern telephone boxes, the 'unholy trinity of newspapers, radio and television', multiculturalism, and, most of all, the feeble-minded, traitorous politicians who were prepared to surrender the country to the European Union. Traitor-in-chief was Edward Heath, the ill-starred Conservative Prime Minister who took Britain into the Common Market by telling what turned out to be a lot of fibs about the limited scope of European ambitions. The editor, and, to judge from the hundreds of letters he gets each week, most of his readers, too, wants Britain to withdraw from the European Community, which he sees as a scam by the Germans to achieve by stealth what they failed to win with Messerschmitt 109s in 1940. 'The whole thing is a racket where we'll end up being a colony of Germany. We won the war, but they'll win the peace.'

We are back in the world of Peter Simple, with the barbarians at the gates and the people of England obliviously asleep inside. That's how the English like it.

CHAPTER SIX

THE PARISH OF THE SENSES

An Englishman thinks he is moral when he is only being uncomfortable.
GEORGE BERNARD SHAW, Man and Superman

We all know God is an Englishman. How else would the English have presided over the first truly worldwide empire? There is the Duke of Wellington surveying the carnage at the end of the battle of Waterloo and remarking 'the hand of God was upon me'. The roots of the English belief to have been chosen by God lie far back with the implausible legend that Jesus had visited the country as a boy (the basis of William Blake's 'And did those feet in ancient time walk upon England's mountain green?') and that Joseph of Arimathea, the man who had begged Jesus's body from Pontius Pilate, had brought to England part of the crown of thorns. In the fourteenth century, religious English people had talked of their country as 'our Lady's Dowry'. In 1554, during Queen Mary's attempt to turn the country back to Roman Catholicism by incinerating Anglicans, Cardinal Pole had arrived with a message from the Pope encouraging her to get on with the frying by saying that England had been uniquely selected by God. The Elizabethan courtier and wit, John Lyly, described the English as 'His chosen and peculiar people'.[1]

By the eighteenth century, as self-confidence grew ever greater, the English had come to believe they were a covenanted people, like ancient Israel. When Isaac Watts set out to translate the Psalms in 1719, the word 'Israel' could easily and thoughtlessly be replaced by 'Great Britain'. Handel celebrated the Duke of Cumberland's massacre of Bonnie Prince Charlie's army of starving Highlanders at the battle of Culloden with the oratorio *Judas Maccabaeus*, comparing 'Butcher' Cumberland to the Jewish guerrilla leader who led the rebellion against invasion by the Seleucids. For the coronation of Cumberland's father, George II, he turned out four anthems, the most famous of which, 'Zadok the Priest' (another Old Testament hero, Zadok was the founder of the priesthood of Jerusalem), has been played at every British enthronement from 1727 to 1953.

The eighteenth-century writer Emanuel Swedenborg, who at one time numbered William Blake among his disciples, went further. Because of their unique genius, the English had a special heaven, reserved exclusively for their use. Nineteenth-century missionaries sent out to convert the colonized peoples of the world sincerely believed they were spreading the word from a New Jerusalem in England. It was only a short step to the crackpot belief propounded by Edward Hine in a lecture in Chelsea in 1879 that Great Britain was Israel, the Americans the lost tribe of Manasseh, the Irish the Canaanites, and that Jacob's Stone was really in Westminster Abbey. It was, his followers claimed, the only explanation for the extraordinary success of the English people. According to this theory, the Jews of ancient Israel had been captured by Assyrians led by King Sargon, had migrated across Europe and eventually emerged as the Anglo-Saxons. As late as the 1960s, an American, Herbert W. Armstrong, was repeating the 'chosen people' theory:

Certainly there can be no mistaking the identity! Take a map of Europe, lay a line due northwest of Jerusalem across the continent of Europe, until you come to the sea, and then to the islands in the sea. This line takes you direct to the British Isles! Proof that our white, English-speaking people today – British and American – are actually and truly the Birthright tribes of Ephraim and Manasseh of the 'lost' House of Israel.

There is nothing unique in the belief that a nation has God on its side: the sight of army chaplains on either side of a conflict urging on their troops with the lie that they are doing the Lord's work is a constant feature of warfare. But what is perhaps most curious about the English experience is the way in which a belief that they had been chosen by God could have produced a version of religion so temporizing, pliable and undogmatic. After all, orthodox Judaism, which is built upon the assertion that the Jews are the chosen people, is one of the most demanding, prescriptive religions on earth. But there is scarcely anything prescriptive about the Church of England.

I once asked the Bishop of Oxford what you needed to believe to be a member of his Church. A look of slight bafflement crossed his face. 'An intriguing question', he answered, as if it had not occurred to him before.

You cannot imagine an orthodox rabbi, or a Roman Catholic priest replying like that. When the bishop went on, he opened with an inevitable English preface, 'Well, it rather depends.'

'It depends on which church you go to. An evangelical church will say you need to be sincerely converted. A traditional Anglo-Catholic church will teach you a Christian orthodoxy virtually indistinguishable from Roman Catholic teaching.'

It doesn't add up to a very coherent set of rules of belief, does it?

'The Church of England doesn't believe in laying down rules,' he said. 'It prefers to give people space and freedom. It's enough to make the effort to attend and take communion. That shows you believe.'

This is the sort of woolliness that drives critics of the Church of England to distraction. If required by bureaucracy to declare their religious affiliation on a questionnaire, millions will tick the box marked 'C of E'. The rest is silence. What kind of an organization is it that makes itself as available as a local post office and requires virtually nothing of its adherents? The most characteristic English statement about belief is 'Well, I'm not particularly religious', faintly embarrassed by the suggestion that there might be something more to life. It sometimes seems the Church of England thinks God is just the ultimate 'good chap'.

And yet it was the Church of England that provided the moral authority for the model Englishman and -woman. Early in Henry Fielding's *Tom Jones*, an argument develops between the humanist Mr Square and Tom's lash-wielding teacher, the Reverend Thwackum. The question is whether humankind is capable of being virtuous without being religious. Square points out that Moslems and Jews each claim that their religion imparts virtue. To which an angry Mr Thwackum responds with 'When I mention religion, I mean the Christian religion; and not only the Christian religion, but the Protestant religion; and not only the Protestant religion but the Church of England'.[2] The self-confidence of the assertion that Anglicanism was the only way of moulding primeval Anglo-Saxon clay into an honourable English person sounds so well practised that perhaps Fielding had heard it from real-life parsons. He could well have done so, for the Church of England is such an odd invention that it can only be explained in its own terms.

This is *not* the same as anti-Catholicism, though. It is true that many popular post-Reformation festivals were explicitly sectarian. The first of August celebration of the beginning of Protestant Hanoverian rule, the November 5th bonfires to celebrate the thwarting of the plot by Guy Fawkes and his co-conspirators to blow up Parliament, and celebrations marking the 1688 landing of William of Orange to deliver the country from James II (coincidentally, he arrived in England on 5 November), all had an anti-Catholic element to them. Bonfire Night, in particular, often turned into something approaching a riot, with mobs demanding money and attacking the homes of Roman Catholics. At an institutional level, recusancy laws forced Catholics to pay fines if they failed to attend Anglican church services and right through much of the eighteenth century they faced harsh taxation, were denied access to education and banned from owning weapons. Well into the nineteenth century Catholics were barred from Parliament, from offices of state and even from voting. Twice – in 1688 and 1714 – the rules for dynastic succession were broken to avoid the horror of a Catholic taking the throne. The 1701 Act of Settlement prevented a Catholic, or anyone married to a Catholic, from ever taking the throne, so that by the time George Lewis, Elector of Hanover, acceded in 1714, over fifty people with a better claim had been passed over. He might have been a dreary lumpen individual with bad English. But at least he wasn't a papist. The Act is still in force.

Both the popular celebrations and the acts of Parliament were not so much religious in inspiration as political: when the historic enemies France and Spain were both Catholic countries, an assertion of Protestantism was a declaration of nationalism. But there is something more profound than politics at work, too. In World War One, Rupert Brooke reported one private encapsulating his suspicion of the Continent by saying, 'What I don't like about this 'ere Bloody Europe is all these Bloody pictures of Jesus Christ an' 'is Relatives be'ind Bloody bits of glawss.'[3] It was not just that the Church of England has no grottoes, no relics of holy cloth, no rotten old tooth or shard of bone said once to have belonged to St Peter and venerated as a cure for sickness. All that was smashed or discarded in the Reformation. There is something else, too, a sense that because Anglicanism has always owed more to Erasmus than to Luther, it is rooted in the everyday world. As a result, it has found it a good deal easier than the Roman Catholic Church to adjust to the scientific discoveries which changed the world: the Catholic catechism predates not only Darwinism but the Enlightenment.

In developing a sense of national identity, the achievement of the Church of England was not so much what it proclaimed but what it made possible. There is a case for saying that the invention of the Church of England *was* the invention of England. However, this is not to say that the English are a churchy people. They prefer their religion as they used to like their clothing and cars, understated and reasonably reliable, there when you need it. In a sense, England is hardly a Protestant country at all. As every schoolchild knows, its national church was invented so that Henry VIII could get a divorce. As Ralf Dahrendorf, a shrewd observer of his adopted country, puts it, 'a falling out with the Pope is not the same as a true Reformation'.

The Church of England is the maddening institution it is because that is how the English like their religion – pragmatic, comfortable and unobtrusive. Small wonder that so many English writers have preferred the dramatic certainties of Catholicism. You simply couldn't write a novel like Graham Greene's *The Power and the Glory* about a church built on the conviction that anything can be settled over a cup of tea. It is nearly four centuries since the heyday of Anglican sermons, and the last flowering of literary Anglicanism – Rose Macaulay, Dorothy L. Sayers, John Betjeman, Stevie Smith – has none of the force of a Catholic poet like Gerard Manley Hopkins. No one can read Trollope or even Barbara Pym and believe the Church of England has a mission to the poor and oppressed. It is what it has always been, a convenience cooked up by Tudor monarchs for political purposes, where the conventional Trinity has been amplified to Five, including the monarchy and Parliament. The cleverness of the achievement of Anglicanism has been to tame a deep anti-clericalism in the English (one of my favourite village names, Bradfield Combust, commemorates the burning-down in 1327 of Bradfield Hall, owned by the Abbot of Bury St Edmunds, by a furious crowd said to number 40,000) by knitting the Church into the fabric of the state.

This profound integration of sect and state is seen every afternoon of the parliamentary year, as, just before two-thirty, a little procession totters through the central lobby in the Palace of Westminster. To the cry of 'Hats Off, Strangers!', the policemen remove their helmets as the column passes. First comes a man in funny gaiters, clicking his heels on the tiles, followed by a retired general carrying the gold Mace, then the Speaker of the House of Commons in black-and-gold gown, and behind the Speaker, the Speaker's chaplain. It is like something out of a Gilbert and Sullivan comic opera. Inside the chamber, for the benefit of the handful of MPs who have bothered to turn up, the chaplain recites the prayers that commend the political deliberations, name-calling and point-scoring of the day to God. What, you wonder, has God got to do with it? Yet something similar is going on in every army, navy or air-force unit, and is recognized in the Archbishop of Canterbury's notional place as the pre-eminent commoner in the land, the man who lays the crown on the monarch's head at the coronation. The everyday liturgy, with its insistence upon prayers for the monarch and 'all those set in authority under her' is the voice of a church a knows its deeply conservative and semi-secular place in English society.

So it would be a mistake to see the historical animosity towards Catholicism as proof of enthusiasm for Protestantism. You have only to look at the hostility shown towards non-conformists for taking the Bible too seriously: John Bunyan, author of the most famous devotional novel of all time, *Pilgrim's Progress*, spent the best part of twelve years in Bedford gaol for preaching without a licence. Anti-Catholicism came from the belief that once the country had gone through the Reformation, it was impossible to be both a Roman Catholic and a patriot. Yet the Church of England's founder, Henry VIII, was a most Catholic sort of Protestant. (Two of the distinguishing elements of Anglicanism, the abolition of clerical celibacy and the creation of a liturgy in the vernacular, did not occur until after he was safely in his coffin.) In the ensuing centuries the Church of England has managed to encompass Puritanism, Anglo-Catholicism, Celtic mysticism, Evangelicalism, Christian Socialism and half a dozen other doctrines. The Church is there because it's there, sensible, adaptable, a comforter of the comfortable. The only sensible conclusion to draw from the uniquely privileged position of the

Church of England – its official status, the bishops' seats in the House of Lords, the Prime Minister's right to appoint senior clerics and so on – is not that it represents some profound spirituality in the people, but that it suits mutually convenient purposes for state and Church. Many a bishop or dean will tell you privately that it would be better for the Church if it severed its formal links with the state, and became 'disestablished'. It is often said that it would better reflect the new Britain, where an average Sunday will find more Roman Catholics in church than Anglicans, a country of large numbers of Asian Moslems and Sikhs and Caribbean Pentecostalists, if the Church of England was just another sect. (Privately, many leaders of these other faiths are much less keen on the idea – they like the idea of *some* spiritual presence near the heart of the constitution, and the woolly old Church of England is better than most, because it worries so much about seeing that other faiths and denominations get a shout.)

The eighteenth-century ballad about the Vicar of Bray, who changed his beliefs to fit in with whomever was on the throne at the time,

> And this is the law, I will maintain,
> Unto my dying day, Sir,
> That whatsoever King shall reign,
> I will be the Vicar of Bray, Sir!

is usually used to tease the Church. But, in truth, trimming represents the true spirit of Anglicanism. Its enthusiasts see something wholly admirable in its refusal to take up extreme positions. 'The *via media* is the spirit of Anglicanism,' wrote T. S. Eliot of the sixteenth century. 'In its persistence in finding a mean between Papacy and Presbytery the English church under Elizabeth became something representative of the finest spirit of England of the time.'[4] The former Archbishop of Canterbury, Dr Robert Runcie, saw the vagueness for which it is castigated as a strength. 'There are other churches in Christendom which take pride in their lack of ambiguity – in doctrine or leadership, or in monolithic interpretation of the Gospel. Anglicanism, by contrast, is a synthesis, and a synthesis necessarily unites thesis and antithesis.'[5]

A more cynical way of putting it might be to suggest that it is the Church of England which gives the English their extraordinary capacity for believing they can have it both ways. The capacity for hypocrisy among this people who have liked to claim that they are straightforward is stunning. Take as one example the question of abortion. Thirty years after it was made legal in the United States, the issue was still the source of angry and sometimes violent confrontation on the steps of abortion clinics across the country. In England, it is not that the issue is any less ethically charged, merely that no one likes to make a fuss about it. The English know that abortions take place on a staggering scale in their country – 177,225 in 1996 – which means that for every four children born, one foetus was destroyed. There is a 'thesis' and an 'antithesis' in the issue all right. But the English simply prefer not to notice.

The nineteenth-century Prime Minister Lord Melbourne got it right. He once complained about his duty of appointing Church of England bishops, saying 'Damn it all, another bishop dead – I verily believe they die to vex me.' He also remarked that 'Things have come to a pretty pass when religion is allowed to invade the sphere of private life.'[6]

During World War Two someone in the BBC had the idea of inviting a group of writers to record a series of morale-boosting radio talks which would be broadcast on the Empire Service to troops serving around the world. J. B. Priestley, Somerset Maugham, Hugh Walpole, and Philip Gibbs all contributed, as did a nowadays largely forgotten writer called Clemence Dane. It was the pen-name of a former actress, Winifred Ashton: she had adopted it twenty-five years earlier from her local church, St Clement Danes in the Strand.

She began her talk with the words 'You know, Britain is an extraordinarily permanent country'.

Despite having taken her name from a church in the Strand and spent most of her adult life in Covent Garden, the author followed this opening with the time-honoured English example of permanence:

Last week-end I drove past my old home in Kent, and, slowing down to look at it, I wondered to see that it was quite unchanged in the forty years, although it lies not twenty-five miles from the heart of London. One still drove to it through cloth-of-gold fields – England is all buttercups this week – the deer were still grazing in the park opposite, and the little paths on to the common trekked round the same heavy-laden pink and white May trees.

Thus far we are in familiar territory: the Luftwaffe may be raining bombs down on London (St Clement Danes had been hit on 10 May 1941), the army may be embattled, but the heart of England beats steadily in tens of thousands of country villages. But then she changed tack. 'What is Britain, to mean so much to us?' she asked, and answered, 'I think the answer is the English Bible!'

After a conventional history of the translation of the Bible into English, Clemence Dane concluded by describing a meeting with the wife of a countryman who, having fought in the First World War, had signed up to fight again, and was currently serving in South Africa. The author had been shown his last letter home,

asking after his two grown daughters and his little son, giving what news he could, worrying over some neglected ploughing, and ending with love and kisses. And then, after his signature, he has added a postscript. In that heavy hand, so much more accustomed to a spade than to a pen, he has written: 'So be of good cheer, my dear ones!'

Dane identified the phrase as coming directly from Matthew's Gospel in the Authorized Version, where Christ appears to his disciples, walking on water.

Be of good cheer; it is I; be not afraid [more lamely rendered in the New English Bible as 'Take heart!']. And that 'Be of good cheer!' has echoed down the centuries [she ended her talk, crackling across the ether to servicemen worldwide], so that today an English working-man can still use it, and so become the voice of the whole Island speaking to all the British World. It is the voice of Caedmon, the voice of Alfred, Wycliffe, Tyndale, Elizabeth, Cromwell, Nelson, Gordon – all the countless known and unknown men and women who made, who are, Britain. And the message still runs – 'Be of good cheer, my dear ones!'[7]

You could not write anything like that nowadays for all sorts of reasons; because England hardly shares even a common faith, let alone a common liturgy, because knowledge of the Bible is so much more restricted, because modern-language versions of the scriptures have such reduced resonance, because while most of the audience might recognize the name of Nelson or Cromwell, they'd be hazy about Gordon, baffled by Wycliffe and shrug at Caedmon.

Thinking that perhaps I might be wrong, I called on the Secretary of the Prayer Book Society at her home in the London suburb of Edgware. Margot Lawrence fights a tireless struggle to preserve the liturgy of the Book of Common Prayer, which, apart from being the cornerstone of Church of England worship almost since its foundation, was for so long the second great reservoir from which the English draw so many of their figures of speech. She had just had a Clemence Dane sort of experience and was in sprightly form. The plumber had reassured her that her hot-water system would soon be working again with the words 'we'll soon have you back in the land of the living'.

'You see, that expression, "the land of the living", comes directly from the Book of Common Prayer!' she exclaimed excitedly.

The Prayer Book Society is neither a wealthy nor a fashionable pressure group. You get the impression that its eight or ten thousand members (there are no central records, but their journal goes out to 7,000 addresses) are mainly men and women like her – sensible, decent folk in the autumn of their lives driving elderly British-made cars). Their campaign has a religious purpose, but the cause has a much greater cultural significance. The 1662 Book of Common Prayer, largely the work of Thomas Cranmer over a century earlier, was devised, as its name suggests, to provide a shared ('common') experience. It did so in plain yet dignified language in the proper register so that even the most tongue-tied vicar could be borne aloft by the words. They became so familiar that 549 of the Prayer Book's phrases occur in the *Oxford Dictionary of Quotations*. 'Moveable feasts', 'the old Adam', 'the jaws of death', to 'lead a new life', to 'pass man's understanding', to be 'at death's door', to 'give up for lost' and many other expressions still in current use are lifted straight from the Prayer Book.[8]

Officially, the Book of Common Prayer is still the cornerstone of Church of England worship. But it is another polite fiction. Candidates for ordination are required to show 'sufficient knowledge' of the book and the church's doctrine in the Thirty-nine Articles. In practice, new vicars are emerging from theological college unaware of anything but the new forms of service.[9] In churches across the country, the old black-bound prayer books have been piled up in a corner of the vestry and in their place are thin red, green or yellow paperbacks, often with some stick-man drawing on the front, which the congregation stumbles through every Sunday.

I know people who have to drive thirty miles to get to a Prayer Book service [says Margot Lawrence]. And the clergy are so manipulative. Sometimes they're downright dishonest. I heard on Monday from a man in Portsmouth whose daughter was getting married. The couple had discussed the wedding with the vicar and made absolutely clear that they wanted the Book of Common Prayer to be used. It was only when she walked up the aisle on her father's arm that she heard him begin another form of service altogether. She was distraught. But what could she do?

The Society claims that it is 'holding the line' against the extirpation of the old liturgy. But every year another few dozen of the remaining parishes where the Book of Common Prayer survives, find a new vicar arriving. He or she introduces 'as an experiment' alternative forms of service. There is nothing so permanent as a Church of England experiment.

In removing the Book of Common Prayer, the clergy are merely trying to make the Church 'relevant'. But in so doing, they are chipping away at a body of language that has been shared by the English people for centuries. While there is nothing inherently wrong with trying to make religion more easily available, the 'experimental' alternatives adopted by the Church of England have no durability: their purpose is to be relevant only in a particular time. 'A prayer is not the same as *the* Prayer Book', is the way one historian puts it.[10] All communities need resonant phrases, touchstones of expression, and instead of the shared language of the Anglican Church, the English have only a series of slogans they have picked up from television: 'Nice to see you, to see you nice', 'And finally', 'It's just for fun'.

When I asked the Very Reverend David Edwards, the author of over thirty books on modern Christianity, for his assessment of the state of spirituality in England, he just told me bleakly that 'The English have lost any sense of what religion is'.

Perhaps he's right. But one is bound to ask whether the mass of the English *ever* had any profound sense of religion. The heyday of the Church of England was 200 years ago, when Jane Austen was born the sixth of seven children in a Hampshire rectory. (Nowadays, the rambling rectories are all occupied by successful businessmen and novelists: the vicars live in red-brick bungalows at the bottom of what was once the vegetable garden.) English religious fervour had by then long blown itself out in the Civil War, after which the nation settled back to mutter its way through a largely passionless set of rituals. Rather than any messianic ambition of leading the English people to salvation, the church authorities who presided over these comfortable slumbers seem to have been much more concerned with putting 'a gentleman in every parish'. Even the best-remembered Anglicans are recalled for something other than their spirituality. They are diarists like Francis Kilvert and James Woodforde, naturalists like Gilbert White, Great and Good figures like Cosmo Lang, or philosophers like Sydney Smith.

The greatest dereliction of this uniquely privileged Church was its inability to put down roots in the city. The archetypal Church of England parish – the one affectionately satirized in television's *The Vicar of Dibley* – is rural, the archetypal bishopric a cathedral close in Salisbury, Hereford or Winchester. Too late, the Church woke up to Dostoevsky's furious denunciation that

Anglican ministers and bishops are proud and rich, live in wealthy parishes and dioceses and wax fat with an entirely untroubled conscience ... It is a religion of the rich, and undisguised at that ... They travel all over the earth, penetrate into darkest Africa to convert one savage, and forget the million savages in London because they have nothing to pay them with.[11]

It may sound like propaganda, but when the Victorian journalist Henry Mayhew asked a London costermonger (fruit-and-vegetable seller) if he knew what St Paul's was, the vendor replied that he'd heard it was a church, but 'I never was in church'. A survey on Sunday 30 March 1851 showed that two thirds of the population of London did not go to church and other samples bore out the pattern of paganism. East and south London had the lowest rate of church attendance in the country.

So when people speak of the Church of England being 'the established Church', they have only ever really been referring to its constitutional privileges, to the monarchy and to its position in the shires. Most of the time, in most of the cities and suburbs, where most of the English people live, the Church of England is almost absent. There *are* Anglican vicars heroically toiling away in poverty-stricken inner-city slums, helping people with their benefit claims,

running soup kitchens and drop-in centres for the elderly or un-
employed. But they are working as social workers – on half the pay.
Their lives are witnesses to a faith, but it is one they are embarrassed
to proclaim, for fear it 'gets in the way' of their work. In David Hare's
play, *Racing Demon*, the Reverend Lionel Espy is summoned to see his
bishop to answer charges that he is neglecting the sacramental side of
his work. He tells the bishop, 'In our area I wouldn't even say the
Church was a joke. It's an irrelevance. It has no connection with
people's lives.'[12] As his evangelical colleague explodes later in the
play, 'Inner-city priesthood? It's a cartel. Based on a massive failure
of nerve. You've become enlightened humanists.'[13]

When I suggested to Canon Donald Gray, chaplain to the Speaker
of the House of Commons, that the Church had lost the cities, he
replied, 'It's not that the Church has *lost* the Inner Cities. We never
had them.' He is right: it was non-conformist denominations from
the Methodists to the Salvation Army who tried to meet the challenge
of urban life, while Irish immigrants brought their own Catholic
faith with them. In the few areas where popular urban Toryism took
root, the Church of England broadened its base. But, for the most
part, those vast, echoing buildings built by the Anglicans on street
corners throughout the great industrial cities as an instinctive
response to mass migration from the countryside have *never* been
filled, not even when originally built. Small wonder they look cold
and uncared for over a century later, waiting to be bought up and
turned into a Sikh temple or nightclub. The Reverend Lionel Espy
and others like him are doing their best. But so long after the event,
they have no chance at all of making up the ground lost.

As things stand, the Church of England has the worst of all worlds.
Admittedly, the virtues of the Church, its gentleness, tolerance and
compassion, are undermined by a complete lack of intellectual rigour.
Because so much of the churchgoing population has still not got
beyond the Enid Blyton Book of Bible Stories, priests are condemned
to stand up each Sunday and preach as if every word in the Bible is

fact when so much is clearly fiction or allegory. Theologians who dare to suggest things may be more complicated, like John Robinson in *Honest to God* or David Jenkins when Bishop of Durham, set themselves up for a howling-down. And because it is 'established', everyone feels they have a right to criticize. More thoughtful members of Parliament may take a vow of silence, feeling themselves unqualified to meddle in issues like the liturgy, but that leaves the floor to boneheads. Even Prince Charles, who will inherit the role of Defender of the Faith that the Pope originally gave to Henry VIII, seems to have lost any will for the job. 'I hope to be the defender of *faiths*,' he once said in an interview, as if Sikhism, Jainism, Catholicism, Druidism and a belief in the healing properties of astral projection were all of equal importance. He was, doubtless, well intentioned, but it is symptomatic of muddle. Religious education in schools – taught by graduates of teacher-training colleges into which the Church of England has ploughed millions – is a bland and passionless blancmange of everything from Guru Nanak to creationism.

The word 'religion' has doubtful origins, but is thought to derive from the Latin *religare*, to bind: the nation that prays together stays together. A pessimist might conclude that the fact that there is no longer any common body of expression reflects the fact that there is no longer any common body of belief and that a society which has lost its most binding ties was destined to fail. But there is another sense in which the Church of England has profoundly shaped the English people.

Everyone knows that the break with Rome involved the wholesale sacking of the Catholic Church, an event registered in school history textbooks as '1536: the Dissolution of the Monasteries'. But stripping the Roman Catholic Church of its earthly power was much more than the appropriation of land, buildings and treasure. This most enormous act of collective vandalism, involving the smashing of thousands of works of art, had profound cultural consequences.

Andrew Graham-Dixon has argued quite persuasively in his *History of British Art* that an entire medieval tradition of painting and sculpture which survived elsewhere in Europe was in England more or less wiped from the slate. Certainly, there is no doubting the scale of the vandalism. Between the dissolution of the monasteries in 1536 and the death of Oliver Cromwell over 120 years later, hardly a corner of England was untouched by a zealotry that decreed that devotional art was a form of Romanist idolatry. There was even talk at one point of razing Stonehenge to the ground. The evidence that this was the moment when England exiled itself from an artistic tradition is scant, for the obvious reason that very little of the Roman Catholic artistic heritage survived the binge of destruction. A single stone sculpture, the Christ discovered by builders working on Mercer's Hall, London, in the 1950s, exquisite in the surviving details, proclaims, says Graham-Dixon, 'two deaths, the death of God and the death of an entire tradition of British art . . . this is a work created on the cusp of an English Renaissance that was never to be'.[14]

If this was the moment when the English cultural tradition cut itself off from the rest of Europe, you could not find a more striking signal of the new direction in which English creativity was to turn than the tearing-down of altar screens and their replacement in many churches by bare boards listing the Ten Commandments. Here, literally, was the replacement of the visual by the verbal. Measured by its consequences, this was not so much 'an English Renaissance that was never to be' as an Anglo-Saxon Enlightenment that predated its Continental counterpart by a century or more. The English not only came to a new way of appreciating the Word, they came to an appreciation of words. We cannot know whether there would ever have been an English Titian, Raphael or Michelangelo. But we are sure that the Reformation and its aftermath threw up William Shakespeare, Christopher Marlowe, John Donne, John Bunyan and John Milton.

The literary tradition that followed them has become the most sustained and distinguished in the western world. We cannot know, of course, how it, and its branches in North America and Australasia, would have evolved had England remained a Catholic country. But the English certainly became a people obsessed by words, while interest in – and facility with – both music and art has varied wildly. At one time England is being called 'the land with no music', at another, the German-born Handel is being fêted by the court, and in 1905, Elgar is lamenting he 'had inherited an art which has had no hold on the affections of our own people, and is held in no respect abroad'.[15] The contrast with the English love of words could not be starker. It shows itself in the absurdly overproductive British publishing business, which turns out 100,000 new books a year – more than the entire American publishing industry – in the fact that the country produces more newspapers per head of the population than almost anywhere else on earth, in the unstoppable flow of Letters to the Editor, in the insatiable appetite for verbal puzzles, anagrams, Scrabble, quizzes and crosswords, in the vibrancy of British theatre, in the secondhand bookshops in half the market towns in the land. 'Books are a national currency,' concluded one recently departed foreign ambassador.[16]

And as for painting? Even in portraiture, the great painters who lived through or followed the Reformation – Holbein, van Dyck, Lely and Kneller – were foreigners. You might argue that the climate was the enemy of much other painting, that grey skies make for gloomy landscapes. But if so, why should not the same argument apply to Holland, which has produced such a roll-call of superior artists? And anyway, northern light is more varied than the bleached heat of southern Europe. The answer seems to have to do with the fact that the English Reformation was about politics, rationality and choice, and the theological stimulus behind it was concerned with *meaning*: therefore words are the medium of choice.

Even before the upheaval, English art had been preoccupied with natural observation: cathedral misericords and illuminated manuscripts were all adorned with scenes from everyday life – animals, farming, even games of football. It was not merely because the aristocracy rather than the Church now became the main patrons of art that the English tradition developed with portraiture and landscape rather than baroque allegory. It was also something in the English cast of mind. 'I would rather see the portrait of a dog that I know, than all the allegorical paintings they can shew me in the world,' said Dr Johnson,[17] and English art is preoccupied with telling stories. 'Nearly all of the greatest painting of the British school is either man observed or nature observed, either portrait or landscape: Constable and Turner, and the water colourists from Cozens to Cotman, and Gainsborough, Reynolds, Romney and so on,' wrote Nikolaus Pevsner in *The Englishness of English Art*.[18] If he had been frank, he might have conceded that it is also one of the least distinguished traditions of visual art in Europe. The English were too busy writing to paint.

Becoming a people of the word also had profound political consequences. The ambition to have a bible in English had been a revolutionary one. In 1407 the Archbishop of Canterbury had made translation punishable by excommunication and Wycliffe's Lollards acquired their name from the Dutch word for 'mumbling', as they met to hear illicit English versions. So that when it was achieved by William Tyndale[19] and Miles Coverdale, the English version was a victory of radicalism over vested interest. The first casualty was the standing of the Church; who needed a hierarchy of clergymen to interpret the Bible when they could read it themselves? But it went further: the Bible was, after all, the Word of God, and it was the Word of God that gave the king or queen their authority. Making the scriptures available to everyone had great subversive potential. An order that every parish was to have its own English Bible displayed in church was rescinded in 1543 because the right was being abused by 'the lower sort'. It was decreed that 'no women, nor artificers, prentices, journeymen, servingmen of the degrees of yeomen or under, husbandmen nor labourers shall read the Bible or New Testament to himself or any other privately or openly'.[20] (The restrictions were lifted after Henry's death.)

The Authorized Version, or King James Bible, whose echoes Clemence Dane heard in the letter from South Africa, appeared in 1611, the fruit of three and a half years' work by forty-seven scholars but, essentially, the work of Tyndale.[21] It had the immediate effect of democratizing learning and created a stock of memorized stories and sentences that became a shared currency among the English people. They may never have been racially monolithic, but now they had a shared intellectual inheritance. Hugo Grotius, the Dutch philosopher, wrote of England in 1613 that 'theology rules here', and the seventeenth century was the heyday of the English sermon. But the most important consequence of the translation of the Bible was to embed in the English mind a belief in the rights of the common man. For the Puritans, the Bible was the supreme authority on everything; the idea would never have occurred to them it was anything other than the direct Word of God. 'Nothing [should] be done in this or any other thing, but that which you have the express warrant of God's word for', as Thomas Wilcox put it.[22] But the power of the Word extended much further. By offering a direct relationship with God, unmediated by popes or bishops, the common language of devotion gave the individual all sorts of rights he might never have otherwise thought he had.

The emphasis on the importance of the individual implicit in the new covenant may also be one of the explanations for the English talent for nurturing utopian romanticism. From the seventeenth-century Diggers to the twentieth-century Labour party, by way of William Blake, Robert Owen and dozens of others, a belief in the perfectibility of mankind has flourished. The vulnerability of America to every passing conman in a shiny suit and a bogus smile comes from its British origins: the founding fathers, after all, were making their own attempt at Utopia. As a historian of the movements discovered, in mid-Victorian Lancashire alone 'Manchester had incubated the ecstasies of Mother Anne, foundress of the Shakers. Accrington kept the Swedenborgian metaphysic warm. Ashton had provided a temple for John Wroe. Salford had provided, with Rochdale, recruits for Manea Fen [a 'communionist' settlement in East Anglia]. Now at Preston, it was the turn of Heber C. Kimball and his fellow missionaries to harvest souls and bodies for their new revelation'.[23] (Mr Kimball was boasting that he would not die until Christ's second coming and prophesying that, within ten or fifteen years, the sea between Liverpool and America would dry up. It didn't, and Mr Kimball's second coming is still awaited.)

Would the English have had their revolution a century or more earlier than much of the rest of Europe, had these beliefs in the rights of the individual not taken such firm hold? Unlike the secular uprisings of the eighteenth, nineteenth and twentieth centuries, the English rebellion did not spit out religion, it turned to it for support. When John Milton sought to justify chopping off the king's head, he cited the belief that God had created man in his own image: therefore all authority from kings and princes is 'what is only derivative, transferred and committed to them in trust from the people to the Common good of them all'.[24] The English belief that 'I know my rights' owes a lot to this profound conviction that it is liberty, not kingship, that is divinely ordained. When England was split by civil war, the rebels identified themselves with the Hebrews, and Cromwell became a Joshua or Moses figure. He wasn't afraid to make the comparison himself: the English people had been blessed by God, he said in 1654, and 'The only parallel of God's dealing with us that I know in the world ... [is] Israel's bringing out of Egypt through a wilderness, by many signs and wonders towards a place of rest'.[25] It is in the fight with Church and state, first to get access to the Bible in their own language, and then to use the scriptures to establish their own relationships with one another and with authority, that we see the spirit of English individualism at work. It is one of the reasons that it has never been necessary for an Englishman or Englishwoman to submerge their identity within the state. And it is one of the reasons that the country has produced so many eccentrics.

CHAPTER SEVEN

HOME ALONE

English life at home is complementary to life at sea:
security and monotony are its essential characteristics.[1]
ELIAS CANETTI, Crowds and Power

In 1835, a young Englishman named Alexander Kinglake decided to mature himself between leaving Cambridge and taking up a law career by travelling across the Syrian desert on a camel. He was making for Cairo, accompanied by 'a brace of pistols and a couple of arab servants'. After several days' travelling there emerged from the desert three other camels, coming towards him. As they drew nearer it became clear that two of the camels carried riders, while the third was laden with baggage. Nearer still, and he could see that one of the riders wore an English shooting jacket and had a European face. The closer they drew, the more agitated Kinglake became:

As we approached each other, it became with me a question whether we should speak. I thought it likely that the stranger would accost me, and in the event of his doing so, I was quite ready to be as sociable and chatty as I could according to my nature; but still I could not think of anything particular that I had to say to him . . . I felt no great wish to stop and talk like a morning visitor in the midst of those broad solitudes.

Luckily for Kinglake the man on the other camel was also English, an army officer making his way back to England overland from India. As, at last, the strangers met in the middle of nowhere, 'we lifted our hands to our caps, and waved our arms in courtesy, we passed each other quite as distantly as if we had passed in Pall Mall'. Not a word was said.[2]

In the end, the inhibitions of England were defeated by the camels of Arabia, which, having passed each other, refused to go any further. The two men turned around and walked their mounts back towards one another.

He was the first to speak; too courteous to address me, as if he admitted the possibility of my wishing to accost him from any feeling of mere sociability or civilian-like love of vain talk, he at once attributed my advances to a laudable wish of acquiring statistical information, and accordingly, when we got within speaking distance, he said, 'I dare say you wish to know how the Plague is going on at Cairo?'

Where did the English acquire this curious reluctance to engage with one another? It is the repeated complaint of one foreign visitor to England after another that they have found the English impossible to get to know. If they are good-natured, like Max O'Rell in late Victorian England, they will simply find it amusing. 'If you remark to an Englishman, in a smoking compartment, that he has dropped some cigar-ash on his trousers, he will probably answer: "For the past ten minutes I have seen a box of matches on fire in your back coat pocket, but I did not interfere with you for that."'[3] But it is just as likely that what the English see as no more than respect for privacy looks to others like disdain. It was arrogant when the English dominated an empire which dominated the world. It is extraordinary in the nation's reduced status. A century after the incident on the train, another American, happily shaking the dust of England from his shoes in 1992, decided that the reason the country hadn't been invaded for a millennium was that it simply wasn't worth the trouble. After eight years of trying and failing to make friends, he had discovered that the only way to gain social acceptance in England was to feign indifference. 'What does it say about your society that it admits only those who do not care very much to belong? For a start, it suggests that the English don't much care to be liked. They prefer the company of other misanthropes. Since no misanthrope worth the name would actually want to join a club, eager applicants must be snubbed.'[4]

He cannot imagine the exquisite pleasure his outburst will have given some English people; Britannia may no longer rule the waves, but the English can still make foreigners feel small. Yet he has hit upon a truth, too. What he calls misanthropy others might call privacy. It is one of the defining characteristics of the English; foreign visitors are forever complaining at it. The abiding memory of the Sherlock Holmes adventures is not of the great detective solving any individual murder mystery but of him and his friend Dr Watson sitting in amiable doziness at home in Baker Street, when their peace is suddenly disturbed by a visitor desperate for help. That's the trouble with the outside world. It keeps on intruding on domestic peace.

Even foreigners sent to work in the country can find that the only time their English colleagues invite them into their homes is on the eve of their departure. Unlike some other countries, where casual socializing can take place in the home, the English have a very protective sense of their hearth and prefer the restaurant or pub. One consequence of this reticence is that an invitation to an English home really means something, unlike in, say, America. But it also means that you may entertain the most unspeakable ideas about what is going on inside someone's house, without ever acting upon them. So, although they have never visited them, a series of addresses are etched in the English mind: 10 Rillington Place, the grimy rooming house in Notting Hill, west London, where the necrophile John Christie murdered half-a-dozen women; 23 Cranley Gardens, Muswell Hill, and 195 Melrose Avenue, Cricklewood, where Dennis Nilsen dismembered fifteen young men and put them down the drain; 25 Cromwell Road, Gloucester, where Fred and

Rose West tortured and murdered at least ten females. All of these cases assumed the dimensions they did because neighbours subscribed to the English belief in keeping themselves to themselves. 'I didn't like to pry', they told curious reporters, as police in black overalls carried out box after box of human remains.

A truly comparable word for 'privacy' simply does not exist in French or Italian, yet in England it is one of the country's informing principles. At first glance it seems curious that the country has no law that enshrines the principle of a right to privacy. But constitutional protection is only necessary in a society in which it is presumed that the individual is subsidiary to the state. The importance of privacy informs the entire organization of the country, from the assumptions on which laws are based, to the buildings in which the English live. Among the wealthy, it is noticeable that with a few deliberately monumental exceptions like Vanbrugh's Blenheim Palace, the English country house does not shout its presence: such places are more likely to incite Pope's quizzical appreciation

> Yes sir, 'tis very fine.
> But where do you sleep
> And where do you dine?

More often, the country house lies hidden away, at the very least behind high walls or dense shrubbery, often using the folds of hillsides to make it more obscure.

In the lives of ordinary people, the discretion continues. In much of continental Europe, you live on the street. It is the place where you eat, drink, commiserate, flirt, laugh and pass the time of day. The English answer to the street is the back garden, in which socializing is by invitation only. Because the English dream is privacy without loneliness, everyone wants a house. Given a choice between their own back garden and life in a communal living project where they might share the benefits of a common swimming pool or playground, most will choose their own plot of ground. In France,

Germany and Italy, about half the new homes being built in the 1990s were apartments. In England, the best estimate was about 15 per cent. It reflects a belief that at the end of the day, instead of sitting on the street chatting, the English would rather go home and slam the door.

In October 1896 the German Embassy in London received a new member of staff. Alongside the diplomats studying British political life, the country's armed forces and her overseas trade, there was to be a special attaché. Nominally, Hermann Muthesius was to write reports for the Prussian Board of Trade on how the British supplied gas, electricity and railways to their cities. What he really planned to do was to study something he believed to be uniquely English. Muthesius, an expert architect, wanted to produce an analysis of how the English built their houses. As he wrote to Grand Duke Carl Alexander of Saxe-Weimar, 'There is nothing as unique in English architecture as the development of the house . . . no nation is more committed to its development, because no nation has identified itself more with the house'.[5] The Grand Duke wrote back enthusiastically encouraging him to get on with his project, because 'Such a publication would be of great value, especially here in Germany. Because of history, the notion of homeliness and home comforts is less developed here, in our less fortunate Fatherland, than in England'.[6]

It was seven years later, on returning to Germany from London, that Muthesius finally published the results of his investigations. *Das englische Haus* appeared in three volumes in Berlin in 1904 and 1905. Although a second edition appeared between 1908 and 1911, it was not until 1979 that a condensed version appeared in English – a mark of how little regard the English pay to the comments of foreigners on their way of life, perhaps.

Muthesius was a tremendous enthusiast for England. It was not an uncritical enthusiasm: the cities had more than their share of 'tasteless speculative housing, with whole acres covered with wretched, absolutely uniform small houses', while suburbia was often full of 'trivial façades, designed without understanding'. Yet for all that, England was the only advanced country in which most of the population still lived in houses as opposed to the apartments of Continental cities. As a result, it had many hundreds of times more artistically worthwhile houses than Germany. The thing he admired most about them was what he admired most in the English character, their unassuming naturalness. The fact that such a prosperous people could design for themselves a way of domestic life that insisted upon the greatest possible comfort without succumbing to an obsession with luxury or showmanship demonstrated, he thought, that the English were a superior civilization.

Although he concentrated, inevitably, on the work of architects like Lutyens, Bidlake and Norman Shaw, Muthesius had some acute observations to make about why English home-building had developed as it had. Like many another foreign visitor, he too commented on the importance of the climate: 'the damp English air and perpetually overcast sky' made the English family seek refuge indoors when in other climates they might have wanted to socialize outdoors. More important was a long-standing English self-sufficiency and independence of mind – 'these people ask relatively little of external life' – which made the house their ideal habitat. Added to an innate conservatism, which saw no charm in change, the English were well suited to this atomized style of living: 'the pronounced lack of sociability which makes the Englishman so different from the continental prevents him finding anything objectionable in the seclusion of his lonely abode.'[7] He rightly noticed that one of the consequences of owning houses was that the English took a more permanent view of their homes: accommodation from which eviction was possible in a matter of weeks or months was hardly likely to engage domestic interest. It would be like expecting someone to be interested in furnishing or decorating a hotel room.

The point is partly a class one, of course. At the time when Muthesius was lauding the genius of the English house, there were millions living in multiple-occupancy terraces, for whom the sort of relationship with property which he found so impressive was the remotest fantasy. The most they could aspire to were places like the curious little street of late Victorian terraced houses which still stands in Manchester, near the site of the world's first mechanized factory. The cobbles are now covered in asphalt, but in most other external respects, it is as it was built, two little red-brick terraces facing each other, the kind of housing that once you could find in every industrial town in England. The most curious thing about it is its name, 'Anita Street', for there is not one Anita Street in the whole of Greater London. The explanation is that at the time it was built, the street was a showcase for the Manchester city fathers, because every single house contained proper internal plumbing, an untold comfort for labourers in the cotton mills. The city fathers proclaimed their pride in the name of the terraces: Sanitary Street. Later inhabitants, uneasy at having their bowel movements trumpeted to the world, insisted on dropping the first and last letters.*

The greatest psychological benefit that Muthesius saw in the English addiction to the house was 'the greater spiritual health' that came from the fact that it had contact with the ground, was more likely to have access to fresh air and, through the presence of a garden, would prevent the natural hardiness which had been built up through country life being 'squandered in the maelstrom of city life'.[8] Englishmen who saw the cities as destroyers of traditional moral values would not share his enthusiasm, but Muthesius had certainly made an accurate hit on one of the great English characteristics.

---

* But for those who could afford it, the English house offered watery convenience on an enviable scale. So advanced were the country's manufacturers that, in the nineteenth century, they dominated the European market for baths, washbasins and lavatories; though not bidets, which many of the English still believe to be a place for washing their socks.

As wealth has slowly become more fairly distributed in England, more and more people have taken the opportunity to become property owners. Two thirds of English people now own the places in which they live. It is well above the European average, and nearly twice the rate of owner-occupation in Germany. Fewer than half the homes in the Netherlands are lived in by their owners, only just over half in France. It would be rash to draw any conclusions from the figures (the European countries with higher rates of owner-occupation include Greece and Norway – what can they have in common?), but the fact that English people choose to burden themselves with a massive commitment of which many fellow Europeans are free illuminates something. It has to do with a sense that they are making an investment, that money borrowed to buy bricks and mortar is money that is working for them, unlike money spent on rent, which is working for the landlord. But it speaks to some deep sense of the importance of individual possession, too.

Historically, participation in the political life of the country depended upon owning your own home. Before 1832, you could only vote if you had property valued for land tax at more than forty shillings a year; and every time the franchise was extended in the nineteenth century, the right to participate in democracy was dependent upon being a male householder. The Abbey National Bank, originally a building society, began life as two organizations, one of which, the Abbey Road, had the declared ambition of enabling young men to buy their homes, in order that they could vote, while the National Building Society additionally hoped to convince them there were better things to spend money on than drink. It was a mark of Margaret Thatcher's deep understanding of some of the instincts of the English (neither the Scots nor the Welsh ever took to her in quite the same way) that she recognized the power of the urge to own property, forcing municipal authorities to give their tenants the right to buy.

The consequences of this obsession can be seen in every town in the land. Drive through an English suburb – any suburb – and the thing that strikes you is the fact that almost everyone has given their house a name. Why? There's a perfectly adequate numbering system, which would make sure the mail got to the right address a lot more easily than any randomly ordered list of Shady Leas, Mon Repos or Dunroamins. But naming a building implies an emotional attachment to the place in which people live. Names express individuality. A number implies communality or anonymity.

And then look at what they do to their houses. Perfectly presentable Edwardian terraces are turned into riots of pebble-dash plaster, bottle-windows and mock-Tudor cladding. Every weekend across the land, husbands abandon wives, fathers leave children, to hammer, saw, drill and paint their stamp upon the bricks and mortar in which they live. Do-It-Yourself is a true national obsession. The phenomenal growth of this dusty passion since World War Two had some rational early explanations – the great growth in owner-occupation, the make-do-and-mend ethic fostered by wartime rationing, the high prices charged by professional builders after the war, and a general desire for the modern among young people stuck in run-down housing. But that sort of analysis ignores the most potent factor, which is the English love-affair with their homes. The greater the opportunity the English had to own their own homes, the greater their desire to improve them. By the 1960s, television had made household names of boring men in tank-tops who could advise viewers on how to grout around the bath. The first DIY superstore opened in 1969, and by the mid-nineties, the two owners, Richard Block and David Quayle, had 280 of the places. By then, the British were spending over £8,500 million per annum Doing It Themselves.

The fixation with owning their homes is a physical expression of the English belief in privacy. Are the three things – the insularity of the nation as a whole, a collective belief in domesticity and an individual preoccupation with privacy – differing expressions of the same phenomenon? And if so, where did it come from? In Ralph

Waldo Emerson's 'English Traits' I came across a meteorological explanation of the Englishman's character. 'Born in a harsh and wet climate, which keeps him indoors whenever he is at rest,' he writes, 'domesticity is the taproot which enables the nation to branch wide and high. The motive and end of their trade is to guard the independence and privacy of their homes.'[9] I wondered whether the English weather might really be the key.

From Paramaribo, Casablanca, Port Moresby, Ascension Island and McMurdo Sound, the electric message comes, this much rainfall, that much cloud. Thousands upon thousands of other places around the world – weather balloons and satellites, ships and aircraft and elderly sub-postmistresses in the Scottish Highlands – scan the skies and file their reports at the ordained minute of the ordained hour. And what happens to this mass of information about the world's weather, from jungles and deserts and icecaps? It goes to Bracknell; Bracknell, Berkshire, a town which isn't really a town at all, just a collection of dual carriageways and carparks. Its claim to fame is as distribution centre for the Waitrose chain of supermarkets, but then it's the sort of town where they have supermarkets for every taste – DIY supermarkets, gardening supermarkets. Probably, at the end of some vast carpark, there's a supermarket selling guides to supermarkets.

I had gone to the town on what I ought to have guessed would be a fool's errand. Common sense says that, because weather affects behaviour, it may also have *some* effect on character. Could the English preoccupation with privacy and 'home' have an explanation as simple as the fact that their climate obliged them to spend a lot of time indoors? It's a reasonable supposition that cold wet weather, which forced teenagers to stay indoors in winter instead of going to the beach or skiing, probably has something to do with the country's capacity for inventive rock music. But is there something more profound? Has a mild and gentle climate, rarely too hot and rarely extremely cold, played a role in producing a moderate, pragmatic people? The Anglophile philosopher George Santayana believed that

England is pre-eminently a land of atmosphere . . . English landscape, if we think only of the land and the works of man upon it, is seldom on the grand scale. Charming, clement, and eminently habitable, it is almost too domestic, as if only home passions and caged souls could live there. But lift the eyes for a moment above the line of roofs or treetops, and there the grandeur you miss on the earth is spread gloriously before you.[10]

Santayana wrote a lot of near-incomprehensible stuff, but you can almost see what he was getting at. Sometimes, the English do seem to lack intensity. It is true they have demonstrated a remarkable facility in producing fine literature. But there is scarcely a single passionate English-born composer in the two centuries between Purcell and Elgar. England has produced one stunning, revolutionary artist, J. M. W. Turner, but no Michelangelo, no Rembrandt, no Dürer, Velasquez, El Greco, no Van Gogh or Picasso. Yet every summer the country bursts out in a rash of exhibitions of amateur drawing and paintings in church halls across the land. It is a country of watercolours rather than oils, miniatures rather than monuments. It would be curious if the climate in which the English lived had had *no* influence at all.

It is 200 years since Dr Johnson remarked that 'when two English-men meet, their first talk is of the weather'.[11] The comment is as true now as it was then. It says something about a national obsession that television audiences for weather forecasts in Britain, based on the analysis produced in Bracknell and delivered in remarkably low-key, low-tech style by uncharismatic men and women in unglamorous clothes, regularly draw audiences of 6, 7, or 8 million viewers. To those accustomed to the extremes of a continental weather system, this English obsession is baffling.

To an outsider [wrote Bill Bryson], the most striking thing about the English weather is that there isn't very much of it. All those phenomena that elsewhere give nature an edge of excitement, unpredictability and danger – tornadoes, monsoons, raging blizzards, run-for-your-life hail-storms – are almost wholly unknown in the British Isles, and this is just fine by me. I like wearing the same type of clothing every day of the year.[12]

Bryson misses the point. The English fixation with weather is nothing to do with histrionics – like the English countryside, it is, for the most part, dramatically undramatic. The interest is less in the phenomena themselves, but in *uncertainty*.

Dr Johnson understood perfectly why the English are obsessed by the weather. It is the consequence of genuine small-scale anxiety. 'In our island, every man goes to sleep, unable to guess whether he shall behold in the morning a bright or cloudy atmosphere, whether his rest shall be lulled by a shower or broken by tempest', he wrote.[13] So, one of the few things you can say about England with absolute certainty is that it has a *lot* of weather. It may not include tropical cyclones but life at the edge of an ocean and the edge of a continent means you can never be entirely sure what you're going to get. Could it be that readiness for changeable skies has contributed to some of the more stolid aspects of English character? At its simplest, the hypothesis is that, as Johnson put it, 'our dispositions change too, frequently with the colour of the sky', making the English cheerful in sunshine and gloomy in the rain. The English hero, John Bull, invented by Arbuthnot in 1712, had a temper which 'depended very much upon the air; his spirits rose and fell with the weather-glass'. (For many it is quite the reverse; English suicide rates actually rise as the weather improves in April, May and June.) And in their caricatures of other races, the English seemed to believe that their own climate had made them vigorous and resourceful while Arabs, for example, had been reduced to fatuous indolence by the effect of the sun. (The same is true in reverse, incidentally: French visitors to England in the eighteenth century commented that a combination of too much meat and a wet and gloomy climate had made the English peculiarly vulnerable to melancholy.)

But my attempts to investigate its influence did not get far. A deadpan professor at Salford University had already told me that while he thought it would make an interesting research topic, established science wouldn't look kindly on it, so 'I am afraid that there would be difficulty funding it'.[14] Hence the trip to the drab, functional buildings of the Meteorological Office in Bracknell, sandwiched between a housing estate and a big roundabout, a memorial to the Protestant soul, which says that public money should only be spent on buildings whose appearance proclaims rectitude. The service gained its status in World War Two, saving the lives of thousands of allied troops, notably aircrew, to whom knowledge of cloud cover meant protection from German flak, and forewarning of likely headwinds meant the difference between having enough fuel to return to base and ditching in the North Sea.

Outside, on a February afternoon, a middle-aged blonde clatters by, pulling her coat tighter around her. 'Ooh, isn't it *cold*?' she says, to no one in particular. There is a faintly Russian look to her dyed hair, with the roots showing black at the parting, and for a moment I wonder whether the Russians ever tried to infiltrate the Met Office, which is still classified as part of the country's defence system. But she cannot be Russian: no true Russian would think it worth saying it was cold in February. It's how things are in Russia in winter. No, the capacity for infinite surprise at the weather is distinctly English. As George Axelrod once complained, 'In England all they ever do is talk about the weather. But no-one does a damn thing about it.'

At the Met Office the English fixation is reduced to number-crunching, performed at the rate of one billion or so floating point calculations per second. Within ten minutes of the sub-postmistress in the Highlands filing her reports of rainfall, temperature and windspeed, an entire picture of the weather in the United Kingdom has been drawn up. Within three hours five minutes of the reports from St Helena, Dar-es-Salaam, Papeete or Cayenne reaching Bracknell, the sixteen-ton cruncher has produced a weather forecast for the whole world. There is something awesome about the ability to sift a series of numbers, match them against a model, and produce a prediction for any corner of the globe. But there is nothing dramatic about lots of chaps in shirtsleeves looking at computer screens. 'They always say we're a bit anoracky,' said the boss when I asked him how obsessive his staff were. It was hard to disagree, looking at this room full of quiet, civilized men with jackets that were a bit too short for their arms and their weekend hobbies of amateur radio and rambling and growing hydrangeas.

As I left, it struck me how terribly British the whole place was, how calm and functional and reticently civilized. It was a crossword-puzzler's sort of place, reducing uncontrollable forces to homely clichés about wrapping up warm. The one time in recent years it had something really out of the ordinary to deal with – an imminent hurricane, which struck in 1987 – Michael Fish, its duty forecaster, had gone on television to tell people they really shouldn't worry themselves about it. After which, the English had even more opportunity to indulge their phenomenal capacity for quiet moaning. The complaints don't trouble the weathermen and -women (any more than long-suffering railway guards are upset by the reaction of delayed passengers on the country's shabby railway services). Even the forecasters are irritated by the prospect of certainty. The boss told me that he got depressed if he saw a change in the weather coming in five days' time. He wanted it now. Which is another reason the English like to complain at the forecasters, too. Deep down, they *like* to be surprised by their weather.

Not all foreigners find the English impossible misanthropes. The American war correspondent Martha Gellhorn arrived in Europe from St Louis, Missouri in 1930 and went on to report the Spanish Civil War, marry Ernest Hemingway, enter the concentration camp at Dachau, file reports from Vietnam and become, at eighty-one, the first foreign correspondent into Panama as the dictator Noriega was toppled. By the time I met her, a year or so before she died, her eyesight had been terribly damaged by a 'damnfool surgeon – the best in London, he said', so she found writing near-impossible. But she still had long, slim legs, natural blonde hair, elegant fingers and spiky opinions on everything under the sun. During World War Two, she had left Hemingway drinking himself stupid in Cuba and come to London to watch from a balcony of the Dorchester as the first of Hitler's doodlebug rockets shot down Park Lane. Later, after living in Paris, Mexico and Africa, she bought a flat in Knightsbridge, dividing her time between there and a remote cottage just over the Welsh border.

I once asked her why she had chosen to live in England. It turned out to be for none of the usual reasons, nothing to do with the standard of the theatre, the good airline connections, the relative quality of the media, or anything like that. She loved England for its absolute indifference. 'I can go away, spend six months in the jungle, come back and walk into a room, and people won't ask a single question about where I've been or what I've been doing. They'll just say, "Lovely to see you. Have a drink."'

I suggested it might be natural reticence or a wish not to intrude. But she called it 'the privacy of indifference'.

'I think the English have a superiority complex. The Germans are always asking, "What do you think of us?" They care, you see. The English don't give a damn. They're certain they're superior to everyone else, so they couldn't care less what others think.'

The 'privacy of indifference' rang a bell somewhere and a couple of days later I remembered why. The French writer, André Maurois, had used a similar phrase. In World War One Maurois had served as a liaison officer with the British army and as a result of his intimate experiences wrote a friendly picture of the national character, *Les Silences du Colonel Bramble*. His advice was never to be shy about saying anything to the English: they were too proud to be touchy. The long history of prosperity meant that 'England has no inferiority complexes ... Thanks to God and her navy, she has never been invaded. The only feeling inspired in her by foreign nations is one of immense indifference'.[15] If Maurois could come to that conclusion in 1918, was it not likely to be even more true after victory in another world war?

They say it's impossible to believe two mutually contradictory ideas at once. But the English seem to manage happily enough. They have long since adjusted to their reduced status in the world. Yet an enfeebled body has somehow clung to a belief in its own incomparability. *Égoïste comme un Anglais* was the phrase in the 1930s, and everyone understood the reference at once. Odette Keun was overcome by the small civilities that punctuated every transaction. 'The matter, the real matter, with these people', she decided, 'is that they are polite ... Courtesy, kindness, obligingness, tolerance, moderation, self-control, fair play, a cheerful temper, pleasant manners, calmness, stoicism, and an extremely high degree of social civilisation, these are the adorable things I discovered in the English.' But they came with a price. A born tendency to compromise meant they were incapable of making up their minds. And worse, they were insufferable snobs.[16] (Miss Keun claimed to have stood in front of a public lavatory that proclaimed GENTLEMEN ONE PENNY; MEN FREE and round the corner LADIES ONE PENNY; WOMEN FREE. As she stood gasping at the implications of this urinary caste system, she was comforted to be approached by a policeman who asked if she was short of a penny.)

At the time of her experience, England was producing a model of citizenship – 'ladies' and 'gentlemen' – that was admired and imitated around the world. But they had been displaying a self-confident pride for centuries. The safety of their island made them look down on less fortunate people who suffered from the chronic disadvantage of not being English. Even by late Tudor times, an astonishing arrogance had emerged. Froissart talked of a people 'so proud that they set store by no nation but their own', Michelet of 'pride personified in a people'. It comes as no surprise to read Emerson remark of the Victorian English that 'they plainly account all the world outside of England as a heap of rubbish'. But even in the 1950s, Harold Macmillan was claiming that 'we know that on the whole, in spite of all our self-depreciation, this is the finest country in the world'.

The enduring, aggressive ignorance of 'abroad' that is still characteristic of this strain of English pride reaches its apogee with the country with whom Martha Gellhorn compared the English, Germany. In many respects it, or Holland, is the country with which the English might naturally have most in common. Germany may be over-regulated and humourless, but it has at least reinvented itself as a prosperous, humane society after two world wars and the evils of Nazism, which is why Germans care what people think about them. The English have conspicuously failed to reinvent themselves and have just got poorer. In 1955 each pound bought 11 marks. By 1995 it bought less than three. It takes a particularly purposeful blindness to see that sort of relative decline as something to be proud of. Yet the national caricatures that Orwell parodied survive, scarcely modified.

In 1990 the then German ambassador in London, sick of the constant Kraut-bashing in the British tabloid newspapers, decided to fight prejudice with knowledge. A meeting was arranged with one of the editors. It was the ambassador's misfortune to be a relative of the World War One flying ace, 'the Red Baron', Manfred von Richthofen. The ambassador deployed all his diplomatic charm as he spent what he thought had been a productive hour or two patiently explaining to the newspaper that his country was not set on creating a fourth reich in which the British Isles would be some offshore slave colony. The following day he opened the newspaper to read an account of his peacemaking under the headline THE HUN TALKS TO THE SUN.

*

Where did the English acquire this remarkable indifference? It helps that they have a well developed sense of humour. The Germanic mind is different, as Wittgenstein discovered when he had to abandon his plan for a book of philosophy written entirely from jokes, realizing he had no sense of humour. German wit, famously, is no laughing matter (although even the German ambassador managed to smile at the headline in the *Sun*. After several days). The English at least have the saving grace of being able to laugh at themselves. Which must be based upon a profound self-assurance. Since the perform-ance of the state as a whole has been less than impressive in the last five decades, its roots must be in the individual. The English do not take pride in the achievements of their governments: they know they consist at best of 'characters' and at worst of charlatans. If a British Prime Minister appeared on television and began addressing them as American Presidents address their people ('Mah feller Meri-cans' as Richard Nixon used to say) their audience would fall about laughing.

Travel to England by the cross-channel train from Paris to London and you can see the English indifference to the nation state at once. It is a journey from a city that, with its grand boulevards and avenues, proclaims a belief in central planning, to one that has just grown like Topsy. Paris remains a city where the government can still plough ahead with *grands projets* like La Défense or the Bastille Opera, whereas London can scarcely agree on a new statue. Even the railway itself testifies to the difference. By December 1994, trains were running directly from Paris to London. Having decided to embark on their *grand projet*, the French government simply willed it to happen. A high-speed railway line was built from Paris to the coast, on which, from the moment the tunnel opened, trains hurtled at up to 186 miles per hour. On emerging into the Kent countryside, the trains cut their speed by nearly half. The English had not got around to building their high-speed rail line. Excuses were given by the authorities about the greater density of population in Kent, the fact that it was in the most prosperous corner of England, as opposed to the relatively deprived north of France. But the real reason was the different relationship between the individual and the state. The French government is simply readier to impose its will: if it wants to build a railway line or nuclear power station, it wills the means, no matter whose back garden it happens to be in. The English not only won't raise the taxes to make it happen, but hold planning inquiries at which every objection from Dunroamin can be weighed. The different priorities – the centrally decreed needs of the state and the individual worries of the citizen – speak volumes. The English expect their high-speed rail line from the tunnel to be finished by 2007. Perhaps it will be.

Belonging to a naturally melancholic people, some of the English found the state of the cross-channel rail link embarrassing. How was it that even something as simple as a collaborative railway line could end up giving the French an opportunity to crow about the superiority of their engineering? A more positive way of looking at it would have been for them to celebrate the fact that they lived in a country where the state cannot do as it pleases and walk all over the citizen. It is tempting to conclude that the French believe the state *is* the people, while in England, the state is something else – 'them'.

If I had to list those qualities of the English which most impress me – a quizzical detachment, tolerance, common sense, bloody-mindedness, willingness to compromise, their deeply political sense of themselves – I think I should praise most this sense of 'I know my rights'. The attachment to certain hard-earned freedoms lies deep. The same spirit runs through the struggles to achieve the Magna Carta, Habeas Corpus, trial by jury, freedom of the press and freedom of election. The heroes of this struggle, whether they be John Hampden, John Pym, John Lilburne, Algernon Sydney or John Wilkes, stand in a line of campaigners unafraid to demand liberties which elsewhere could only be bought by wholesale revolution. The point about these struggles is that, if they were not won uniquely by individuals, victory was the consequence of the state's willingness to accommodate individual struggle. Every fight has its Robespierres, but in England, the state enclosed them, with more or less reluctance.

Even that great authoritarian Napoleon seems to have recognized the sedimentary quality of English liberty. He scribbled in the margin of his translation of John Barrow's *A New and Impartial History of England, from the Invasion of Julius Caesar to the Signing of Preliminaries of Peace, 1762* that 'For a long spell of years, the King can doubtless arrogate to himself more authority than he ought to have, may even use his great power to commit injustice, but the cries of the nation soon change to thunder, and sooner or later the King yields'.[17] When Napoleon's own attempts to arrogate supreme European power to himself were defeated at the battle of Waterloo, he threw himself on the English sense of liberty, surrendering to them because he said, with 'any other Allied power, I would have been at the mercy of the whims and will of a monarch. In submitting to England I put myself at the mercy of a nation'.[18] On being told the British government planned to repay this confidence by packing him off to the island of St Helena, he was outraged. 'I demand to be received as an English citizen,' he said. 'I know indeed that I cannot be admitted to the rights of an Englishman at first. Some years are requisite to entitle one to be domiciled.'[19] For sheer nerve it takes some beating.

One consequence of this English obsession with privacy and individualism has been to create a people who are not easily led. They distrust exhortation, and the further away they are from metropolitan life, the stronger their cussedness. In the Fens, for example, they simply don't give a damn. The Bishop of Norwich was told by his predecessor, 'Welcome to Norfolk. If you want to lead someone in this part of the world, find out where they're going. And walk in front of them.'

Some sort of liberal atavism seems to have been at work for centuries. It produced John Locke and Thomas Hobbes; it gave the English the confidence to get their revolution over early; to dethrone a king and then behead him; to exchange one ruling family for another when it suited; it bore fruit in the American Revolution with its glorious insistence upon the liberty of the individual. It nurtured Adam Smith, Jeremy Bentham, Herbert Spencer and John Stuart Mill. The English demonstrated time and again that they could disentangle the personal frailty of the individual (Wilkes, for example, was an ugly dissolute with an almost xenophobic loathing of the Scots) from the nobler cause they represented.

The sixteenth-century radicals, the Levellers, proclaimed a mythical time before 'the Norman yoke' enslaved freeborn Englishmen. There is evidence that long before the Norman invasion, there was already a long tradition of belief in the rule of law and the rights of the individual and English kings were ruling not by diktat but in consultation. Alfred of Wessex's codification of laws in 871 attests to the English taste for freedom. Not only did it recognize that without the ability to rely on people when they gave undertakings, society could not function ('Every man should strictly hold to his oath and pledge'), it also incorporated the idea of individual freedom. 'If a man binds a free man who has no sin, he shall pay ten shillings. If he beat him, he shall make compensation with twenty shillings.'[20] The habit of law was so deeply engrained in the English that even when William the Conqueror invaded in 1066 he merely asked his new subjects to continue abiding by the laws of Edward the Confessor, with the additions he had made to them.

The historian Alan Macfarlane has argued that, contrary to Marxist interpretations of history, the country had a sense of personal liberty long before the Reformation because the English enshrined individual property rights in English law;[21] since property could be acquired by purchase, relationships were based on contract rather than status. And because individuals could buy and sell land quite easily, there arose the idea of personal rights enshrined in law, which has been embedded in the English consciousness for centuries. Compared with the rigid feudal and semi-feudal class structures that survived in countries like France, England had invented for itself a system of social organization that, because of its flexibility, was robust enough to survive all manner of shocks. In England, despite the class stereotypes, there existed for centuries a remarkable degree of social mobility. England has had her share of class revolts, from Wat Tyler's peasants' revolt in the fourteenth century to the Chartists in the nineteenth. But they were very civilized affairs by comparison with the bloodletting which accompanied similar events on the European continent.

By Tudor times, England had become economically, socially and politically distinct from the rest of Europe, not least because this small population (half that of Spain and one quarter that of France) was so prosperous. Wealth grew on the backs of sheep: the English were the main producers of high-quality wool in Europe and one jealous traveller, looking at the opulence of the wool merchants, talked of the country's 'golden fleece'. What had determined England's salvation had been the fact that she was prepared effectively to mortgage future wool crops to fund a superior army in the Hundred Years War. The great Renaissance poet and humanist Francesco Petrarch, who had been born in 1304, wrote that 'In my youth the English were regarded as the most timid of all the uncouth races, but today they are the supreme warriors; they have destroyed the reputation of France in a series of startling victories and the men who were once lower even than the wretched Scots have crushed the realm of France with fire and steel'.[22]

The evidence of this period of wealth can be seen in the hundreds of mansions which survive from Tudor days. While it may be true that snobbery became the English disease, the barriers between the English classes were never as unbridgeable as Marxists have tried to suggest: had they been, the upper classes would either have been murdered or have died out ages ago. As it was, the élite was constantly replenished with new blood, which had made its way by individual enterprise. What the Reformation did achieve, particularly with the sacking of the monasteries, was to remove – sometimes literally, when a monastery was taken from the Church and given to one of the *nouveaux riches* – an idea of earthly power based upon the authority of the Pope and to replace it with a model based on the evidence that enterprise worked. As tyrannies have discovered the world over, when wealth is spread about, the people demand rights. The model Englishman (see Chapter Nine) was the product not of breeding but of grooming. Alan Macfarlane cites the remarks of people like Archbishop Cranmer, who spoke of admitting pupils of all social backgrounds to Christ Church School, Canterbury, remarking 'I take it that none of us here, being gentlemen born as I think, but had our beginning that way from a low and base parentage.' It might be added that the institutions which mass-produced gentlemen, be they the great grammar schools or the colleges of Oxford and Cambridge, were generally created by individual benefactors rather than the state.

One of the consequences seems to have been that the English became a deeply political people. The German traveller Carl Philip Moritz, visiting England in 1782, made an unfavourable comparison with the way things were directed in Germany. He wrote home,

My dear friend, when one sees here how the lowliest carter shows an interest in public affairs; how the smallest children enter into the spirit of the nation; how everyone feels himself to be a man and an Englishman – as good as his king and his king's minister – it brings to mind thoughts very different to those we know when we watch the soldiers drilling in Berlin.[23]

At first sight, this seems to be at odds with the phenomenon of English individualism. After visiting England in the 1830s, Alexis de Tocqueville concluded after long thought that the 'spirit of individuality is the basis of the English character'.[24] But how, he wondered, did the English manage to be simultaneously so highly singular, yet to be forever forming clubs and societies: how could the spirit of association and the spirit of exclusion be so highly developed in the same people? He decided that the English formed associations when they couldn't get what they wanted by individual effort. They then wanted to keep for themselves the gains they had made, which was why they cultivated exclusivity. Because individuality drove people to ever greater competition, the need to pool resources also grew. He once asked John Stuart Mill, author of *On Liberty*, whether he thought the English would ever opt for a centralized system of government. The Englishman replied that 'Our habits or the nature of our temperament do not in the least draw us towards general ideas; but centralisation is based on general ideas; that is the desire for power to attend, in a uniform and general way, to the present and future needs of society. We have never considered government from such a lofty point of view.'[25]

When you look at how English life is organized, not much has changed from Mill's day. It is true that the responsibilities of the state have proliferated, and the amount of money taken from the citizen in taxation increased hugely. But the post-war promise of the potential of government to build utopia has been shown to be so much hot air, and Margaret Thatcher's counter-offensive in the 1980s equally discredited. The belief remains in a common-sense middle way, in which as much as possible is left to individual discretion. One of the reasons the English have never been much interested in either fascism or communism is that they have a very sensible scepticism about what the state can achieve.

It is instructive that the lowest rank in the British army is a 'private soldier', a term which goes back to before Shakespeare. His counterpart in France is called a 'soldat de 2e classe'. The English soldier does not swear allegiance to his country, and certainly not to his government, but to his king or queen and his first loyalty is to his regiment, which is still likely to be based on ancient counties.

It was the instinctive English suspicion of standing armies that led the authorities to dress the Metropolitan police force in blue, in a uniform designed to resemble civilian more than military dress. By the 1880s, *The Times* was able to hold forth that 'The policeman, who is in foreign cities regarded as an enemy, not only by the criminal classes but by the working classes generally, and who in times of social disturbance is made the first victim of popular hatred, is in England rather the friend of the people than otherwise.'[26] This was a class comment at the time it was made and seems a barmy view from the perspective of a century later, when the country had seen Margaret Thatcher deploy police to break the coal miners' strike, television series portrayed hard-drinking tough-guys, and the evidence of the citizens' own eyes showed police careering around the streets of the big cities in fast cars, always arriving too late to do anything. Yet still the cry goes up that the way to deal with crime is to 'put the "bobby" back on the beat'. It is not the demand of a people estranged from their police.

In a society of individuals, loyalties are to groups of kindred spirits. Instead of the easy-going, random meetings of street life, the English do their socializing by choice and form clubs. 'Who runs the country?' asked John Betjeman rhetorically. 'The Royal Society for the Protection of Birds. Their members are behind every hedge.' And he was speaking long before the RSPB membership reached its present vertiginous levels of well over 1 million. There are clubs to go fishing, support football teams, play cards, arrange flowers, race pigeons, make jam, ride bicycles, watch birds, even for going on holiday. Many Europeans adopted medieval guild systems, but it took the English to develop honorary membership of the stonemasons' guild into Freemasonry, and to create the first Grand Lodge or association of lodges in 1717. Though much reduced in strength, by the late 1990s the organization was still boasting 350,000 members. Other organizations founded by the English – the Boy Scouts or the Salvation Army, for example – have been exported worldwide.

Even the great political and humanitarian campaigns, like William Wilberforce's fight to abolish slavery through his Anti-Slavery Society, have been the consequence of voluntary association. Still, the main organization working to protect children is the charity the NSPCC. The point about all these organizations is that you choose whether to belong.

'Home' is what the English have instead of a Fatherland. The notion of a *Vaterland* or *Patrie* is too hedged around with a sense of the importance of the state and ideas of race and breeding. 'Home' is where the individual lives, but it is also something imagined, a spiritual resting place. But, curiously, it can also mean that the idea of 'England' which the English carry in their minds is different to the reality they see around them.

CHAPTER EIGHT

THERE ALWAYS WAS
AN ENGLAND

An acre in Middlesex is better than a principality in Utopia.
LORD MACAULAY

On the eve of St George's Day 1993, the then British Prime Minister, John Major, had a tricky speech to deliver. He needed to convince his party they could trust him to defend the country when negotiating with the European Union. Party discipline was already badly fraying, as an increasingly voluble right-wing caucus refused to accept his assurances. The issue of Britain's relations with the rest of Europe split the party from the top of the cabinet to the humblest constituency association, with opinion getting increasingly 'anti-Europe' the further you got towards the party's grassroots. Within four years, the parliamentary party would be in more or less open warfare on the subject, squabbling among themselves as the Conservative government spiralled out of the sky to electoral oblivion in May 1997.

Major could sense all this. His own attitude to Europe suffered by comparison with his right-wing critics, with their easy and scary slogans, because it was essentially pragmatic, with little clear ideology. His beliefs, in the sovereignty of nation states and the importance of free trade, were no different from those of most of his party. But he was not prepared to demonize the rest of the European Union, most of whose leaders he knew and respected. What was he to do? This most English of men was a decent chap who ought to have had an instinctive understanding of the worries of 'his' people. But he had been trapped in the narrow world of Westminster politics for years. And he had few rhetorical skills; a reporter who had seen him mount his soapbox during the 1992 election campaign had described him as sounding, when he tried to declaim, like some 'angry nerd in Woolworth's returning a faulty toaster'.[1]

Much of the speech could write itself. There would be a recital of the government's achievements, the usual credit-taking that is the small change of political opportunism. There would be a lot of nonsense about the government's determination to be 'at the heart of Europe' when so much of its own behaviour made it seem less like a heart and more like an appendix. There would be claims that nothing in Britain's involvement in Europe endangered the country's sovereignty. There would be the blunt suggestion that, frankly, the country had no alternative. But he needed a peroration to end with and an image of Britain's security to leave with his audience. What emerged was an extraordinary word portrait. 'Fifty years from now,' he said, 'Britain will still be the country of long shadows on county grounds, warm beer, invincible green suburbs, dog lovers and pools fillers and – as George Orwell said – "old maids cycling to holy communion through the morning mist".'[2]

Where on earth did all this stuff come from? Which corner of England was the Prime Minister talking about where life proceeded in this quaint, prelapsarian way? The last time we heard a Prime Minister wax lyrical about an England of smiling milkmaids and warm beer was in the 1920s. Stanley Baldwin claimed to speak 'not as a man in the street, but as a man in the field-path, a much simpler person steeped in tradition and impervious to new ideas'. (At the time he was chosen to lead the Conservative party in 1923 Baldwin claimed to have been preparing to return home to Worcestershire where he said he would 'lead a decent life and keep pigs'.) Despite having a Scottish grandfather and a Welsh grandmother, Baldwin presented himself as a thoroughbred Englishman. With what metropolitan snobs considered to be a studied sub-urbanity of cherrywood pipe and tweed suit, his appeal to the people was that of a stolid, God-fearing yeoman (another sleight of hand: he was a third-generation ironmaster who never owned more than a handful of acres within sight of the family forge).

To me, England is the country, and the country is England [Baldwin said in a characteristic speech]. And when I ask myself what I mean by England, when I think of England when I am abroad, England comes to me through my various senses – through the ear, through the eye and through certain imperishable scents . . . The sounds of England, the tinkle of the hammer on the anvil in the country smithy, the corncrake on a dewy morning, the sound of the scythe against the whetstone, and the sight of a plough team coming over the brow of a hill, the sight that has been England since England was a land . . . the one eternal sight of England.[3]

It was pure fantasy. There was absolutely nothing eternal about any of these sights or sounds. The scythe was already being replaced by harvesting machines, and as the internal combustion engine moved in, the blacksmith was reduced to making shoes for the ponies of the children of the businessmen who were buying up the cottages of farmworkers driven from the land. By the time of this speech, England had been a predominantly urban society for seventy years. The vast majority could no more have recognized the *rerrk-rerrk* call of a corncrake than they could have parsed Sanskrit. By the time John Major stood up to deliver his Baldwinesque speech seventy years later, the corncrake appeared in England only as an occasional summer visitor – its breeding habitat had been destroyed by intensive farming. Major had modified the idyll a little, to draw in suburbs as well as countryside. But they are 'green suburbs', the comfortable places which exist as a refuge from the city.

The speech was manna from heaven for the satirists, who seized with metropolitan disdain on the antediluvian imagery as another sign of the Prime Minister's fading hold on reality. When I asked John

Major why on earth he had chosen these sub-Baldwin metaphors, the memory was clearly still painful three years later. He felt he had been misunderstood (characteristically he added, 'my fault, perhaps'). As he saw it, he had 'quoted some poetry' about 'warm beer and English maids cycling to communion', 'to illustrate that the essential characteristics of our country would never be lost by a deepening relationship with the European Union. The intended message was, to put it bluntly: the French and Germans will not take over, as so many people fear!'

The fiction must be maintained that political leaders write their own speeches (although Major's belief that he had 'quoted some poetry' gives the game away). But the truth is that, for all the lampooning, it worked. John Major's audience *did* recognize the picture of England he painted. Why?

Something remarkable has happened to the English perception of the land in which they live. Major was like the man at the top of a well lowering a bucket to snatch up water. In the collective unconscious from which John Major drew his pictures, there exists another England. It is not the country in which the English actually live, but the place they *imagine* they are living in. It touches the reality they see around them at various points, but it is something ideal, like the 'other country' of Spring-Rice's patriotic hymn: 'her ways are ways of gentleness and all her paths are peace'. What has happened is that the English have become exiles from their own country. Their relationship with this arcadia is that of some emotional remittance-man.

The picture of England that the English carry in their collective mind is so astonishingly powerful because it is a sort of haven. The critic Raymond Williams once wrote that romantic ruralism was connected with imperial exile, a refuge conjured up in the longing for home of a chap stuck deep in the bush, serving his queen:

Its green peace contrasted with the tropical or arid places of actual work; its sense of belonging, of community, idealized by contrast with the tensions of colonial rule and the isolated alien settlement. The birds and trees and rivers of England; the natives speaking, more or less, one's own language: these were the terms of many imagined and actual settlements. The country, now, was a place to retire to.[4]

By the time of John Major's speech, the same idea could be applied not merely to the overseas victims of the English Tourist Board's propaganda, but to millions of native English people living their lives in the suburbs and dreaming of a return one day to the Land of Lost Content.

The idea becomes strongest when times are most stressful. In World War One, soldiers were despatched to the Front by the trainload from industrial cities and towns around Britain. Their loved ones sent them postcards showing churches, fields and gardens, above all, villages. 'This', the unstated message went, 'is what you are fighting for.' The protection of this arcadian 'home' was invested with a greater nobility than any amount of flag-waving. Sir Arthur Quiller-Couch, whose immensely popular anthology *The Oxford Book of English Verse* was in many a kitbag on the Western Front,[5] claimed that English patriotism drew on the spirit of Merrie England. It was not, he said, the English way, to throw back 'Rule Britannia' at 'Deutschland über alles'. Blithely ignoring the fact that, for most Englishmen, the countryside was a place from which their ancestors had escaped and of which they had only the haziest knowledge, 'Q' claimed that the private soldier in the trenches looked to 'a green nook of his youth in Yorkshire or Derbyshire, Shropshire or Kent or Devon; where the folk are slow, but there is seed time and harvest'.[6] There was more in a similar vein from the editor of the 1917 YMCA anthology produced for soldiers, *The Old Country: A Book of Love and Praise of England* (how characteristic that it is England, not Britain), who believed that from his trench the soldier, 'in imagination, can see his village home'.

By the outbreak of the Great War, the British navy was the most powerful on earth and her army had accumulated battle honours in most corners of the world: German soldiers reported facing massed machine guns, when they were really just the well drilled rifles of the British Expeditionary Force. At no stage did the British field a European-style 'peasant army'. When Kitchener realized that a vastly expanded mass army would be needed, it was drawn mainly from the urban proletariat. Yet it was often portrayed as a force of ploughmen, shepherds and market gardeners: when you saw it like that, it became some sort of moral militia.

The most famous evocation of this idea is Rupert Brooke's *The Soldier*. Brooke seemed the distillation of the English hero, handsome, athletic, sensitive and brave, a man, in Henry James's words, 'on whom the gods had smiled their brightest'. The most famous of his war sonnets was written at the end of 1914, after he had volunteered for service with the Royal Naval Division:

> If I should die, think only this of me:
>   That there's some corner of a foreign field
> That is for ever England. There shall be
>   In that rich earth a richer dust concealed;
> A dust whom England bore, shaped, made aware,
>   Gave, once, her flowers to love, her ways to roam,
> A body of England's, breathing English air,
>   Washed by the rivers, blest by the suns of home.
>
> And think, this heart, all evil shed away,
>   A pulse in the eternal mind, no less
>   Gives somewhere back the thoughts by England given,
> Her sights and sounds; dreams happy as her day;
>   And laughter, learnt of friends; and gentleness,
>   In hearts at peace, under an English heaven.

The poem was acclaimed immediately. Its marriage of some of the strongest ideas of Englishness – goodness, home, the countryside – encapsulated exactly how the English wanted to see themselves. They contrast starkly with the poet's nasty death of blood poisoning aboard a French hospital ship in the Dardanelles. The timing is significant, too. At the end of 1914 the British Expeditionary Force was losing 80 per cent of its strength – nearly 3,000 officers and over 55,000 men – at the Battle of Ypres. Already, another poet, Charles Sorley, had written 'England – I am sick of the sound of the word', and once the scale of the casualties and the paltriness of the gains had sunk in, pastoral whimsicality rang hollow. The dreams of clean-limbed heroes dying for a land of rose-scented hedgerows had been replaced by something altogether darker, in the verse of Wilfred Owen or Siegfried Sassoon. The writers who emerged from the war – Eliot, Graves, Huxley and the rest – had a blacker view of humanity than this dream of clean-limbed youth suggested.

But somehow the English mind kept alive the idea that the soul of England lay in the countryside. A. E. Housman's *A Shropshire Lad*, first published privately, had, by 1922, sold 21,000 copies. The whole country was soon pining for his 'blue remembered hills'. Writers like H. J. Massingham – a townie who had escaped to the Chilterns – produced book after book (his own score was forty in thirty years) telling the English people that the Industrial Revolution had 'destroyed the true England', while the countryside was 'a source of our daily bread and the indispensable foundation of our national well-being'.[7] People who should have known better, like Sir Philip Gibbs, who had been one of only five war correspondents officially accredited to the British Expeditionary Force in 1915, were soon back in this agrestic wonderland. Despite being London-born and -bred, Gibbs's celebration of the 1935 Silver Jubilee of George V, *England Speaks*, begins 'England is still beautiful where one slips away from the roar of traffic and the blight of industrialism . . . All this modernisation is, I find, very superficial. I mean, it has not yet bitten into the soul of England or poisoned its brain'.[8]

A visit to any secondhand bookshop will show the enthusiasm with which readers – many, if not most of whom, of course, lived in suburbia – grasped again at this idea that the modern world they lived in was a poison, that the real England was 'out there'. By 1930, there were a million cars on the roads and a torrent of books began to appear celebrating the English countryside as a place to visit or to dream about. Batsford's *Face of Britain* series was phenomenally successful. Arthur Mee, inventor of the *Children's Encyclopaedia* and the *Children's Newspaper*, produced forty-one volumes describing *The King's England*. The Shell Oil company invited John Betjeman to edit its series of *Shell Guides* to the counties of England. Recognizing the way that urban sprawl was gorging upon the countryside, the Council for the Preservation of Rural England was founded in 1926 to protest against the spread of tar. Putting footwear upon this interest, the Ramblers Association was established in 1935, a crusade to allow urban walkers to stroll where they pleased across the countryside. They could find cheap and wholesome accommodation with the Youth Hostel Association, which had been founded in 1930 and within five years had nearly 50,000 members.

Those who didn't run to knapsacks, boots and baggy shorts could read accounts of the travels of others. H. V. Morton's hugely successful *In Search of England* was published in 1927: it had been conceived as he lay ill in Palestine, convinced he was dying of meningitis. It never seems to have struck him as odd that when he thought of the England he imagined he would never see again he didn't conjure up St Paul's Cathedral or the townscapes of his youth, but villages, church bells, thatched cottages and woodsmoke rising in the clear air. J. B. Priestley, who had been born and raised in industrial Bradford, travelled the country in his Daimler in 1933 to produce *English Journey*. While conceding that preserving an England of 'cathedrals and minsters and manor houses and inns, of Parson and Squire' would require killing off nine tenths of the existing population, he gave it as his opinion that 'nearly all Englishmen are at heart country gentlemen'.

On the bandwagon rolled, reassuring the English in a belief that 'England is the country and the country England'. In 1932 the

English Folk Song Society merged with its Folk Dance counterpart, the better to protect the rural cultural heritage. Edward Elgar was portrayed as drawing his inspiration from some mystical power in the Malvern Hills and Worcestershire. The country village became a paradigm of English life: the title of C. Henry Warren's 1940 morale-booster, *England is a Village*, says it all. 'England's might is still in her fields and villages, and though the whole weight of mechanized armies rolls over to crush them, in the end they will triumph. The best of England is a village.'[9] Virginia Woolf's last novel *Between the Acts* is set in a village where virtually nothing had changed in a hundred years: '1833 was true in 1939. No house had been built; no town had sprung up. Hogben's Folly was still eminent; the very flat, field-parcelled land had changed only in this – the tractor had to some extent superseded the plough.'[10] The village is never named in the novel: there's no need, as it is 'the very heart of England'. Agatha Christie's first Miss Marple novel, *Murder at the Vicarage*, published in 1930, even included maps of the nameless village where a retired colonel is murdered in the study. The abundance of 1930s thrillers in which colonels are done to death in picturesque hamlets – the 'Mayhem Parva' school of writing as Colin Watson puts it – have a very particular kind of village in mind. It is in the Home Counties, 'where there's a church, a village inn, very handy for the odd Scotland Yard inspector and his man who come to stay for the regularly recurring crimes'.[11]

So by the time the next world war rolled around, the idea that England is a garden had somehow regrown, not so much like a perennial flower as some peculiarly invasive weed. The sons of those who had survived the horrors of the trenches were marching off to war again, singing,

> There'll always be an England
> While there's a country lane,
> Wherever there's a cottage small
> Beside a field of grain.

A couple of wartime broadcasts will be sufficient to make the point. On Easter Day 1943 Peter Scott, the naturalist son of the imperial hero who had frozen to death in Antarctica, gave a talk for the BBC. At the outbreak of war Scott had joined the Royal Naval Volunteer Reserve, where he served in destroyers, on anti-invasion patrols in the Western Approaches. 'For most of us,' he said, England means 'a picture of a certain kind of countryside, the English countryside. If you spend much time at sea, that particular combination of fields and hedges and woods that is so essentially England seems to have a new meaning.' He recalled how he felt when, on patrol, he looked from his destroyer to the English coast:

I remember as dawn broke looking at the black outlines of Star Point to the northward and thinking suddenly of England in quite a new way – a threatened England that was in some way more real and more friendly because she was in trouble. I thought of the Devon countryside lying behind that black outline of the cliffs; the wild moors and ragged tors inland and, near the sea, the narrow winding valleys with their steep green sides; and I thought of the mallards and teal which were rearing their ducklings in the reed beds of Slapton Leigh. That was the countryside we were so determined to protect from the invader.[12]

It does not seem to have struck Scott as odd that while he thought it was the valleys and hedgerows he was fighting to defend, it was the cities and ports that had Hitler's bombs raining down upon them.

A couple of months earlier, John Betjeman had given another talk on the BBC Home Service, in which he described a visit during the Battle of Britain to a village in Kent at which the Women's Institute was staging a competition to find the best decorated table centre:

Bombs and aeroplanes were falling out of the sky; guns thundered and fragments of shell whizzed about. 'I am afraid we have not *everybody* here,' said the head of the Institute. 'You see, several of our members had to be up all night, but we have quite a little show all the same': and there they were, the raffia mats, the bowls of bulbs, the trailing ends of smilax writhing round mustard and pepper pots. God be praised for such dogged calm.

He went on that

For me, England stands for the Church of England, eccentric incumbents, oil-lit churches, Women's Institutes, modest village inns, arguments about cow-parsley on the altar, the noise of mowing machines on Saturday afternoons, local newspapers, local auctions, the poetry of Tennyson, Crabbe, Hardy and Matthew Arnold, local talent, local concerts, a visit to the cinema, branch-line trains, light railways, leaning on gates and looking across fields; for you, it may stand for something else, equally eccentric to me as I may appear to you, something to do with Wolverhampton or dear old Swindon or wherever you happen to live. But just as important. But I know the England *I* want to come home to is not very different from that in which you want to live. If it were some efficient ant-heap which the glass and steel, flat-roof, straight-road boys want to make it, then how could we love it as we do?[13]

Well, at least he conceded the possibility that people might live in Wolverhampton or 'dear old Swindon', but his touchstones of Englishness are all about tranquillity, simplicity and village pursuits. In the half-century which has followed that broadcast, the 'glass and steel, flat-roof, straight-road boys' have elbowed whimsicality aside. The real destroyers of Betjeman's England have turned out not to be the Luftwaffe but the town planners, the accountants who pronounced sentence of death on railway branch lines and the cowardly politicians who bent the knee to pile-'em-high-sell-'em-cheap retailers and rapacious developers demanding the right to build wherever they liked. By the 1990s, according to the Council for the Protection of Rural England, British roads covered an area the size of Leicestershire and carparks a space twice the size of Birmingham. The consequence was to make the English people more convinced than ever that wherever England was, it was certainly not what they saw around them.

Here is an amusing game. Stand in the middle of a High Street in the Surrey stockbroker belt and allow the crowds of Saturday morning shoppers to drift past. Count them as they pass, and look closely at every seventh person. Statistically, you will have found a member of the National Trust. It is an astonishing fact that one seventh of the entire population of this wealthy county, be they window-cleaners, policemen, pensioners, criminals or lunatics, belongs to this organization devoted to preserving the past.

It would be Surrey, of course. Surrey, with its half-timbered, half-a-million-pound Edwardian mansions, its well-watered golf courses, its endless procession of nameless Conservative MPs. It cannot be a truly representative cross-section of the population, this one-in-seven, for preserving the past is the hobby of the wealthy. The poor are more worried about a better future. The key to the National Trust's success in Surrey is to make members feel they belong to a club, and that if they don't belong, their social life will be the poorer. The formula also works well in West Sussex, where the figure is nearly one in ten of the population of the county, and even in Surrey's northern cousin, Cheshire, where in the wealthier enclaves membership approaches the same level.

The National Trust has travelled a long way since its foundation in 1895. Then, its business was to protect those picturesque areas of countryside the landed gentry didn't want for their field sports. The intention was to create a series of 'outdoor sitting rooms' for the poor to escape the foul air of the Victorian cities. In doing so, it would provide a shield for parts of 'old' England, which Thomas Hardy's novels showed being eaten alive by the demands of the machines. It was very much part of the mood of the time, the height of the country's industrial greatness, glancing backwards to a vanishing 'real' England. *Country Life* (founded two years later) offered a fond look back at country piles: it was so successful that its founder, Edward Hudson, was able to do what generations of his readers have only been able to dream of, and buy a succession of country houses, ending up living at Lindisfarne castle. The English musical renaissance, led by composers like Edward Elgar, Ralph Vaughan Williams and Frederick Delius, involved the rediscovery of sixteenth- and seventeenth-century music and (despite Elgar's splendid put-down 'I *am* folk music') the reclaiming of folk melodies. In architecture, Edwin Lutyens's British Pavilion at the Paris Exhibition of 1900 was a faithful copy of a seventeenth-century country house, while at home, the rash of fake half-timbering was soon to crawl out along arterial roads the length of the country.

The theme of the destruction of 'old' England had already been around a good while by the time of the National Trust's invention. In 1822, the Vicomte de Chateaubriand, then French ambassador in London, had written about the 'melancholy vertigo' that overtook him as he thought about the passing of pre-industrial England:

Today, its valleys are hidden beneath the smoke of its forges and its factories, its lanes transformed into iron tracks, and along the roads where Shakespeare and Milton wandered, trundle steaming locomotives. Already, those nurseries of knowledge, Oxford and Cambridge, are assuming an air of desolation: their colleges and Gothic chapels, now half-abandoned, are poignant to behold, whilst in their cloisters, beside the sepulchral stones from the Middle Ages, lie neglected the marble annals of the people of Ancient Greece – ruins guarded by ruins.[14]

By preserving the ruins, the National Trust feeds this belief that the worst is yet to come. Of course, the millions who visit historic houses and gardens have a gentle, undemanding day out, usually involving a cup of tea and a bit of a stroll. But what does the Trust's phenomenal success tell us about the English frame of mind? We must accept, first, that a sense of history runs deep in the English people. It may not be particularly well informed (a surprising number of people are unsure precisely how many wives Henry VIII had), but it is deeply felt and is one of the things that makes the people what they are. The National Trust expresses this sense, as does the appetite for cheap historical romance, a love of Shakespeare and a deep-rooted scepticism about the political leaders of the rest of Europe.

Secondly, it is indicative of a deep conservatism. Every traditional English family home has a room, a cupboard, an attic, cellar or garage piled with everything from ancient prams to odd rolls of wallpaper in the patterns of twenty years ago, old light-fittings to the boxes in which long-broken electrical appliances were sold. They are kept because 'they might come in useful some day'. Really, their pragmatic and sensible owners are just reluctant to part with them. In 1930, after twenty years living among the English, Émile Cammaerts concluded the habit was indicative of an attitude to life: 'The present is not, for them, a hard line of demarcation between two opposite worlds, but a gentle mist through which they wander leisurely . . . They travel through time, as they do indeed through space, dragging behind them a quantity of useless luggage.'[15] He has a point. How else can one explain the survival of so much that is so utterly pointless – barristers' wigs, bearskins, an unelected House of Lords, flummeries from the Trooping the Colour to Swan-upping, or archaic-sounding offices of state like Chancellor of the Duchy of Lancaster or Warden of the Cinque Ports? In the end, it gets to everyone: those who start their adulthood in passionate argument for modernization end up dreaming of a seat in the House of Lords.

Thirdly, of course, the English are class-obsessed and intensely nosy. Part of the attraction for the 160,000 people visiting Churchill's home at Chartwell, or the 140,000 going to the Astors' residence at Cliveden is to see how the other half lived and to imagine themselves in their shoes. The Duchess of Devonshire treasures the baffled comment written in the visitors' book at Chatsworth, their pile in Derbyshire: 'Saw the Duke in the garden. He looked quite normal.'

In the great houses, the staff easily outnumbered the family, often many times over. Yet how many of the tourists at these places call to mind a picture of themselves as a 'tweeny', helping out the cook and housemaid, as the third footman or the twelfth undergardener?

The National Trust's success story tells us something else about the English. It took ten years from the Trust's foundation for membership to reach 500. Even at its Golden Jubilee in 1945, it still had only 800 subscribers. Yet by the time of its centenary in 1995, it had 2 million: the archly smug 'I'm one in a million' bumper stickers the Trust had been handing out only seven years previously now looked decidedly feeble. The growth did not stop there. Within a further two years, it had added another half-million. No similar organization in the world can match its success: even the most popular of the big houses open to the public in history-deprived nations like the United States cater for only a few tens of thousands of visitors. The number of visits to National Trust properties in England and Wales is 10 million. This phenomenal success reflects a growing population of elderly people with time on their hands, as well as a general increase in leisure time. But it also says something about the English. It is surely more than mere coincidence that the membership of the National Trust has exploded at the time when uncertainty about national identity has become most acute?

The English country house has become a metaphor for the state of the country. There are two relevant texts here. The first is James Lees-Milne's elegant wartime diaries recounting his journeys around England from one ancestral pile to another. He would be given appalling food to eat by eccentric old men rattling around in freezing buildings. In exchange, as secretary of the Country Houses Committee of the National Trust, he would listen to their pleas for help in coping with the world they guessed would follow the war: the successful ones would find their houses taken over by the Trust, in a deal which allowed them to continue living there. The second text is Evelyn Waugh's *Brideshead Revisited*, whose immense popularity, both between hard covers and when televised in 1980, attests to the plebs' fascination with the aristocracy, and the power of the bricks-and-mortar metaphor. The book is narrated by Charles Ryder, who finds himself in a wartime billet in the beautiful great house that had once consumed his imagination; at times it reads like a lament for a dead love-affair.

Despite its immense popularity, even Evelyn Waugh became slightly nauseated with *Brideshead* for its necrophiliac obsession with the splendours of the past. He conceded, in a preface to the 1959 edition of the novel, that it was 'a panegyric preached over an empty coffin'.[16] He was right. While it may be true that over 1,000 country houses were demolished between 1875 and 1975, that still leaves over 1,500 big landed estates in England. More profoundly, one might wonder what the decay of the country house has to do with the rest of the population anyway. If its decline was a sign of anything, it was a mark of the inability of the upper classes to cope with taxation, agricultural depression, the loss of a generation in the Great War and, often, their own unworldliness. The extraordinary popularity of the National Trust testifies to contradictory impulses in the English. At one level, it bears out a strong sense of individual freedom. What more vivid example can there be of the triumph of the common people over the landed aristocracy than the fact that their houses are now owned and visited by millions? But at the same time, when the English celebrate these Ideal Homes they are venerating feudalism.

If you had to guess the whereabouts of the lane, small cottage and field of grain where there'll always be an England, you'd decide pretty quickly where it was *not*. You could instantly rule out places like Northumberland or Yorkshire, where the fields would have dry-stone walls and are more likely to be full of sheep anyway. Come to think of it, you could probably rule out anywhere north of a line from the Severn to the Trent. For not only is this imagined

England rural rather than urban, it is southern rather than northern.

At first glance, this seems rather surprising, since, by comparison with places like Yorkshire or Northumberland, the counties of southern England scarcely exist. Who knows – who cares? – where Berkshire ends and Hampshire begins? Any self-respecting York-shireman knows precisely which towns are inside his county and which have the misfortune to lie in outer darkness. Yet the inhabitants of the north did not become more than paradigms of themselves – Yorkshire Tykes, Tyneside Geordies or Liverpudlian Scousers. The wealth of modern England was built on the Industrial Revolution, so how did towns like Preston, Bolton and Blackburn, which produced three cotton-spinning geniuses in Richard Arkwright, Samuel Crompton and James Hargreaves, somehow manage to be exiled from the country the English imagined they were living in?

Some of the reasons are practical. Firstly, they suffer from the significant disadvantage of being a long way from London, where fashions are set. Secondly, no coherent 'north country' has been invented in its own right: it exists mainly in contrast to southern England, which is seen as fat, affected and, above all, 'soft'. The south country is based on counties, market towns and villages of great age, where any rivalries are long dead. The north of England contains a series of mainly nineteenth-century city-states. Manchester and Liverpool may be only thirty miles apart, but they are quite distinct in character, Manchester a Protestant seat of heavy industry, Liverpool a more Catholic dock city, the one an aggressive mill and trading town, the other a gentler, more wise-cracking port. Manchester has more in common with Leeds or Sheffield, its com-mercial rivals across the Pennines, and Liverpool with Newcastle, than either has with the other. The two cities even have quite distinct accents. The virtues of the English character – tolerance, individuality, humour – are more obviously in evidence in either place than in, say, Winchester or Salisbury. They are, in a sense, the truer repositories of 'Englishness'. But because of the intense local rivalries, they have been seen merely as individual cities competitively challenging both each other and the soppy South Country.

The more profound reason is that having invented the Industrial Revolution, the English then invented a mental counter-revolution. Consider the lines which came to Wordsworth as he sat on the roof of the mail-coach rattling over Westminster Bridge for Dover in 1802.

> Earth has not anything to show more fair:
> Dull would he be of soul who could pass by
> A sight so touching in its majesty:
> This City now doth, like a garment, wear
> The beauty of the morning; silent, bare,
> Ships, towers, domes, theatres, and temples lie
> Open unto the fields, and to the sky;
> All bright and glittering in the smokeless air . . .

The 'smokeless air'? The lines could not have been written sixty years later, by which time sittings of Parliament had to be suspended in summer because of the appalling stink from the Thames. At the time Wordsworth crossed Westminster Bridge, London was the biggest city in Europe, shortly to become four times larger than Vienna and six times the size of Berlin. Yet it could still touch the Romantic poet's heart. But as the people drained away from the countryside, the capital and the other big conurbations grew at a staggering pace. In 1801, only a quarter of the English population could be called urban. By the middle of the nineteenth century, England had become the first country in the history of the world to have most of its population living in towns. Immigration from Scotland and Ireland and a staggering rate of reproduction meant that a population of 9 million in 1801 had doubled by 1851 and doubled again by 1911.

The cities grew as inelegant sprawls with a purely functional intent. As a result, England contains some of the most exceptionally hideous towns in Europe. They sprang up like a plague of warts. When Queen Victoria took the throne in 1837 there were only five places in England and Wales with a population of more than 100,000 outside London (thirty years earlier, there had been none). By 1891 there were twenty-three and the process of urbanization was irreversible.[17] It was an Englishman, Thomas de Quincey, who first noticed the new phenomenon of reddish city skyscapes caused by industrial pollution. In some of the bigger places – Manchester, Leeds or Birmingham – local industrialists who had made their pile gave a little of their fortune back to the huddle of gimcrack housing around their mills. When Joseph Chamberlain became mayor of his adopted city of Birmingham in 1873 he demolished slums, took over the gas and water companies and municipalized the sewage farms. Health improved as a result, but, in Birmingham as elsewhere, the occasional city-centre art gallery or library merely accentuated the unrelieved grimness all around.

H. G. Wells, who had been born above his father's unsuccessful hardware shop in the High Street of Bromley, Kent, speaks for all: 'It is only because the thing was spread over a hundred years and not concentrated in a few weeks,' he wrote, 'that history fails to recognize what sustained disaster, how much massacre, degeneration and disablement of lives was due to the housing of people in the nineteenth century.'[18] Friedrich Engels, whose father had taken advantage of the Industrial Revolution to found a textile mill in Manchester, travelled from one northern city to another to produce *The Condition of the Working Class in England*. It presented a picture of blackened buildings, streets rank with rubbish and shit, stinking rivers and vermin-infested tenements. Charles Dickens's Coketown in *Hard Times*, written after a visit to Preston, Lancashire, 'had the painted face of a savage', with 'a black canal in it', endless chimneys trailing 'interminable serpents of smoke' and 'a river that ran purple with ill-smelling dye'. Who would choose this diabolical place as an emblem of England? As to the inhabitants,

It contained several large streets all very like one another, and many small streets still more like one another, inhabited by people equally like one another, who all went in and out at the same hours, with the same sound upon the same pavements, to do the same work, and to whom every day was the same as yesterday and tomorrow, and every year the counterpart of the last and the next.[19]

Is it any wonder that the English did not wish to see these places as the heart of England?

They turned instead to tales of the 'real' country – pure and breezy and full of clean-limbed artisans uncorrupted by the filth of the cities. The delightful books of Richard Jefferies provide some of the better examples. This most English of writers, the son of a small farmer, first won success in 1878 with his detailed and highly idealized evocation of *The Gamekeeper at Home* (it begins, 'The keeper's cottage stands in a sheltered "coombe", or narrow hollow of the woodlands, overshadowed by a mighty Spanish chestnut, bare now of leaves, but in summer a noble tree'[20]). His very popular *Wild Life in a Southern County*, which he narrates from a vantage point high up on Wiltshire downland, spreading out to cover all animal and human life in the locality, offered its readers an England in which life was based on seasonal and circadian verities. By contrast, his novel *After London* (1885) imagines a capital city which has been turned into a poisonous swamp inhabited by cruel dwarfs.

Struck down by illness when still a young man, Jefferies died at the age of thirty-eight, having for the previous two years eked out a living dictating his essays to his wife. Among the many people with whom his work struck a chord was Edward Thomas, whose 'accidental Cockney nativity' had been in Lambeth in March 1878. He spent many childhood holidays in the vanishing Wiltshire that Jefferies had spent so much energy memorializing. Thomas belongs to a school of writers – Thomas Hardy and W. H. Hudson are two others who spring to mind – who saw England as increasingly populated by people who had no sense of belonging anywhere. The new England was the England of the suburbs, in which a baffled and listless citizenry had lost all rootedness. Like so many others, Thomas perished in the First World War, killed at Arras in 1917. When his friend Walter de la Mare introduced his posthumous *Collected Poems* in 1920 he wrote simply that 'if one word could tell his all, that word would be England . . . When Edward Thomas was killed in Flanders, a mirror of England was shattered, of so true and pure a crystal that a clearer and tenderer reflection can be found in no other than these poems.' Of course, it is not England that is reflected in his poems. It is a *part* of England. Thomas's England, the England of rolling hills, village greens and hedgerows is what he called The South Country. When he explained what he meant by the term, he spoke of it as being below the Thames and the Severn and east of Exmoor: it included Kent, Sussex, Surrey, Hampshire, Berkshire, Wiltshire, Dorset and part of Somerset.[21] To all intents and purposes, this is the essential England. Over time, it has expanded, to include counties like Oxfordshire, and stretched as far north as A. E. Housman's Shropshire.

There was one particularly big hole in this pastoral idyll: London. Its slums were as bad as anywhere, but they were offset by the city's status as capital of the Empire. One foreign visitor after another spoke in reverential tones about the splendour of the place, and was stunned on seeing the squalor of its underbelly. Fyodor Dostoevsky came away with a bundle of contradictory impressions, bowled over by the city's grandeur, energy and public amenities and appalled by the drunkenness, prostitution and general sordidness of the place. He recorded his impressions under the title Baal, in recognition of the false gods that ruled the place. He found that 'in London you no longer see the populace. Instead you see a loss of sensibility, systematic, resigned and encouraged.'[22] On a Saturday night he saw taverns where 'everyone was drunk, but drunk joylessly, gloomily and heavily'. 'Gloom never forsakes the English', he wrote. Tender English spirits agreed: John Ruskin wrote of 'the great foul city of London', William Morris called it 'hideous'.

It fitted with the growing idea that cities dehumanized the people, but London was, as it remains, exceptional. More now even than in the days when it was the centre of a world empire, the place remains an oddity. The British and English capital is, increasingly, a city which belongs to neither country but to the world. London is a centre for international organizations, its most profitable activity, the trade in money, beating to a pulse that knows no national borders. For the rest, it conforms to the English belief that the 'real' country is somewhere else. When they want to praise London the English say it is 'a collection of villages', a description which, while it may explain much of its chaotic charm, would never be uttered by a truly proud urbanite. Londoners were willing to build monuments, like Trafalgar Square, but not to plan a coherent, liveable whole.

Having invented the modern city, not only did the English monied élite recoil in horror, they pretended it had nothing to do with them. 'Take the people away from their natural breeding grounds,' Lord Walsingham told H. Rider Haggard, the author of *King Solomon's Mines*, 'thereby sapping their health and strength in cities such as nature never intended to be the permanent home of men, and the decay of this country becomes only a matter of time. In this matter, as in many others, ancient Rome has a lesson to teach.'[23] Instead of engaging with this deracinated, brutish horde, the educated classes just walked away. When Gustave Doré was looking for inspiration for his illustrations of Dante's Inferno, his idea of hell was inspired by an English city, and the theme that urbanization and industry corrupted the human spirit runs unbroken through late Victorian and early twentieth-century literature. 'Gloomy, noisy and dirty Birmingham' wrote Thomas de Quincey in *The English Mail Coach*[24] in 1849. For every Joseph Chamberlain in places like Birmingham trying to develop a civic pride, there were thousands content to take the money and run.

The contrast is again with France, which had the great advantage of industrializing later than the British and therefore being able to learn from their mistakes. It meant that the French were able to develop towns and cities that were both planned and invested with a sense of pride. More than that, the revolution gave the cities a deep suspicion of much of the countryside for its supposed royalist sympathies: the new republican France was aware of its peasant roots but determinedly and sophisticatedly urban. In England, too, there was a political dimension to the division between the conservatism of the country and the radical ideas born in cities. It was in Manchester that the agitation began that led the Anti-Corn Law League to campaign for fairer grain prices. Birmingham nurtured the Liberal caucus. The Independent Labour party was founded in Bradford. Apart from a few leafy enclaves of prosperity, cities like Manchester, Bradford and Newcastle became the sort of places where you could have pinned a red rosette to a donkey and seen it elected.

The intriguing question is why this rock-solid powerbase did not result in a new idea of England. After all, not only did most of the people now live in conurbations, but they possessed, in the Labour party, a coherent focus for their ambitions. That they failed to invent an alternative to the roses-round-the-door, thatched cottage and village-green impression of England is due to a combination of factors. For a start, there was the fact that socialism was, by definition, internationalist: the new Jerusalem was to be a city where citizens from all over the world would rub along in fraternal solidarity. There was the additional awkwardness that so many of the Labour movement leaders were Scottish or Welsh and the party's parliamentary majorities were built upon the over-representation of the Celtic fringe at Westminster: it was therefore always much more 'British' than English. Thirdly, the political division of the country, with the Conservatives holding the rural 'shire' counties, while the cities belonged to Labour, meant that those who did well in trade moved to live in areas which carried a different political banner: a fatal association was thus cemented between political affiliation and social aspiration. Fourthly, there was the fact that so many of the early idealists, from Morris onwards, were strongly anti-urban and hostile to industry. And fifthly, there was the fact that so many leaders of the Labour movement – Harold Wilson with his cottage in the Scilly Isles, or James Callaghan with his farm in Sussex are two who spring to mind at once – themselves obviously aspired to escape the city.

Those – the great majority of Labour voters – who were denied the chance of release were condemned to live in places that had been thrown up in a hurry a century ago by speculative builders to meet the needs of manufacturing. The only difference today is that so many of the industries no longer exist. Urban socialism seems to have spent so much of its energy trying merely to mitigate the effects of capitalism. 'Gas-and-water socialism', the efforts by city authorities to provide heat, light and sanitation to the urban masses, was a noble aim. But it sought essentially to improve what already existed rather than to invent something new. The same was true of the vast post-war slum clearance programmes, which ended up decanting the masses from back-to-back terraces into cheaply built high-rise towers.

The cities do have their fans, who see in their energy, their industry, railway stations and tramlines, their great civic monuments, something awesome. But even socialists have found it hard to imagine that their country's heart could beat there. When H. V. Morton went to Leeds to write a piece for the *Daily Herald*, later reprinted as a pamphlet for the Labour party in 1933, he noted bleakly that 'to be quite frank, the whole of Leeds should be scrapped and rebuilt . . . [It] is the creation of the big commercial booms of the nineteenth century, when no-one cared for anything but profit and exploitation. It is a nasty, dirty old money box'.[25] D. H. Lawrence's return to the Nottinghamshire mining country of his childhood led him to think that the real tragedy of England, as I see it, is the tragedy of ugliness. The country is lovely; the man-made England is so vile ... The great crime which the moneyed classes and promoters of industry committed in the palmy Victorian days was the condemning of the workers to ugliness, ugliness, ugliness: meanness and formless and ugly surroundings, ugly ideals, ugly religion, ugly hope, ugly love, ugly clothes, ugly furniture, ugly houses, ugly relationship between workers and employers ... The English character has failed to develop the real *urban* side of a man, the civic side. Siena is a bit of place, but it is a real city, with citizens intimately connected with the city. Nottingham is a vast place sprawling towards a million, and it is nothing more than an amorphous agglomeration. There *is* no Nottingham, in the sense that there is Siena. The Englishman is stupidly undeveloped as citizen. And it is partly due to his 'little home' stunt, and partly to his acceptance of hopeless paltriness in his surroundings ... The English are town-birds through and through, today, as the inevitable result of their complete industrialization. Yet they don't know how to build a city, how to think of one, or how to live in one. They are all suburban, pseudo-cottagey, and not one of them knows how to be truly urban.[26]

The scorn is as well deserved now as it was when Lawrence wrote it. Even new supermarket branches for the suburbs are half-timbered. A visit to one of the dozens of craft fairs every summer will give some idea of how deeply rooted is this belief in pseudo-cottageyness. The clientele are parents and grandparents; teenagers are, not surprisingly, absent. They watch displays of wattle-making, weaving, potting and dry-stone walling in the warm August sunshine with polite interest. But they reach for their wallets inside the marquees. Here, some atavistic impulse has them lining up in their hundreds to buy ornamental pottery light-pulls, wooden bedroom nameplates, wrought-iron names for their houses ('Castaway Cottage', 'Miller's Rest', 'Hazel Haven'), tiny wooden model villages, complete with pub, church and village green. Even, heaven help us, patchwork loo-roll covers.

What is it they all appeal to? Some inner belief that the great swathe of suburbia sprawling across the South Country in which they live is not really their home at all.

So how did John Major's evocation of the English idyll seem to the few people who actually live in it? The Dorset town of Beaminster, whose creamy limestone houses and shops, central square and dazzling sixteen-pinnacled church tower are almost unchanged from Thomas Hardy's day (it is the 'Emminster' of his Wessex novels), was as good a place as any to find out. I was sitting on the terrace of a farmhouse high above the town, on one of those glorious late-summer days when the English countryside seems to exhale after the heat of the day and the fields and hillsides relax into their richest green. Butterflies danced around the flowers in the garden, buzzards wheeled lazily in the sky. A blue heat haze had still not quite evaporated in the valley and the tower of Beaminster church struck upwards through it, like a pencil on a sketchpad. If John Major had anywhere in mind, it surely must have been here, the quintessence of the imagined South Country.

From her terrace, Georgia Langton looks down on this glorious panorama with a cup of tea in her hand. She is a handsome, grey-haired woman of fifty-four, aware that as a relatively wealthy widow she is infinitely privileged to live in this picture of the ideal England. From the fields behind the house come the distant bleat of her sheep. On the hillside below, the beech trees rustle in the evening breeze. So what did she and her neighbours think when they heard John Major's speech?

'We all fell about with laughter. We laughed ourselves silly.'

Why?

Because it's all packaging. It's all an illusion. The farmers around here can only live on subsidies. You know who's paying to keep this alive? You are, the taxpayers. And because the farmers don't need half the staff they once needed, the farmworkers have all been driven off the land. Their cottages get sold – unmodernized – for hundreds of thousands of pounds.

Which means country people simply can't afford to live here any more. So new people move in. Then they start complaining about the mud on the roads, the fact that there aren't any pavements or streetlights. And soon it's all just another suburb. The whole country's just one big suburb now.

If they are honest, most country people will agree with her: where the English countryside remains, it exists only as scenery. North-east of Beaminster, on Cranborne Chase, is the place where an eccentric group of back-to-the-land romantics tried to act out the idea of England as some earthy dream. On a walking tour in 1924 the composer Balfour Gardiner had come across Gore Farm, a run-down part of an old Dorset estate. Before the First World War, Gardiner had, with Percy Grainger, Norman O'Neil, Roger Quilter and Cyril Scott, been part of the 'Frankfurt Group' of musicians who were to do much for English music. But he discovered that after the war the appetite for his romantically inspired work had almost disappeared, to be replaced by a taste for something altogether more austere. As the well-off son of a London merchant, Gardiner could afford the gesture that followed, and he renounced music. It also meant he had the means to buy Gore Farm, where with his nephew, Rolf Gardiner (an 'English patriot' who was part Austrian-Jewish and part Scandinavian), he created a back-to-the-land community. The idea was to act out D. H. Lawrence's incoherent urgings about escaping the horrors of industrialism ('we'll have to establish some spot on earth that will be the fissure into the under-world, like the oracle at Delphos', the novelist wrote to Gardiner[27]). The principles of this curious group had a millennialist feel: they believed in organic farming, small communities, self-government and the beneficial power of folk-custom. To the bafflement of local people, tented work camps sprang up in the summer, where, beneath a Cross of St George, young people would emerge to sing English folk-songs and prance around Morris-dancing before being sent off to plant trees.

Now, only the husk of an idea is left. Gardiner had fought the death of country life as best he could. He bought land, applied visionary ideas of organic farming, planted 4½ million trees to raise the water table and encouraged local people to take an interest both in their folk history and contemporary democracy. Many of Gardiner's ideas were bizarre – a belief in the purifying power of folk-dancing for one – but his legacy lives on in the Soil Association and in the forests that have, as he planned, saved Cranborne Chase from becoming a scrubby, sheep-cropped temperate desert. But even this eccentric dedication was not enough to stop the rot. Thirty local people worked for Rolf Gardiner. His son, the celebrated conductor John Eliot Gardiner, still spends lambing, calving and harvest times at Gore Farm. But he employs only two men, one of whom has to live on a housing estate in a nearby town because it is the nearest affordable accommodation.

Talking drivel about life in the countryside is a staple of the propagandists' idea of England, a good example being the work of Arthur Bryant, author of patriotic histories with titles like *English Saga* and *Set in a Silver Sea*.[28] But the strength of such myths is so great that in February 1996 the Council for the Protection of Rural England (its name had altered slightly since its foundation seventy years earlier) persuaded all three of the major party leaders to sign a letter to *The Times*. This joint appeal was not unprecedented: Tony Blair, John Major and Paddy Ashdown were consciously echoing a joint appeal from Stanley Baldwin, Ramsay MacDonald and Lloyd George, who had all signed a letter to the same newspaper on 8 May 1929 arguing for the countryside to be protected from unplanned development. The 1996 version contained similar platitudes ('the full confidence that the necessary development can and should be directed with thoughtful and scrupulous attention' . . . etc., etc.) to the 1929 version, and committed none of them to anything. No one really doubted the importance of the issue: in the twelve years to 1990, 20 per cent of hedgerows, 10 per cent of dry-stone walls, 10 per cent of ponds, and up to 14 per cent of plant species had disappeared.[29] It will, no doubt, turn out to have achieved nothing: the 1929 appeal was followed by an explosion of housing developments across the green fields of southern England.

Drafted by the dead hand of bureaucracy, the letter was not significant for what it said, but for the fact that all three party leaders felt it worth their while to sign it. You cannot imagine them getting together to argue that England's cities should be preserved. But the obsessive English belief that the only 'real' England is some other version of Arthur Bryant's land of singing milkmaids is dangerous for three reasons. Firstly, it is counterproductive: the consequence of a belief that the only 'proper' way of life for an English person is to live in a house with a garden and access to what's left of the countryside will eventually turn most of England into one vast suburb. Secondly, it does nothing to improve the conditions in which the vast majority of people live. And thirdly, it necessarily excludes most of the population from an idea of what their country is about.

None of this is to deny the extraordinary enchantment of the English countryside. Who could resist the lure of the extraordinary names of England's villages? High Easter, New Delight, Kingston Bagpuize, Sleeping Green, Tiptoe, Nether Wallop, Nymphsfield, Christmas Common, Samlesbury Bottoms, Ryme Intrinseca, Huish Champflower, Buckland-tout-Saints, Wyre Piddle, Martin Husingtree, Norton-Juxta-Twycross and so on, a gazetteer of dreams. More, the landscape of England is the landscape of its imaginative inheritance. The Chilterns are Bunyan's Delectable Mountains, Langland's Field of Folk lies beneath the Herefordshire Beacon, Dorset belongs to Hardy, Sussex to Kipling, George Herbert claims Wiltshire as powerfully as Wordsworth the Lake District, Jane Austen Hampshire or Emily Brontë the moors of west Yorkshire.

It is the charm of small things; there is scarcely a geographical feature in the land that has any claim on world records. It is a place of tended beauties; the country lane, the cottage small, the field of grain, belong to a landscape that has been shaped by generations of labour. Its appeal is charted in fields and acres. 'All is measured, mingled, varied, gliding easily one thing into another, little rivers, little plains ... little hills, little mountains ... neither prison nor palace but a decent home', as William Morris wrote, linking the landscape again to that most powerful English idea.[30] It is still a place of short perspectives. Yet increasingly in southern England, that is *all* it is. Unlike France, where a peasant culture survived the twentieth century, in England, it died out at the time that agricultural workers were turned over to their landlords' cash crops of wheat or milk: at evening they returned not to their own smallholding but to tied cottages where the best they could hope for was the room to raise a chicken or three. The real rural life has long gone, to be replaced with suburbanism that affects farmers almost as much as it affects the commuters who live around them, for agriculture is a business, too.

The pressure on remaining undeveloped bits of England is intense, because of the belief that the only way for an English person to live is to have their own little piece of Arcadia. The apartment is either for the rich, somewhere to stay while sojourning in town, or places where the poor are dumped, on vast soulless estates. Rich and poor differ in their expectations, but they share the same ambition. It is a *house* with a *garden*. Not all Englishmen can live in a castle. But they all want their moats and drawbridges. Where else in the world would you hear it seriously argued that living in flats causes riots? The resultant pressure on the land is worst in what is left of Thomas's South Country. George Walden, who retired from the House of Commons in 1997 because he thought being a backbench politician was a waste of his life, represented Buckingham in Parliament. 'I can tell you,' he says, 'there *is* no country life any longer. There's just a memory of the country, because there's so little of it left.' The people who now occupy this rural suburbia are not country people at all and have little sympathy for the way country people behave. A planning application is made for the local pub to build an extension so that it can improve business, or for permission to convert disused farm buildings into low-cost housing. Parish councils across the country report the same split: the long-time villagers will support the plans because they want the pub to survive and they want somewhere affordable for their children and grandchildren to live, the suburbanites will fight the application tooth-and-nail, to preserve the place as it was when they first arrived and maintain the value of their property. They bring with them, too, the prejudices of the town. The letters column of the *Daily Telegraph*, where once one found the English shires in full cry on anything from bad manners to the best way to deal with verdigris, reflects the change. The Letters Editor, David Twiston-Davies, told me that 'The single most noticeable thing about the letters we get now is the number which arrive from Group Captain So-and-So saying what a disgrace hunting is'.

Most of the English people left the land because they were driven away by the enclosures and the erosion of common rights, or because they wanted to better themselves. Those who can make the return journey are a privileged minority. If England is to avoid its fate of becoming one vast suburb in which there may, perhaps, be a few national parks surviving, it has to develop the art of urban living. Yet it seems incapable of recognizing an opportunity when it arises. From this point of view, the most recent calamity to befall England was for her cities to be half-bombed in the war: the measure of misfortune not so much what was lost as what replaced it. When the Luftwaffe gave the English the opportunity to rebuild their cities more graciously, they merely recreated worse versions of what had been there before. German cities that had been flattened by Allied bombing were able to reinvent themselves from scratch with the aid of the Marshall Plan.

By contrast with the English inability to create desirable metropolitan living spaces, the Dutch project to reclaim sufficient land from the sea around Amsterdam to build a community of 28,000 homes is breathtaking. The most ambitious project of its kind since the seventeenth-century has as its principal architect an Anglo-Sri Lankan, raised in Ealing, west London, and educated at Leeds University. Ruwan Alivuhare left England because, he says,

I fell in love with Amsterdam, and I couldn't stand being spat at four times a day in Leeds . . . I could never do what I do here when I was in England. It just doesn't happen. Here we are called Steden Bouwers – city builders, who form the urban landscape. We just don't have them in England, as I notice only too clearly every time I go home to London.[31]

A visit to town centres in most counties of England will show he is right and demonstrate that the redevelopment of English cities has been left in the hands of stupid, short-sighted and sometimes corrupt local councils, aided and abetted by third-rate architects and get-rich-quick builders. If ever evidence were needed of English contempt for the urban way of life, it is there in concrete and steel.

Which brings us to the third and most damaging of the consequences of believing that the 'true' England is the England of the shires. It excludes the vast majority of the people who live in England. The country they see around them is one of blacktop streets, cars and concrete and occasional parks. The best they can hope for is some imaginative association with the land of warm beer and old maids cycling to church, but it is bought at the price of making them feel shut out and convincing them that 'England' happened years ago.

Periodically, someone will write a letter to *The Times*, pointing out that England (as distinct from Britain) has no national anthem and that it needs one. There are, perhaps, four national songs which the average Englishman can stagger through (this anthem business is a rather male preoccupation). Three of the songs are political; the National Anthem, which is really a profession of loyalty to the monarch, 'Rule Britannia', a dated and faintly embarrassing chant about imperial expansion ('When Britain first, at heaven's command . . .') and 'Land of Hope and Glory', which is another glory-days-of-empire declaration of a divine mission to rule the world. All three are really about Britain. But the fourth, William Blake's 'Jerusalem', is something else altogether.

Blake had been an ardent disciple of Emanuel Swedenborg, whose bizarre prophecies had been translated into English by Thomas Hartley in 1778. Of the sixty original subscribers to the resolutions setting up the Swedenborgian church to propagate this whacky theology in London, William Blake was number 13 and his wife number 14. She was later to complain that 'I see so little of Mr Blake now. He is always in Paradise.' Swedenborg told his English disciples that he had visited the spiritual world, which, in physical appearance, he found to be organized strikingly like our own. The angels, for example, 'dwell in contiguous habitations, disposed after the manner of our cities and streets, walks and squares. I have had the privilege to walk through them, to examine all round about, and to enter their houses, and this when I was fully awake'.[32] In this idealized garden city Swedenborg was told that the Last Judgement had been carried out in 1757 and every earthly society was heaven on a smaller scale. There was a special, select heaven reserved exclusively for English people.

The eccentric genius of his disciple, Blake, could, perhaps, only have been nurtured in an island culture. His best-known work is short (only sixteen lines) and begins with a question.

> And did those feet in ancient time
> Walk upon England's mountains green?
> And was the holy Lamb of God
> On England's pleasant pastures seen?

It is a reference to the legend, for which not a shred of evidence exists, that Jesus visited England in his youth. It was set to music in 1916 when the country needed all the moral encouragement it could find, and is the best-known apparently English song in the country, sung in schools, at weddings, funerals, and Women's Institutes. Yet it feeds precisely the same prejudice against urban life. Blake's second verse goes on to ask,

> And was Jerusalem builded here
> Among these dark Satanic mills?

The question seems to conjure up some possibility of national redemption. But the contrast between the green and pleasant land and the Satanic mills peddles the same old propaganda. It is merely a more mystical version of the English aphorism that 'You are closer to God in a garden'.

It infuriates those English people, including clergymen, who have chosen to live in the cities. 'It is massively dangerous. It perpetuates the belief that God doesn't have anything to do with the horrible urban environment,' exploded Canon Donald Gray, when I asked him whether he thought it would make a good national anthem for the English. As a man who infinitely prefers pavements to footpaths, he finds the English rejection of the city baffling and depressing. 'As a nation, we simply don't affirm urban life at all. The idea is just to extract the maximum amount of wealth from industry and commerce in order to enjoy the delights of the countryside.'

It is not as though the English cities have failed to develop their own cultural heroes. Whether in the music-hall tradition, through George Formby and Gracie Fields, to the Beatles and the generations of would-be Beatles, or on the football field, from Stanley Matthews to Paul Gascoigne, urban colossi have been produced (all the aforementioned, incidentally, coming from somewhere that was very obviously, and audibly, not part of the South Country). Because of where they came from, and the fact that their speech identified them with their birthplace, all became working-class heroes, even when hugely rich. But, uniquely among the peoples of western Europe, those who set the social and intellectual tone have failed to develop an urban ideal. Authors like Martin Amis, Peter Ackroyd or Julian Barnes engage with metropolitan subject-matter, but the books that sell by the container-load are historical romances. The upper classes may have lost their political power, but they still manage to set the social tone and determine the aspirations of the ambitious. So, when the successful businessman makes his first £10 million, he starts scanning the pages of *Country Life* for a manor house to buy. There is nothing *necessarily* harmful in this – you could make a case for saying that the fact that the socially ambitious want desperately to acquire country seats is one of the few safeguards the countryside has. But it won't do any longer. John Major's speech was more canny than he was given credit for, but the chasm between the imaginative England and the real England won't do any longer because it fails to reflect the lives of the majority.

It is time to explore where this 'traditional' ideal Englishman and -woman came from.

CHAPTER NINE

THE IDEAL ENGLISHMAN

I like a man to be a clean, strong, upstanding Englishman
who can look his gnu in the face and put an ounce of lead in it
P. G. WODEHOUSE, Mr Mulliner Speaking

'Before the war Derek Vane had been what is generally described as a typical Englishman,' wrote 'Sapper' in his story 'Mufti'.

That is to say, he regarded his own country . . . whenever he thought about it . . . as being the supreme country in the world. He didn't force his opinion down anyone's throat; it was simply so. If the other fellow didn't agree, the funeral was his, not Vane's. He had to the full what the uninitiated regard as conceit; on matters connected with literature, or art, or music, his knowledge was microscopic. Moreover, he regarded with suspicion anyone who talked intelligently on such subjects. On the other hand, he had been in the eleven at Eton, and was a scratch golfer. He had a fine seat on a horse and rode straight; he could play a passable game of polo, and was a good shot. Possessing as he did sufficient money to prevent the necessity of working, he had not taken the something he was supposed to be doing in the City very seriously . . . He belonged, in fact, to the Breed; the Breed that has always existed in England, and will always exist to the world's end. You may meet its members in London and Fiji; in the lands that lie beyond the mountains and at Henley; in the swamps where the stagnant vegetation rots and stinks; in the great deserts where the night air strikes cold. They are always the same, and they are branded with the stamp of the Breed. They shake your hand as a man shakes it; they meet your eye as a man meets it.[1]

Oh, the Breed, how we miss them. Fearless and philistine, safe in taxis and invaluable in shipwrecks, they were the embodiment of the ruling class, men you could send to the ends of the earth and know they would dominate the natives firmly but fairly, their needs no more than the occasional months-old copy of *The Times* and a tin of their favourite pipe tobacco. Their uncomplicated view of the world divided into decent chaps and the 'Bolshevists, Anarchists and members of the do-no-work-and-have-all-the-money brigade', as 'Sapper' had his more famous hero, Bulldog Drummond, describe them.

'Sapper' was Colonel Herman Cyril McNeile, who had retired from the army with a Military Cross in 1919, and *Bulldog Drummond* is subtitled 'the adventures of a demobilised officer who found peace dull'. It tells us all we need to know: the Breed was bred for action. Drummond was 'six feet in his socks . . . hard muscle and clean bone . . . a magnificent boxer, a lightning and deadly shot with a revolver and utterly lovable'. He was also exceedingly dim, hated foreigners and was prodigiously ugly: anyone who had encountered this sort of person at their public school would recognize him at once, probably with a shudder. Richard Hannay, the hero of John Buchan's *Thirty-Nine Steps* is another cut from the same timber: this story tells us that the villain behind all the villains in the world is 'a little white-faced Jew in a bathchair with an eye like a rattlesnake'. The enemy was set upon undermining the Empire and selling women into White Slavery.

Of course, neither Derek Vane nor any of the others was ever a 'typical Englishman'. That remark about the private income gives it away, as does the comment about belonging to the 'eleven' at Eton: elevens only have eleven members, so he wasn't even typical at school. What the Breed represented was a certain ideal, a carefully selected number of the strengths and weaknesses of the male taken and raised to Platonic heights. They were bold, unreflective and crashingly pragmatic, men you could trust. It has been the misfortune of the English male that, just as he found himself living in a country different to the one he imagined himself to be living in, so the so-called English ideal excluded most of the population from the identity with which they had been born.

Imitations of the Breed were mass-produced by the private schools, which proliferated throughout the nineteenth century. They were all-male institutions and the world of the Breed remained male for ever. If the Breed reproduced (presumably by some sort of virgin conception), their children existed only as putative adults who were to be packed off to school as soon as possible. One can only guess at the sort of emotions which must have gone through a mother's heart at the little she was allowed to learn of her child's experiences. At Radley, the boys were reduced to scratching around in the dirt for bulbs and plants to eat (cowslips were a great delicacy), and acorns were cooked in the flames of candles. One letter home from an eighteenth-century Eton schoolboy mentions the black beetles which appeared in the food. It reads:

My dear mama,

I wright to tell you I am very retched, and my chilblains is worse agen. I have not made any progress and I do not think I shall. i am very sorry to be such expense to you, but i do not think this schule is very good. One of the fellows has taken the crown of my new hat for a target, he has burrowed my watch to make wheal, with the works, but it won' act – me and him have tried to put the works back, but we think some wheels are missing as they won't fit. I hope Matilda's cold is better i am glad she is not at a schule. I think I have got the consumption the boys at the place are not gentlemen but of course you did not know that when you sent me hear, i will try not get into bad habits . . . I hope you and papa are well and dont mind my being uncomfortable because i don't think i shall last long please send me some money as i owe 8d . . .

Your loving but retched son[2]

It is so perfect in its depiction of the horrors and so cunning in its attempts to extract sympathy before the appeal for cash that it reads like a parody. Certainly, a century later the wise schoolboy would know there was nothing to be gained from a recitation of the horrors of his school: that was what his parents were paying for, as the price of turning him into one of the Breed.

Once away from home, a good thrashing was accepted as an essential part of the process of turning out a gentleman. The champion flogger was the Reverend Dr John Keate, appointed headmaster of Eton in 1809, who beat an average of ten boys each day (excluding his day of rest on Sundays). On 30 June 1832 came his greatest achievement, the thrashing of over eighty of his pupils. At the end of this marathon, the boys stood and cheered him. It says something about the spirit of these places that he was later able to tell some of the school's old boys of his regret that he hadn't flogged them more often. When the time came for him to retire the Eton pupils subscribed large amounts of money for his testimonial. In the circumstances, is it surprising that the products of these schools were skilled at hiding their emotions?

The traditional English system of education certainly did its best to channel the hormonal urges of young people into other outlets. The predictable adolescent hobby of masturbation was particularly challenging. A Doctor Acton, author of *Functions and Disorders of the Reproductive Organs* (published in 1857 and still in print forty years later), painted a horrifying picture of the effect of masturbation upon a boy who discovered to his cost that 'the large expenditure of semen has exhausted his vital force'. As a result, he had become a walking wreck.

The frame is stunted and weak, the muscles underdeveloped, the eye is sunken and heavy, the complexion is sallow, pasty or covered with spots of acne, the hands are damp and cold, and the skin moist. The boy shuns the society of others, creeps about alone, joins with repugnance in the amusements of his schoolfellows. He cannot look anyone in the face, and becomes careless in dress and uncleanly in person. His intellect has become sluggish and enfeebled, and if his evil habits are persisted in, he may end in becoming a drivelling idiot or peevish valetudinarian.[3]

Although many a modern parent might recognize their own spotty teenage son in this picture, the portrait is reminiscent of nothing so much as contemporary government attempts to warn young people off drugs. The best way to avoid temptation was to keep them fully occupied, which was one of the reasons for the obsession with school sports. Dr Acton advised adults trying to prevent boys from succumbing to masturbation that 'the essence of this training of the will, however, lies in beginning *early*. If a boy is once fully impressed that *all* such indulgences are dirty and mean, and, with the whole force of his unimpaired energy, determines he *will* not disgrace himself by yielding, a very bright and happy future is before him'.[4]

The advice obviously worked for a number of distinguished members of the Breed, for it is noticeable that a good proportion of the more distinguished men who left England to build the empire seem to have more or less discarded their sexuality as baggage not needed on voyage. A. C. Benson, the author of that hymn of empire 'Land of Hope and Glory', confided to his diary that 'for me the real sexual problem does not exist'. The explorer Wilfred Thesiger wrote in his autobiography that 'Sex has been of no consequence to me, and the celibacy of the desert left me untroubled . . . with no sense of deprivation'.[5] Others, like General Gordon, who wished he had become a eunuch at fourteen, or Field Marshal Montgomery, simply tried to squash whatever sexual feelings they had: during a House of Lords debate to legalize homosexuality, Montgomery suggested the age of consent be set at eighty. The vehemence of some of these denials may have had something to do with latent or repressed homosexuality: both Gordon and Montgomery, like Field Marshal Auchinleck, had a fascination with boys. But in many cases, sex was simply not a priority. Cecil Rhodes, who added great tracts of Africa to the Empire, neither married nor showed the slightest interest in sex of any variety. Emotionally, Lord Kitchener seems scarcely to have grown out of pre-puberty. Others married late in life; the explorer Henry Morton Stanley at fifty-one, the founder of the Boy Scouts, Robert Baden-Powell, at fifty-five, the colonial governor, Lord Milner, at sixty-seven.

These were all driven men, with great ambitions, for themselves and for the Empire, often living in harsh conditions under a spartan code. But self-control extended much beyond the mortification of the flesh. Late in the British war against the Boers in South Africa, the writer Ford Madox Ford (another 'Englishman', this time with a German father) was at an English railway station when he ran into a friend, a retired major. The major was waiting for his son, 'a young man who had gone out to the war as of extraordinary promise. He had fulfilled this promise in an extraordinary degree; he was the only son, and, as it were, the sole hope for the perpetuation of an ancient family – a family of whose traditions old Major H was singularly aware and singularly fond'. As they waited on the platform, the two men chatted about the weather, the crops and the lateness of the train, anything to keep their minds 'studiously averted from the subject that was continuously present in both our minds'. For the son was returning from the war a casualty. He had been caught in a shell-blast and lost an arm, one leg and the entire side of his face. Ford described the meeting between father and son thus: 'When, at last, the crippled form of the son let itself down from the train, all that happened was the odd, unembarrassing clutch of left hand to extended right – a hurried, shuffling shake, and Major H said: "Hullo, Bob!" his son, "Hullo, Governor!" – And nothing more.'

Who knows what private tears the major may have wept later? But in public, all was stoicism. The writer commented that 'it was a thing which must have happened, day in, day out, all over these wonderful islands; but that a race should have trained itself to such a Spartan repression is none the less worthy of wonder'.[6]

Worthy of wonder and worthy of respect, too. Imagine the distress of the great poet of empire, Rudyard Kipling, in the First World War. One year he was standing on a flag-draped platform appealing for volunteers to join the crusade against Hunnish evil, and the next, his only son John was listed 'wounded and missing' at the Battle of Loos. The boy, who had appalling eyesight, had only been accepted for military service because Kipling had pulled strings with friends in the army. The last person to see Lieutenant Kipling alive had watched him weeping with pain as he tried to fasten a field dressing around his shattered mouth, but his brother officers conspired to keep the details of his son's agonized last minutes from Kipling. The father wrote bravely to a friend, 'I don't suppose there is much hope for my boy and the little that is left doesn't bear thinking of. However, I hear that he finished well ... It was a short life. I'm sorry that all the years' work ended in one afternoon, but lots of people are in our position, and it's something to have bred a man.'[7] That consoling pride in having 'bred a man' perhaps persuaded Kipling that he had done something he could be proud of, something his country expected of him. What else was there to clutch at in the senseless slaughter of the war?

The Breed represented a class, of course. But it was not necessary to be English to belong. John Buchan's hero, Richard Hannay, was a white Rhodesian mining engineer. And the English public schools offered the opportunity to others – boys of non-aristocratic background or even foreigners – to become part. As a young boy from Ghana, the MP Paul Boateng used to visit his grandparents in the west of England. 'I remember, I used to pore over an old book they had, a Jubilee album I think it was,' he recalls. 'There were all these pictures of the Aga Khan, or the Maharajah of Jodhpur, all looking like quintessential Englishmen. They were nothing of the sort, but they had become Englishmen.'

And yet they had not. The patina of the Breed was English, but it really belonged to the Empire rather than to England. The Breed lived at one remove from their emotions, as a consequence of their education: as the businessman Roger Cooper explained on leaving Iran in 1991, anyone who had been through his experiences at Clifton

College in Bristol could have survived the time he spent in Tehran's notorious Evin prison after a conviction for spying. It was not just the bad food and general hardship, but the fact the education allowed the individual to live at arm's length from the physical reality around them, whether it be in Bristol or in darkest Sudan. But the Breed was bred for empire and action and not for post-war England.

In 1964, the great-grandchildren of Derek Vane were looking back on the Breed with scorn. In a sketch for their student revue, *Beyond the Fringe*, Jonathan Miller and Peter Cook conjured up a scene on a wartime airfield. The conversation went like this:

PETER: Perkins! Sorry to drag you away from the fun, old boy. War's not going very well, you know.

JON: Oh my God!

PETER: We are two down, and the ball's in the enemy court. War is a psychological thing, Perkins, rather like a game of football. You know how in a game of football ten men often play better than eleven –?

JON: Yes, sir.

PETER: Perkins, we are asking you to be that one man. I want you to lay down your life, Perkins. We need a futile gesture at this stage. It will raise the whole tone of the war. Get up in a crate, Perkins, pop over to Bremen, take a shufti, don't come back. Goodbye Perkins. God, I wish I was going too.

JON: Goodbye sir – or is it au revoir?

PETER: No, Perkins.[8]

The Britain of the Breed had become the Britain of the Pointless Gesture.

Stereotypes are comforting, save us the trouble of fresh thought. Just as 'Sapper' presented the Breed as the essence of the imperial ruling class, so, in the mind of the headline-writer or farceur, every Swede is lugubrious, every German humourless, every Frenchman a garlic-breathing fop. It says something that the caricature of themselves to which the English had clung for the two centuries before the Breed was neither glamorous nor dashing, nor even particularly heroic.

The English might have chosen anyone to be their national symbol, from a mariner to a poet. Instead, they chose a tradesman. The jowly figure of John Bull still occasionally surfaces in newspaper cartoons – not bad going for a character invented in 1712. Like so many apparently authentic aspects of Englishness, John Bull was the creation of a foreigner, John Arbuthnot, the son of a Kincardineshire clergyman who had taken the High Road to England. Even so, Arbuthnot could not resist the opportunity for propaganda in the Scottish cause, so that while the English hero was 'ruddy and plump, with a pair of cheeks like a trumpeter', his sister Peg

look'd pale and wan, as if she had the Green-Sickness [anaemia]; and no wonder, for John was the darling, he had all the good bits, was cramm'd with good pullet, chicken, pig, goose and capon, while Miss had only a little oatmeal and water, or a dry crust without butter ... Master lay in the best appartment, with his bed-chamber towards the south-sun. Miss lodg'd in a garret, expos'd to the north wind, which shrivel'd her countenance.[9]

But John Bull's indifference to his sickly Scottish sister is nothing by comparison with his more important preoccupation, which is to sort out the dishonest and scheming Continentals. A doctor by training and a friend of Pope and Swift, Arbuthnot portrayed the jockeying for influence which led to the Treaty of Utrecht as a lawsuit brought by a cloth-dealer, John Bull, against Lewis Baboon. John Bull is 'an honest, plain dealing fellow, choleric, bold and of a very unconstant temper', unafraid of anyone, but liable to quarrel with his neighbours 'especially if they pretended to govern him'. His mood

depended very much upon the air; his spirits rose and fell with the weather glass. John was quick and understood his business very well, but no man alive was more careless in looking into his accounts, or more cheated by his partners, apprentices and servants. This was occasioned by his being a boon companion, loving his bottle and his diversion; for to say truth, no man kept a better house than John, nor spent his money more generously.[10]

Here we have a self-portrait more honest than many English might like to admit. John Bull is, as befits a nation of shopkeepers, a tradesman. He is fiercely independent and proud, drinks heavily and possesses a truly bovine stolidity. He is also temperamental, whining, insensitive and, in his attitude to 'Nicholas Frog' ('a cunning sly whoreson, covetous, frugal, who would pine his belly to save his pocket') sneeringly disdainful of foreigners. Although John Bull subsequently went through numerous modifications, becoming slower to anger and posher, some features remained constant. He is always pot-bellied, solid, peaceable and a bit dozy. He is more given to assertion of what he takes to be blindingly obvious than to reasoning. He believes in Law and Order and is instinctively conservative. He is home-loving, reliable, jolly, honest, practical and fiercely attached to his freedoms.

There have been other attempts to invent an archetypal Englishman – Joseph Addison's Worcestershire baronet, Sir Roger de Coverley, enjoyed a short celebrity – but none has lasted as well as John Bull. It is curious that this not particularly attractive character should have endured so long. After all, he is neither physically appealing nor even particularly intelligent. His longevity comes from his very solidity. In cartoons, he was soon being portrayed not as bull but bulldog, so that nearly two centuries after his invention he could fit with Arthur Reece's jingoistic music-hall anthem 'Sons of the Sea, All British born', at the time of the great naval rivalry with Germany, which coined the phrase 'Boys of the bulldog breed'. By the time of the Second World War, the country had, in Winston Churchill, a man whose physiognomy seemed to blend bulldog and John Bull into one.

*

Just as the English kept alive the belief that they belonged not in the cities where they found themselves living, but in the countryside where they didn't, there remained a sense that the true Englishman was a countryman. 'It becomes a gentleman to be adept at blowing hunting horns, to be skilful in the chase, and elegantly to train and carry a hawk', explained one seventeenth-century authority.[11] Sir Robert Burton in his *Anatomy of Melancholy* makes a similar point, talking of the nobility's obsession with hunting: '´Tis all their study, their exercise, ordinary business, all their talk'. The principle was still true three centuries later: it is only very recently indeed that country gents have attached any importance at all to academic qualifications, and then not for the things themselves but because having them may make it easier for their children to earn the money to keep up country life.

The fictional model for the country gentry is the hard-riding, heavy-drinking, red-faced, Hanoverian-damning, 'Pox!'-exclaiming, no-nonsense Squire Western in Fielding's *Tom Jones*. None of life's mysteries is so complex that it cannot be reduced to comparison with a pack of foxhounds or the behaviour of a badger at bay. But Squire Western existed in real life, too. Lady Mary Wortley Montague wrote of the breed that 'Their mornings are spent among the hounds, their nights with as beastly companions – with what liquor they can get'.[12] The paradigm is Jack Mytton, born in 1796 and said to be heir, by the age of twenty-one, to £10,000 per annum and £60,000 of ready money. Mytton's father had died when he was two and his education never flourished: he was expelled first from Westminster, then from Harrow. The private tutor subsequently engaged quit after Mytton punched him to the ground. An army career was cut short when he was obliged to quit the Seventh Hussars because of obsessional gambling. An undistinguished year as Tory MP for Shrewsbury gave way to his true talent, which was for making mayhem, and having fun.

Mytton's reckless courage was legendary. He galloped a horse at full speed over a rabbit warren to see whether it would take his weight: the warren collapsed, so did the horse, which then rolled on him. For a bet he drove a two-horse carriage across country at night, leaping a ditch, two hedges and a three-yard-wide ha-ha. He picked fights at the drop of a hat, once going twenty rounds against a Welsh miner, before the man surrendered. On another occasion, while duck-shooting in the middle of winter, he crawled naked across a sheet of ice, so as to keep his clothes dry. He never carried a handkerchief, gloves or watch. When a passenger in his gig told him he had never been involved in an accident, Mytton exclaimed 'What a damn slow fellow you must have been all your life', drove the vehicle up a bank and turned it over. Guests who came to dinner and hogged the fire would find he had slipped red-hot coals into their pockets. Later, as they rode home after dinner, he was in the habit of dressing up as a highwayman and robbing them – victims included his own butler. One guest who stayed the night and fell asleep dead drunk, awoke to find that Mytton had put a live bear and two bulldogs in his bed.

In the end, he was undone by his extravagance. A daily intake of between four and six bottles of port, the first of which accompanied his morning shave, didn't help matters. (His pet monkey, who shared his enthusiasms and regularly went out hunting with him on horseback, also had a taste for the bottle, and died after mistakenly swallowing a container of boot polish.) In the last fifteen years of his life, according to 'Nimrod', he got through half a million pounds. Eventually, his debts had piled up so much that he was forced to flee to Calais, where one night he had a sudden attack of wind. 'Damn this hiccup', he swore, and to frighten it away set fire to the tail of his cotton nightshirt. It went up like paper.

The vast quantities of brandy Mytton was now drinking helped to deaden the pain, but at a cost. He died of delirium tremens in the Kings Bench prison on 29 March 1834.

*

Jack Mytton was, of course, exceptional, even by the standards of his own time. But whether in the age of the Whigs, or the more 'respectable Victorian society', or even in the late twentieth century, one characteristic of the English remains constant. John Bull and his supporters were practical men of action. To say that the English have a severely limited idea of the value of intellectuals would be a very English sort of understatement. 'The study of letters should be left to rustics,' said Richard Pace, Professor of Greek at Cambridge, as long ago as 1525. If attitudes have changed since then, it has not been by much, as George Steiner discovered when he applied for a teaching job at Cambridge University. Almost any institution in the world would have been proud to have had this eloquent, enigmatic and provocative man on their staff. His academic career had taken him through Paris, Chicago, Harvard, Oxford, Princeton and Geneva. He had been publishing books since 1958. He had a list of honorary degrees as long as the small print on the back of a mortgage agreement.

Steiner, however, suffers from one insuperable problem. He is an intellectual. When interviewed for a university lectureship, he made the mistake of declaring his belief in the importance of ideas.

'I said that to shoot someone because of a disagreement with him over Hegel was a dignified thing to do. It implies that these things matter.'

He did not get the job. It was a characteristically Steinerish sort of thing to say, but it showed a profound misjudgement of the English. To believe that any intellectual position is worth dying or killing for is a leap no English academic could make. It is a cliché that there are no intellectuals in England. It is also untrue. But if you are going to be an intellectual in England, you had better do it discreetly, and certainly not call yourself an intellectual. It does not do to grow passionate about your beliefs or to believe that every problem has a solution. Above all, don't look clever.

I had met George Steiner at Cambridge, where, after the

university's refusal to recognize his talents, he was offered an Extraordinary Fellowship by Churchill College, which allows him to make the occasional lecture to corrupt the minds of students. We had made the date by juggling diaries on the telephone. April 23rd, I suggested.

'Oh, April 23rd. Birthday of William Shakespeare, Vladimir Nabokov, Sergei Prokofiev, J. M. W. Turner, and Max Planck. And George Steiner.'

As we walked down the college steps he pointed to the house next door and said in hushed tones,

You see that upstairs window? Wittgenstein's death room.

You know what happened on Wittgenstein's last birthday? He was working at his desk. Mrs B. came in carrying a cake. She said, 'Many happy returns, Ludwig!' He turned to her and said, 'I want you to think precisely about what you have just said.' She burst into tears and dropped the cake.

I wondered whether Steiner saw himself as another Wittgenstein. Both were *émigrés*. Both had trouble with Cambridge (Wittgenstein called being Professor of Philosophy there 'a living death'). But it doesn't work. Steiner is altogether too keen on the limelight and has published much too much. The reason Steiner didn't fit in with Cambridge is because he insists on seeing English literature in the context of other literatures. And he takes ideas altogether too seriously.

Do you know [he went on], there are 45,000 people buried under the Rue Faubourg St Honoré? Forty-five thousand men, women and children! They died in the Commune. They died for an idea. You English simply haven't a clue how important ideas, ideology, are in the rest of Europe. All you've had in this country is a rather civilized little civil war. You export your hatred to Ireland. There is a deep social contract with tolerance and an instinctive distrust of cleverness or eloquence. If the Lord God came to England and started expounding his beliefs, you know what they'd say? They'd say 'Oh, come off it!'

Providing you aren't Irish, I thought it not a bad thing that by and large the English don't believe in killing people for their beliefs. Steiner agreed, in a Steinerish sort of way.

'Yes, this land is blessed with a powerful mediocrity of mind. It has saved you from communism and it has saved you from fascism. In the end, you don't care enough about ideas to suffer their consequences.'

He is right. Occasional fashions may take hold, like the 1980s flirtation with monetarism and privatization, but deep down, the English distrust isms, which is why Tony Blair had such difficulty asserting his credo of 'The Third Way' to be anything more than pragmatism dressed up as a slogan. There are some practical explanations: the education of the Breed was not designed to turn out young men who were particularly thoughtful or reflective. The French philosophy professor, Hippolyte Taine, visiting England in the 1860s, noted that the public schools put a lot more emphasis on sport, and a good deal less on book-learning than the French *lycées*, which, being in towns, had little room for sports fields, anyway. He made the acute observation that English schools tended to produce people who were instinctively conservative; at a religious level, the steady din of Victorian Anglicanism meant that most emerged from their schooldays 'defenders, not as opponents of the great ecclesiastical establishment, the national religion'. Above all, the system had prized integrity above intellect; 'learning and cultivation of the mind come last, character, heart, courage, strength and physical address are in the first rank'.[13] The consequence has been that the English have approached any promised panacea in a spirit not of enthusiasm but of profound scepticism.

Intellectuals appear disdainful in England because they suffer from the most corrosive of inferiority complexes: no one takes them as seriously at they take themselves. Behind their backs, people like George Steiner are – his words – 'mocked up and down the land' for being intellectuals. (That said, he is politer about the English than some other continental Europeans. Richard Wagner could think of no creature more objectionable than the authentic Englishman. 'He is like a sheep, with a sheep's practical instinct for sniffing out its food in the field.')

Why is it that England has no place for mental Brahmins? After all, the country has one of the most distinguished intellectual traditions in the world. By the late seventeenth century, the Royal Society of London had become the acme of European science. 'England may justly lay claim to be the Head of a Philosophical League, above all countries in Europe', wrote Bishop Sprat in his 1667 *History of the Royal Society*, 'Nature will reveal more of its secrets to the English than to others, because it has already furnish'd them with a Genius so well Proportion'd, for the receiving and refining of its mysteries.'[14] Others have been far more ready to recognize the English genius than the English have been themselves. Voltaire, in many senses the apotheosis of the eighteenth-century 'Enlightenment', fell in love with the English intellectual tradition, using his *Letters from England* to compare Isaac Newton with René Descartes. He observed that the Cartesian belief in pure thought was 'ingenious, at the best only plausible to ignoramuses' and simply shouldn't be spoken of in the same breath as the genius of Newton. 'The first is a sketch, the second a masterpiece.' The distinction continues: until very recently Newton's Alma Mater, Trinity College, Cambridge, had produced more Nobel Prize winners (twenty-nine) than the whole of France.

But the point is that the English do not make a song-and-dance about it. When three Frenchmen were awarded Nobel Prizes in the same year recently, the French government declared a public holiday and gave the nation's schoolchildren a day off. When Aaron Klug was telephoned at the molecular biology laboratories in Cambridge to be told he had been awarded the 1982 Nobel Prize for Chemistry, he threw his arms in the air and sighed happily, 'I can afford a new bicycle!'

The English seem hardly to notice the quality of their intellectual achievements. Shakespeare is probably the greatest writer in the world. Yet when Victor Hugo came to London to pay homage to the man, he searched in vain for a monument. He listed those who did qualify for remembrance:

Statues for three or four Georges, one of whom was an idiot ... For having drilled the infantry, a statue. For having commanded the Horse Guards on manoeuvres, a statue. For having defended the Old Order, for having squandered England's riches propping up a Coalition of Kings against 1789, against Democracy, against the Enlightenment, against the upward movement of the human spirit – set up a pedestal, quickly, a statue for Mr Pitt. To find the nation's tribute to England's greatest genius, you have to penetrate deep into Westminster Abbey, and there, overshadowed by four or five enormous monuments where, in marble or bronze, unknown royal personages stand in splendour, you are shown, on a tiny pedestal, a little figurine: beneath this figurine you read the name: WILLIAM SHAKESPEARE.[15]

Things have changed a little in the century and a half since Victor Hugo's visit, although not as much as many of the country's cultural élite like to pretend. Shakespeare is now commemorated by theatres in London and Stratford that perform his works, although without the contributions of the British government and foreign tourists, none could survive. New writers are periodically beatified by their inclusion in the crowded little poets' corner of Westminster Abbey. But Hugo's essential objection remains valid: as far as officialdom is concerned, when it comes to commemorating achievement, one second-rate general is worth a dozen poets. Just look at the twice-yearly honours lists issued by Buckingham Palace: you are more likely to be honoured for writing up the minutes of a municipal council than for any volume of poetry.

The English approach to ideas is not to kill them, but to let them die of neglect. The characteristic English approach to a problem is not to reach for an ideology but to snuffle around it, like a truffle hound, and when they have isolated the core, then to seek a solution.

It is an approach which is empirical and reconciling and the only ideology it believes in is Common Sense. The English mind prefers utilitarian things to ideas. As Emerson put it, 'They love the lever, the screw, the pulley, the Flanders draught-horse, the waterfall, wind-mills, tide-mills; the sea and the wind to bear their freight ships.'[16] You can see why they have produced so many great scientists.

But none of this completely explains why the English should have conceived such a distrust of intellectuals. I am inclined to think it may have something to do with their borders. Living on an island, the English developed as a comparatively homogeneous people. They have had a degree of insulation from the theoretical tides that swept the rest of Europe. And since the boundaries of England were defined by the sea and Celtic neighbours, the English had a very clear sense of their own identity. A history of relatively few political upheavals meant they had no need to reinvent themselves: like their law, their national personality was essentially sedimentary. The intellectual, by contrast, flourishes in a more changeable world where anything seems possible; the greatest thoughts become theories for reordering the world, and the grandest of theories are ideologies. While many of the countries of continental Europe have been through unifications, separations, wars, reunifications and reinventions, the institutions of England have changed gently, incrementally, and often at the last minute. In the last two centuries, France has been through one monarchy, two empires and five republics. In half that period of time, Germany has gone from a monarchy to a republic, to a Reich, to partition between communism and capitalism and finally to reunification as a Federal Republic. In all that time, Britain has remained a parliamentary monarchy. There has been no appetite for wholesale upheaval: the greatest social change of the twentieth century, the invention of the Welfare State, was a practical project built on ideals rather than ideology. It may simply be that the English have not needed intellectuals to tell them who they are.

*

When the French class structure exploded in revolution, a new model Frenchman and -woman was born. 'Subjects were told they had become Citizens;' writes the historian Simon Schama, 'an aggregate of subjects held in place by injustice and intimidation had become a Nation. From this new thing, this Nation of Citizens, justice, freedom and plenty could be not only expected but required.'[17] The Revolutionary ideal, which has lasted ever since, had catastrophic political side-effects, like the thousands mourned by George Steiner in the Paris Commune. But the idea of the Citizen State had been born as a place in which people had clearly defined rights and obligations, guaranteed by constitution. The English, having undergone no similar seismic shock, remained a nation of individuals with no grand expectations of the state. Curiously, before the Revolution a succession of Frenchmen, including Voltaire, Montesquieu and Mirabeau, had crossed the Channel and praised precisely this quality of the English. During the American War of Independence, when French opportunism decreed they side with the revolting colonials, Beaumarchais received a letter from a friend saying that 'The whole world looks to France for deliverance, the one nation well able to beat the English.' But it went on to advise that 'Should you end on the winning side, show respect for England. Its liberties, its laws, its talents are not oppressed there beneath absurd despots. It is a model for every state.'[18] Even bloodthirsty revolutionaries like Jean-Paul Marat admired what he had seen of the English political tradition during his periods of exile in London; it might seem bizarre for John Bull to have been an inspiration for the French Revolution, but it is partly true.

While the French Revolution invented the Citizen, the English creation is the Game. The legacy can be seen any week in schools and stadia anywhere from Spitsbergen to Tierra del Fuego. The word 'soccer', *the* world sport, is public-school slang for Association Football. Baseball is a form of the English children's game rounders, American football a version of rugby, which developed after William

Webb Ellis picked up the ball and ran with it during a game of soccer at Rugby School. Tennis was redeveloped by the Marylebone Cricket Club and the first of the world-famous Wimbledon tournaments was held in 1877. Englishmen set the standard distances for running, swimming and rowing competitions and developed the first modern horse-races. Contemporary hockey dates from the codification of rules by the Hockey Association in 1886, competitive swimming from the formation of the English Amateur Swimming Association in 1869, modern mountaineering can be dated from the 1854 attempt on the Wetterhorn by Sir Alfred Wills. The English invented goalposts, racing boats and stopwatches and were the first to breed modern racehorses. Even when they imported sports from abroad, like polo or skiing, the English laid down the rules. The first padded boxing glove was worn by the English prize-fighter Jack Broughton in the mid-eighteenth century, the Marquess of Queensbury codification of the rules of boxing followed over a century later. The list goes on.

Perhaps you could make a case that whichever nation was dominant in the late nineteenth century would have passed its obsessions to the world. Had there been an empire built by Scottish Highlanders, perhaps everyone would now be playing shinty. Had the indigenous North Americans colonized the globe, it might be lacrosse, except that it would be called by their original name, baggataway. A Basque empire could have produced intercontinental pelota championships. So maybe the world's acceptance of English sports was simply the consequence of political and mercantile power at a time when the world was on the cusp of getting smaller. But that does not explain why the English themselves developed such an obsession. It seems reasonable to suppose that it had something to do with safety and prosperity and the availability of leisure time. Perhaps the fact that duelling was frowned upon earlier than in the rest of Europe meant there was a need to find alternative challenges. Certainly, while urbanization may have meant the end of traditional village sports, the development of the great boarding schools, with hundreds of boys cooped up together in training for the business of running the Empire, made it essential to find ways of exercising the hormonally challenged.

Certainly, sport came to occupy a central position in English culture. In 1949, when T. S. Eliot (another person who became English by choice) was grappling with the question of what defined a national culture, he drew up a list of the characteristic interests of the English. It included 'Derby Day, Henley Regatta, Cowes, the twelfth of August, a cup final, the dog races, the pin table, the dart board, Wensleydale cheese, boiled cabbage cut into sections, beetroot in vinegar, nineteenth-century Gothic churches and the music of Elgar'.[19] Fifty years on we should have to change the list a little, reflecting convenience foods, the mass media and the decline of the pin table. But it would still have its most startling characteristic: out of the thirteen characteristics Eliot identifies as distinctively English, no fewer than eight are connected with sport.

And the language of sport permeated deep into the national consciousness. It has a slightly dated feel to it nowadays, but still, to describe a man or woman as 'a good sport' is high praise. A good sport is the sort of person willing to concede defeat by saying that 'the best man won'. At the height of the Battle of Britain, the pacifist Vera Brittain was walking along Piccadilly when she saw a newspaper-vendor's placard. It read

BIGGEST RAID EVER
SCORE 78 TO 26
ENGLAND STILL BATTING[20]

Vita Sackville-West – no thoughtless admirer of English males – wrote in 1947 that

the English man is seen at his best the moment that another man starts throwing a ball at him. He is then seen to be neither spiteful, nor vindictive, nor mean, nor querulous, nor desirous of taking an unfair advantage; he is seen to be law-abiding, and to respect the regulations which he himself generally has made; he takes it for granted that his adversary will respect them likewise; he would be profoundly shocked by any attempt to cheat; his scorn would be as much aroused by any exultation displayed by the victor as by any ill-temper displayed by the loser ... It is all quite simple. One catches, kicks, or hits the ball, or else one misses it; and the same holds good for the other chap. It is all taken in good part.[21]

What she is talking about is something whose importance cannot be exaggerated. It is the significance to the English of the idea of the *Game*. The thing is loved for its own sake.

The wildness of Jack Mytton and much of the English gentry was partly tamed by the evangelicalism of the early nineteenth century. But the other civilizing influence was the Game. Nowhere is its moral significance more trumpeted than in Henry Newbolt's three-verse epic, 'Vitaï Lampada'. Although Newbolt himself, a slight and spare teenager, never made the grade to play cricket for his school, Clifton College, he understood its importance to the English ruling class. After his death, his friend and fellow poet, Walter de la Mare described him as 'faithful throughout his life to his idea and ideal of England and Englishness'.[22] His poem remains the encapsulation of the belief that all life's problems can be solved by playing a straight bat.

> There's a breathless hush in the Close to-night –
>   Ten to make and the match to win –
> A bumping pitch and a blinding light,
>   An hour to play and the last man in.
> And it's not for the sake of a ribboned coat,
>   Or the selfish hope of a season's fame,
> But his Captain's hand on his shoulder smote –
>   'Play up! play up! and play the game!'
>
> The sand of the desert is sodden red, –
>   Red with the wreck of a square that broke; –
> The Gatling's jammed and the Colonel dead,
>   And the regiment blind with dust and smoke.

The river of death has brimmed his banks,
  And England's far, and Honour a name,
The voice of the schoolboy rallies the ranks:
  'Play up! play up! and play the game!'

This is the word that year by year,
  While in her place the School is set,
Every one of her sons must hear,
  And none that hears it dare forget.
This they all with a joyful mind
  Bear through life like a torch in flame,
And falling fling to the host behind –
  'Play up! play up! and play the game!'

It is hard not to be carried along in its rhythm, even if there is
something so breathtakingly stupid about the poem that it is hard
to imagine how on earth it could ever have been taken seriously.
Yet in the balmy days before August 1914, the idea that life was
essentially a version of the Game seemed almost plausible. 'Such
wars as arose were not general, but only a brief armed version of
the Olympic Games', Osbert Sitwell recalled. 'You won a round;
the enemy won the next. There was no more talk of extermination,
or Fights to a Finish, than would occur in a boxing match.'[23]

It is hard to imagine how anyone could have clung to a belief in
the Game amid the squalor of the Flanders trenches. Yet as late as
1917, old men egging on the young to muddy death were blathering
on about the physical and moral superiority they enjoyed because
of the sports they played. The English élite continued in the fond
belief that the entire population had spent their formative years
charging around sports fields, behaving like Corinthian heroes, which
made them naturally superior to their enemies. One glance at the
medical examinations of the 2½ million young men conscripted in
1917–18 would have shown them how wrong they were: out of
every nine men of military age in Great Britain, three were fit and
healthy. Two were in sub-standard health. Three were nearly physical

wrecks. And one was a chronic invalid. But then, sport was as much about improving the spirit as the body. Lord Northcliffe's propaganda message to the troops that year suggested that British soldiers were naturally better warriors because they possessed a sense of individuality, whereas their enemy had only been trained 'to obey, and to obey in numbers'. The reason for the poor German's inadequacy was that 'He has not played individual games. Football, which develops individuality, has only been introduced into Germany in comparatively recent times'.[24]

Newbolt's poem was the anthem of the Breed, to whom death was, presumably, just another fast bowler. The poet's only son, Francis, might have told him how off-beam he was, having been wounded in the football match which passed for the battle of Ypres. Others had taken the poet at his word. On 1 July 1916, at the start of the battle of the Somme which was to claim 420,000 British casualties, Captain W. P. Nevill, a company commander in the 8th East Surreys, presented his four platoons with a football apiece. One was inscribed 'The Great European Cup-Tie Finals, East Surreys v Bavarians. Kick-off at zero'. Another said 'no referee'. He offered a prize for the first platoon to dribble and pass the ball as far as the German front-line. He was dead before he could present it.[25]

Captain Nevill was clearly mad. What the Game had taught these men was the importance of 'manliness' and self-control and obedience to orders. It could produce the most extraordinary consequences, as the life of C. B. Fry demonstrates. The son of a chief accountant at Scotland Yard, he had played in the FA Cup before he left Repton School in 1890 and appeared for Surrey county cricket team in the time between school and university (Oxford, inevitably, and the top scholarship at Wadham College). By the time of his graduation, he had represented the university at cricket, soccer and athletics, tied the world long-jump record at 23 feet 6½ inches, and only missed playing wing three-quarter for the Oxford rugby team because of injury. He managed, in passing, to win a first in classics. While working as a sporting journalist he represented England both at soccer and cricket (in 1902 he played in an FA Cup Final on Saturday and scored 82 for Sussex on the following Monday). But it was as a batsman that he achieved true greatness. His stroke-play, particularly his on-drive, became the stuff of legend. For five years Fry topped the first-class batting averages and a career total of 30,886 runs included 94 centuries with an average of over 50. His last invitation to play for England came at the age of forty-nine.

Here, surely, is an English hero. Fry's career total of runs may be only half that of Jack Hobbs, but Hobbs, the son of a groundsman, was a professional. Fry seemed to embody the ideal of the gentleman player: there was something particularly appropriate about his most memorable innings, of 232 not out, in partnership with the old Harrovian Archibald MacLaren, to save the Gentlemen from the Players at Lord's in 1903. Handsome, strong, intelligent and clean-living, Fry is the Breed at its best.

Yet his autobiography, *Life Worth Living*, has an entire chapter devoted to the glories of Nazi Germany. In 1934 Fry had been approached by the Germans to see if he could help foster better relations between the British Boy Scouts and the Hitler Youth movement. The Nazis had chosen their willing fool wisely. Arriving in Munich, Fry found the German people 'devoted to the Fuehrer', thought Rudolf Hess handsome and charming – inviting him to come and stay with him in England – and was impressed by more junior Nazis whom he thought 'quiet, attentive and courteous'. What Fry seems to have liked most about Germany was the single-minded vigour of the place:

there was a complete absence of the lounge-lizard type of youth, who looks as if he would break in two in the middle, so frequently seen in the entertainment resorts of London. Nor did one see the kind of girl who looks as if she were presenting herself to the late hours of the night as the whole object of her existence. Berlin in 1934 gave me the feeling of a world swept clean by a fresh wind which had left it stimulated, energetic, and ready to work without losing its capacity to enjoy itself.[26]

In this Aryan wonderland, Fry began to question whether the British Boy Scouts were really up to the job. What impressed him was that whereas England had schools and universities, clubs and voluntary organizations, the Germans had put everything under the control of the Reich Ministry of Kultur, which made for a much more serious approach. When, finally, the great English sporting hero met Hitler he greeted him with a Nazi salute, chatted for an hour and a quarter, meekly accepted the Nazi line about the 'Jewish problem', and concluded that 'this great man' had 'an innate dignity', was 'fresh and fit', 'notably alert' and 'quiet and courteous'. The book was written in 1939. Fry concluded his praise of Nazi Germany by saying that 'such were my impressions and my conclusions when last I saw Herr Adolf Hitler. Whatever may have happened since, I see no reason to withdraw any of them'.

Fry's sympathy for fascism was by no means unique among wealthier English people. Perhaps it is unfair to pillory a sportsman for his political blind-spots. But the point about the Breed is that their sense of fair play and sportsmanship was supposed to have given them qualities of character that fitted them to lead the nation. The other thing to be said about C. B. Fry is that for all the pretence of being a gentleman amateur, his journalism was a way of maintaining the illusion that he played the game just for amusement. The Breed was fine if, like Derek Vane, you had 'sufficient money to prevent the necessity of working'. For anyone who lived in the real world, belonging was an impossibility.

'I myself am not a gentleman,' the writer Simon Raven once said. 'I have no sense of obligation. I am happy to enjoy privilege: I am also prone to evade or even totally ignore its implicit commitments.'[27] This became the post-war attitude to the Victorian ideal, more

Flashman than Tom Brown. And yet, there is something of the English gentleman bred in Simon Raven's bones. Clever and learned, a good cricketer, handsome and popular at school, Raven as a boy must have seemed some sort of flannelled Apollo, a prospective member of the Breed. But he had too much imagination and too little self-discipline.

By the age of thirty Raven had successively won 1941's top scholarship to Charterhouse School, to be expelled four years later for 'the usual thing' (homosexuality); won a scholarship to Cambridge and been invited to try for a fellowship, only to leave in a flurry of debts; and been commissioned in the King's Shropshire Light Infantry and assisted out before the bookmakers could have him court-martialled for bounced cheques. Despite his hostility to marriage and children, on the grounds that 'children use up money which could be better used for high-grade pleasures for oneself', an accidental son arrived, provoking a doomed marriage. Once, desperate for cash, the child's mother telegraphed Raven, 'SEND MONEY. WIFE AND BABY STARVING', to which he is said to have replied, 'SORRY NO MONEY. SUGGEST EAT BABY.'

By the standards of the English gentleman, Raven would have been classed as a bounder or worse. He once said he was too intelligent not to be a rotter. He even carries the rotter's military rank of captain. Yet he was so confident the ideal was finished that in 1960 he wrote:

the traditional gentleman, one, that is, whose life is founded in truth, honour and obligation, has been done to death by certain hostile social pressures, envy and materialism being paramount among them. These pressures have compelled him either to abandon his standards of excellence, or, if he should retain them, to recognise that they are unwanted anachronisms, objects at best of mockery and at worst of hatred.[28]

There is something pretty rich about the sheer nerve of Raven's funeral oration for the English gentleman, as if the ideal were something so frail that it could be extinguished merely by 'hostile social pressures, envy and materialism'. But, even if we disagree as to the causes, it has become received wisdom that the gentleman has indeed been done to death. The evidence cited to support this argument ranges from the rise in adultery to the end of the belief in the City of London that 'my word is my bond'.

Simon Raven arrived for lunch with a gentleman's punctuality, on the dot of twelve-thirty and promptly excused himself to find the loo. 'Crohn's disease. Rather irritating.' Tall, slightly unkempt, a club tie holding his buttonless shirt collar together, tweed jacket, he has the look of a man who spent years living in rented rooms, a short-tempered, retired prep-school master, perhaps. The impression isn't far off the mark: he spent much of his writing career put up by his publisher in a boarding house in Deal, Kent: a weekly wage was the only way of getting anything out of him. The million words of his highly entertaining *Alms for Oblivion* series of novels were the result.

He had answered my request to talk to him about the fate of the English gentleman characteristically: 'As you know, being inter-viewed is tiresome and exhausting. However, if you were to suggest lunch somewhere *very choice and quiet*, I might meet you.' I replied suggesting the Caprice in St James's. There followed a series of postcards, usually with three or four words scrawled on the back. 'Caprice fine. Date?' 'Wednesday fine. 12.30?' '12.30 fine.'

'Haven't been here for years,' he says, ordering a Campari and soda, slightly shabby among the bankers' wives and more opulent Tory politicians who have now colonized the place.

In the event, like so many others who might have been expected to avow certainties about Englishness (his novels are, after all, all about English attitudes and behaviour), Raven was curiously unsure about what constituted the national mentality. 'I think cricket's important' was about as far as we got. But he has a point. It is because the English are, in their hearts, more interested in games-playing than anything else, that cricket is the quintessential English sport. When Robert Winder travelled to India for the 1996 World Cup he was struck by the different responses of the competing nations:

If you are Pakistani or Indian you might just as well commit suicide when the team is humiliated; if you're West Indian, you might feel the world has fallen apart when things go wrong at the Oval. But these are countries where cricket is one of the leading suppliers of national pride. In England, you don't support cricket teams, you follow them. It's the game you support, not the team.[29]

The slow pace of a cricket match played over days has something to do with this curiously passionless devotion. Perhaps it would be different if there were a British cricket team, when the fate of the flag would be tied up with the performance of the team. But there is something else, too.

In the dying days of the Breed, the English cricketing ideal was well summed up in a message from Lord Harris to young cricketers in 1931. 'You do well to love it,' he told them, 'for it is more free from anything sordid, anything dishonourable, than any game in the world. To play it keenly, honourably, generously, self-sacrificingly is a moral lesson in itself, and the class is God's air and sunshine.'[30] It is as clear a statement of the value of the Game as you can get. The spirit of cricket may live on in innumerable matches on school and village grounds. But it was humbug even at the time the words fell from Lord Harris's lips. The following year, the world saw why. On tour in Australia, the England captain, Douglas Jardine, ordered his fast bowlers to aim short-pitched deliveries directly and consistently at the leg stump. For public consumption, this was to encourage batsmen into mistakes which would be snapped up as catches from close-in fielders. But his bowlers, especially Harold Larwood (a former miner and most definitely a 'Player'), were so fast that the effect was simply to batter the batsmen into submission as one ball after another shied up from the pitch at ferocious speed. Quite how Jardine – Winchester, Oxford, captain of Surrey and of the 'Gentlemen' against the 'Players' – squared the clear intimidation of bodyline bowling with the 'moral lesson in God's air and sunshine', we shall never know. He certainly never apologized for the tactic. But it reveals the ethical confusion into which the English were thrown when the ideal of the amateur proved inadequate to the times.

By the time Simon Raven wrote his threnody for the gentleman, English cricket had become the preserve of professionals. The problem was, the English couldn't do professionalism as well as many others. By the 1990s, foreign players, arriving to spend a season with an English county side, were astonished to discover the workaday lack of enthusiasm among the native players, who scarcely seemed to care whether their team won or lost. At a national level, players had picked up the Australian habit of 'sledging', or barracking, batsmen, would tamper with the ball if they could get away with it, and an England captain had even been seen shouting obscenities at an umpire. Maybe Raven was right.

And yet there is perhaps something in the circularity of his own life, too, which tells us about Englishness. Despite being expelled from Charterhouse School, a numberless London address, Charterhouse, EC1, will find him these days.

'When I realized my books were getting worse and worse and selling fewer and fewer copies, I knew I had to do something,' he says. A certain type of Englishman always seems to know useful people, and in his case, 'something' turned out to be contacting the warden of one of the more unusual establishments in London. To pacify his soul after a lifetime of coal trading from the Durham coalfields (a business which had made him the richest commoner in England), in the early seventeenth century Thomas Sutton established two institutions for the benefit of others. The educational establishment he created, Charterhouse School, became too big to remain at its base in London and moved out to Surrey, catering to ambitious Home Counties tradesmen who wanted to turn their sons into gentlemen. His other invention, an almshouse for 'gentlemen soldiers who had borne arms by land or sea, merchants who had been ruined by shipwreck or piracy and servants of the king or queen', remains in Charterhouse Square.

To qualify for admission to Sutton's Hospital, you have to be a 'gentleman', which, since the species was done to death in 1960, must make it an echoingly empty place. Yet not only is it full and lusted-after, Raven himself was admitted. He is anxious not to give the impression that he is some sort of roué who has seen the light and changed his ways: his attitudes to the rest of the human race are as dyspeptic as ever. But, it is the strength of the English Establishment that it can tolerate any amount of mockery and then enfold the culprits in its bosom. No Englishman ever really escapes the institutions which made him.

So in the almshouse cloisters, the Brothers live out their old age, eating their three meals a day, waited on at lunchtimes, supplied with beer and wine, all for £138 a month. Raven would like to earn more money to pay off some of his many thousands of pounds of debts, but doubts he ever will. The only serious inhibition – redolent of the beliefs of the Breed – is a ban on bringing in women. 'But at my age that's not a problem,' he says. The only exception to this rule is the resident matron, there to perform the same role performed by another woman who was not their mother when they were sent away to boarding school as children.

CHAPTER TEN

MEET THE WIFE

Contrary to popular belief, English women do not wear tweed nightgowns.
HERMIONE GINGOLD, Saturday Review, 1955

It is not often you meet someone who has had a bottom transplant. The man in question, jowly, balding, 50ish, in a pinstripe suit and well made shoes, looks the picture of British probity. You know he prides himself that his word is his bond. By day, he runs a merchant bank. At night, he likes to be spanked until the blood runs. His obsession has become known as *le vice anglais*.

The surgery on his backside, which put the best part of a thousand pounds in the hands of a Harley Street cosmetic surgeon, became necessary after a lifetime of corporal punishment. Like a cut on a boxer's eyebrow, there are only so many times the same wound can be reopened before you have to rebuild with fresh skin. His beatings began as a child at the hands of his father. Kissing between father and son had been banned at the age of five, on the grounds that it was effeminate. Corporal punishment was to be 'taken like a man', so when the boy was beaten as a punishment he was expected to show no emotion. If he survived the ordeal without crying, his father congratulated him. Over the next ten years, 'my backside was assaulted by no less than seventeen people, including parents, nanny, teachers, prefects'. He says it with no hint of self-pity, laughing at the recollection. At this stage, the beatings, the common coin of

English private education at the time, had no sexual connotations. They were just part of a schooling system that aimed to achieve Squire Brown's ambition for his son Tom and turn him into a 'brave, helpful, truth-telling Englishman, and a gentleman, and a Christian'.[1]

It was only when the young man got to university that the recollection of childhood and adolescent beatings became the stuff of sexual fantasy. He read Swinburne, *Fanny Hill* and the *Story of O*, but found English girls reluctant to make his compulsion real. Marriage was no better: the thought of caning left his wife cold. There was a succession of treatments with three different psychiatrists to try to 'cure' himself of his obsession. The third eventually advised that he would be better off spending his money to find discreet ways of satisfying his need than passing his whole life feeling bad about it. His wife, with whom he conducted an otherwise normal married life, producing four children, agreed that he could satisfy his tastes elsewhere, on condition no one, especially the children, saw his backside until the weals had healed.

And so his life was divided into compartments. Most of the time he lived the life of a pillar of society, fathering children who were then sent away to the same sort of expensive schools where his bottom had first been tanned, while he travelled the world as a British banker, a pillar of respectability. At night, he would seek out women, preferably muscular black women, who – for a price – would beat him. On a visit to New York he discovered a thriving sado-masochistic club scene, where he met others who liked whipping or being whipped. He found his greatest thrill of all was not merely to be caned but to be caned *in public*. Since then, the merchant banker has indulged his taste as often as he can among groups of friends or at clubs of like-minded strangers.

It is a very hard compulsion to understand. To an outsider nothing seems to bear out the comment of the medieval visitor to England that 'the English take their pleasures sadly'. It is not a uniquely English obsession – Rousseau admits to a taste for spanking in his

Confessions – but it has become known as *le vice anglais*. Try to use any public telephone box in the centre of London and you will find half a dozen prostitutes' calling cards staring you in the face advertising corporal punishment. A Dutch pornography merchant once told the writer Paul Ferris that 'caning is a super-speciality with the English. In England, they say, fucking is not allowed, but spanking is'.[2] It certainly goes back a long way: in Plate Three of Hogarth's *Harlot's Progress*, Moll the prostitute has a cane hanging on the wall. Much of the literature on the subject, under titles like *The Romance of Chastisement*, is English. In the nineteenth century entire brothels were devoted purely to flagellation. The English even invented machines which were capable of whipping several people at once.

Foreign visitors have been baffled by the obsession, assuming at one time or another that the practice was originally Anglo-Saxon, or due to the fact that the English ate too much meat. Conventional wisdom has it that it is an upper-middle-class taste, acquired by boys at their miserable Victorian boarding schools, where caning was the ultimate deterrent. 'Where are the instruments of pleasure?' asks the man of his mistress in Thomas Shadwell's *The Virtuoso*. 'I was so used to it at Westminster School I could never leave it off since . . . Do not spare thy pains. I love castigation mightily.'[3] (Dr Busby, a headmaster of Westminster in the seventeenth century, was 'regarded by flagellants as perhaps the finest expert with the rod that England has ever known'.[4] The school's other great contribution to the sport was to number among its alumni John Cleland, author of *Fanny Hill*, which, with its depiction of beatings, did much to spread the belief that the English were obsessed with being whacked.) Certainly, authors of Victorian pornographic tales of beatings sign themselves with names like 'Etonensis' or 'Old Boy', suggesting that the stories were written by, and intended for, men who had been beaten at school. Apparently, there is a regular gathering of devotees of spanking, all dressed in specially made school uniforms at 'Muir Academy', a club for English fetishists in, of all places, Hereford.

I had, naïvely, assumed that it was really a game, in which women merely pretended to inflict painful beatings, while the victim imagined himself to be a naughty schoolboy. But the merchant banker said I was wrong: 'If there's no pain, there's no point: you might as well be beating the sofa.'

And did he think this compulsion was the result of being beaten as a child?

Well, it was the most plausible explanation the psychiatrists gave. When my father beat me, he was insistent that I didn't cry or flinch. If I managed it, he congratulated me. The shrinks thought I had associated receiving pain with earning love and respect. And as for schools, it's certainly noticeable that English people like to be beaten with a cane, which was what was used in English schools, while Scots seem to prefer the leather tawse, which was what was used in Scottish schools.

It would be silly to claim that 'the English vice' is widespread among the English. It is not. Nor, despite its name, is it unique to the English. *Aficionados* say it is more commonplace in northern European, Protestant countries than in southern European, Roman Catholic cultures. But its central ambiguity – that punishment is reward; pain, pleasure – rings with English hypocrisy. You might expect that with the end of corporal punishment in schools the practice would be in decline. But apparently not. It's thriving. 'There are people of all social classes involved – one of my favourite kindred spirits is a bus driver. And plenty of women, too. I don't know what it is about the Diplomatic Service, but the wives of two senior ambassadors, whenever they are in London, make their first call to me, to come round and spank them.'

There is a scene in Kingsley Amis' novel, *Take A Girl Like You*, where the heroine, Jenny, moves house to take up a teaching job in a strange town in the late 1950s. She is chatted up by a young man. He has a look on his face 'which she had got quite used to seeing on men's faces – some of them quite old men – when they first saw her'. He opens innocently by asking if she's French. He has pressed the wrong button. Jenny's experience of men who ask if she's French – or Italian or Spanish or Portuguese – is that their intentions are more commercial.

'There had even been that time in Market Square at home when a man had accosted her and, on finding she was not a tart after all, had apologized by saying: "I'm awfully sorry, I thought you were French." What could it be like to actually live in France?'[5]

France and 'abroad' are the homes of forbidden pleasures, the place you went to get dirty books (*Ulysses* was produced in Paris) or – the word is, appropriately, French and has no precise English equivalent – to lead a louche life. Kingsley Amis's novel was published in 1960, the year in which, thirty years after its original publication on the Continent, the unexpurgated *Lady Chatterley's Lover* was first produced in Britain. ('Is it', memorably asked Mervyn Griffith-Jones, the prosecutor in the ensuing obscenity trial at the Old Bailey, 'even a book you would even wish your wife or your servants to read?') The English belief that France is a phantasmagoria of endless copulation is rooted far back. 'The French have the reputation for knowing more about love and of making it better than any other race on earth', said Laurence Sterne,[6] two centuries ago, and the belief persists. In the summer of 1997, the *People* published a four page pull-out, *Forbidden French Sex Secrets*, containing 'exclusive extracts' from a suppressed report edited by a Mademoiselle Énorme Poitrine. (The 'enormous chest' reveals the thing as an English invention: as the airbrushed parade of Page Three girls in the cheap newspapers proved every day, English men are obsessed by breasts.) Apart from such useful advice as 'a woman on her knees will be unable to stimulate her own clitoris without taking one hand off the floor and falling over' it provided an opportunity for plenty of photos of models in stockings and suspenders. And French knickers.

This obsession with foreign sexuality conceals a dirty little secret at the heart of relations between the sexes in 'respectable society'. The nineteenth-century institutions that were supposed to turn out 'ideal' English men and women invested the sexes with entirely different expectations of life, ensured they were educated apart from one another, and, even within marriage, obliged them to lead separate and unequal lives until they died. The clubland hero – a solid, unimaginative, pipe-smoking individual who invariably ordered plum duff for his pudding – was always ill at ease in the company of women because he had been brought up in one all-male institution after another. When there was such a profound chasm between the sexes, the hierarchy that existed in public life was bound to continue in the most intimate of relationships.

The sheer hypocrisy of many Englishmen, pretending morality while debauching themselves, takes some believing. The Industrial Revolution created big cities which allowed them to get away with things that would have been impossible in tighter, more ordered communities, and as early as 1793 it was reckoned that there were 50,000 prostitutes in London alone. Forty years later, another investigator listed the backgrounds from which they came:

milliners, dress-makers, straw bonnet makers, furriers, hat-binders, silk-winders, tambour-workers, shoebinders, slop-women or those who work for cheap tailors, those in pastry-cook, fancy and cigar shops, bazaars, servants to a great extent, frequenters of theatres, fairs, dancing-rooms which, with almost all places of public amusement in large towns and cities, are licentious. It is impossible to estimate the number of those addicted to secret prostitution in the different ranks of society.[7]

Often the streetwalkers were dressed by the madam of their brothel, who sent a spy to follow them as they solicited, in case they tried to abscond with the clothes.

By 1859, the police knew of 2,828 brothels in London, a figure the *Lancet* reckoned to be half the true total, calculating that there were about 80,000 prostitutes on the streets. The trade was centred on Haymarket, where many shops displayed the notice 'beds to let'. When Fyodor Dostoevsky walked down Haymarket at dusk, he found it colonized by armies of streetwalkers, the old and the young, the attractive (Dostoevsky thought 'there are no women in the world as beautiful as the English') and the ugly.

The streets can hardly accommodate the dense, seething crowd [he wrote]. The mob has not enough room on the pavements and swamps the whole street. All this mass of humanity craves for booty and hurls itself at the first comer with shameless cynicism. Glistening, expensive clothes and semi-rags and sharp differences in age – they are all there ... In the Haymarket I noticed mothers who brought their little daughters to make them ply that same trade. Little girls, aged about twelve, seize you by the arm and beg you to come with them. I remember once among the crowd of people in the street I saw a girl, not older than six, all in rags, dirty, barefoot and hollow-cheeked; she had been severely beaten, and her body, which showed through the rags, was covered in bruises ... what struck me most was the look of such distress, such hopeless despair on her face that to see that tiny bit of humanity already bearing the imprint of all that evil and despair was somehow unnatural and terribly painful. I went back and gave her sixpence. She took the small silver coin, gave me a wild look of frightened surprise, and suddenly ran off as fast as her legs could carry her, as if afraid that I should take the money away from her.[8]

It is a haunting picture. Defenders of Victorian London – then the greatest city on earth – might point out that Dostoevsky's was a flying visit, so perhaps his account is elaboration heaped on the tiniest basis of fact. But Hippolyte Taine, a French professor of philosophy, recorded similar scenes when visiting London in the 1860s.

Above all [he wrote], I recall Haymarket and the Strand at evening, where you cannot walk a hundred yards without knocking into twenty streetwalkers; some of them ask you for a glass of gin, others say 'it's for my rent, mister'. The impression is not one of debauchery but of abject, miserable poverty. One is sickened and wounded by this deplorable procession in those monumental streets. It seemed as if I were watching a march-past of dead women. Here is a festering sore, the real sore on the body of English society.[9]

In other European countries, the courtesan might acquire respectability; there was an accepted place for the *grande horizontale*. But in Victorian England it was all unbelievably squalid, partly because of the pretence that the trade did not exist, and partly because it represented in its starkest form the commercial nature of the relationship between men and women. The prostitute would never be accepted because she had no existence beyond the reality given to her by her client's wallet. Taine thought that 'what remains, then is nothing but an expression of lust, simple and coarse'.[10]

The thing was so blatant that it is astonishing the English could turn a blind eye. But, unless someone like the campaigning journalist W. T. Stead of the *Pall Mall Gazette* forced it upon their attention, the English preferred to ignore these tasteless facts. In the 1880s, Stead bought a thirteen-year-old girl called Eliza Armstrong and spirited her away to safety in Paris, proving the existence of a trade to satisfy the English appetite for deflowering virgins. The conclusion that 'London, or rather those who carry on the White Slave Traffic, provides the largest market in the world for the sale of human flesh' played a big part in getting the age of consent raised to sixteen in 1885. Newspaper accounts from before World War One tell tales built on the theme that although it was accepted that men had appetites, English women were all roses, pure and incorruptible. The great danger was not at home, but, inevitably, from foreign white-slave traders. Typical was the *News of the World*'s GIRLS SOLD TO INFAMY. LONDON AS CENTRE OF HIDEOUS TRAFFIC, an account provided by a police Assistant Commissioner of the hiring of stage-struck girls by foreign impresarios who took them abroad and sold them into degradation.

But the real degradation was not in France, it was at home. The scale of the industry has declined since the days of such exposés.

But the tatty, sordid nature of English prostitution, the cards in a thousand telephone boxes, the dimly glowing Soho doorbell above a scrawled sign 'MODEL — WALK UP', the frozen children on Birmingham street corners, the kerb-crawlers in their company cars, show how little the spirit has changed. It remains a coarse, cynical transaction between the relatively powerful and the relatively power-less, with dirt, disease and danger its daily concomitants. The contrast is with other European cultures, where the trade is legal, brothels are above-board, registered and regulated. But to introduce such a system in England would be to acknowledge that the trade exists.

On 7 April 1832, Joseph Thompson, a Cumberland farmer, went to market in Carlisle. It was a journey he made regularly, the only difference being that this time he was not planning to buy or sell cattle. He was getting rid of his wife.

The couple had been married for three years, but it had not worked and they had agreed to separate. Thompson held to the popular belief that all legal bonds would be severed if his wife was fairly disposed of at public auction. At twelve noon he sat her on a big oak chair in the marketplace, and, according to the *Annual Register* began his sales pitch in the following unpromising way.

Gentlemen, I have to offer to your notice my wife, Mary Anne Thompson, otherwise Williams, whom I mean to sell to the highest, fairest bidder. Gentlemen, it is her wish as well as mine to part forever. She has been to me only a born serpent. I took her for my comfort and the good of my home; but she became my tormentor, my domestic curse, a night invasion and a daily devil. Gentlemen, I speak truth from my heart when I say – may God deliver us from troublesome wives and frolicsome women! Avoid them as you would a mad dog, a roaring lion, a loaded pistol, cholera morbus, Mount Etna, or any other pestilential thing in nature.

In the unlikely event that this awesome advertisement had not deterred potential bidders, he went on to list Anne's better points:

She can read novels and milk cows; she can laugh and weep with the same ease that you could take a glass of ale when thirsty. She can make butter and scold the maid; she can sing Moore's melodies, and plait her frills and caps; she cannot make rum, gin or whisky, but she is a good judge of the quality from long experience in tasting them. I therefore offer her, with all her imperfections, for the sum of fifty shillings.

This calculatedly frank appraisal did not, apparently, have them waving their arms in the air with bids, and after an hour Thompson settled for an offer from a man called Henry Mears, of twenty shillings. Thompson asked him to throw in his Newfoundland dog, and so the deal was struck. 'They parted in perfect good temper – Mears and the woman going one way, Thompson and the dog another.'[11]

Unless Joseph Thompson was a farmer of quite astonishing eloquence, the story had obviously been embellished. It was clearly unusual – why else would the *Annual Register* have bothered with the details? But it was not unprecedented. The custom of men selling their wives seems to have begun with the Anglo-Saxons, and even then to have baffled other peoples. As late as 1884, men were still at it: in December that year, a reporter for *All The Year Round* listed twenty cases, complete with names and dates. Prices paid varied from twenty-five guineas and half a pint of beer, to one penny and dinner. The best-known story of wife-selling, Thomas Hardy's *The Mayor of Casterbridge*, the maudlin tale of how Michael Henchard gets drunk and disposes of wife and child to a sailor, was published in 1886.

Buying and selling wives provides one of the starkest examples of the relative status of men and women in some areas of English society. The practice owed much of its popularity to the belief that it was a lot simpler and cheaper than going through a divorce. And, providing the sale was properly witnessed, buying a man's wife from him was considered as legally valid as a conventional marriage ceremony; in some places, the purchaser even had to pay tax on his wife, as on any cattle he bought. The practice was an embodiment of the medieval belief that women were by definition inferior to men: as the law-givers explained it, if God had intended women to be equal or superior to men, he would have created Eve not from one of Adam's ribs but from his head. Violence against women, whether in ducking stools for objectionable wives (the last recorded instance of a ducking was in Leominster as late as 1809) or in the whippings seen in medieval manuscripts and misericords, followed naturally.

There was nothing unique to the English in the oppression of women. It was the consequence of things – the importance of combat, laws of inheritance, unequal distribution of wealth, expectations about child-rearing and domestic life – that were common to much of Europe. Resourceful women could find ways around the barriers erected by male society, as the number of women controlling large estates in the late eighteenth and early nineteenth century testifies. Even as far back as the sixteenth century, some accounts of visits to England compare the position of wealthy women very favourably with other European cultures. Emanuel Van Meteren, who first visited England in 1575, noted that

women are entirely in the power of their husbands ... yet they are not kept as strictly as in Spain or elsewhere. Nor are they shut up, but they have free management of the house or housekeeping. They are well dressed, fond of taking it easy, and commonly leave the care of household matters and drudgery to their servants. In all banquets and feasts they are shown the highest honour; they are placed at the upper end of the table, where they are the first served ... This is why England is called the Hell of Horses, the Purgatory of Servants, and the Paradise of Married Women.[12]

The problem was sex. As in most male-dominated societies, the victims of uncontrolled sexual desire were women. But it was the men who made the rules. If men were sexually incontinent, it was the fault of women. Statuary of the Seven Deadly Sins showed Lust as a woman, which was presumably why the received wisdom became that the only good woman was a chaste woman. Women who were sexually self-confident were likely to be trouble. The evidence that such women lived exists mainly by default, in the fact that so many in authority thought it necessary to declaim against them. In 1620, James I ordered the Bishop of London to tell his clergy to preach against 'the insolency of our women and their wearing of broad-rimmed hats, their hair cut short or shorn', which shows that some at least were prepared to ignore the usual rules. And here, at least, there was no chasm between royalist and parliamentarian: during the Commonwealth, which followed the execution of James's son, King Charles I, the Puritans kept up the assault upon women. After the Restoration the theme continued, with people like Bishop Jeremy Taylor preaching that chastity was 'the life of the angels, the enamel of the soul'.

The occasional enlightened male, like the philosopher John Stuart Mill, might protest, when marrying the widow with whom he had been intimate for years, that the laws were offensive. But his was a voice crying in the wilderness. Only in 1870 did Parliament recognize the right of women to control their own finances in the first Married Women's Property Act. It was not that Victorian England, which had refined the ideal Englishman, had no place for women. It had all too clear an idea of a woman's place.

When Victorian scholars began to compile the definitive roll-call of the people who had made the nation great, the twenty-two volumes of the *Dictionary of National Biography*, it turned out to be an overwhelmingly masculine compendium. Of the 28,000 people listed from the beginnings of British history to 1900, only 1,000 were women. Its editor, Sidney Lee, remarked that 'Women will not, I regret, have much claim on the attention of the national biographer for a very long time to come.'[13] There are two possible explanations. Either women genuinely played a very minor part indeed in the nation's history. Or the editors were purblind to their achievements. Certainly, the original *Dictionary* belongs to the heyday of British imperial power, of a piece with other celebrations of Anglo-Saxon achievement, from the Great Exhibition of 1851, through the Royal Albert Hall, the Tate and National Portrait galleries, the National Trust, the *Oxford English Dictionary*, the Victoria and Albert Museum, the Natural History Museum and Science Museum in London, to the great eleventh edition of the *Encyclopaedia Britannica*, and the *Cambridge History of English Literature*. Public life was a male world.

In the hundred years following publication of the first twenty-two volumes, the *Dictionary* produced supplements giving obituaries of the movers and shakers who had died recently. These point to a slow increase in the prominence of women through the twentieth century. They accounted for 3.5 per cent of the entries in the original publication. In the supplement reporting the lives of *illuminati* who died between 1986 and 1990, one in ten of the entries were women. By then, Oxford University Press had decided to revise the entire project for the Millennium. In the politically correct 1990s, it was a high priority to increase reporting of the role of women in the nation's history. After five years of research, the editors had discovered an additional 2,000 women who had been influential in the nation's history. It tripled the number of women singled out for recognition. But it was still a tiny fraction of the whole.

The original *Dictionary* had been blind to the achievements of women because it did not look for them in the right places. At a time when women were excluded from most areas of public life, you would be unlikely to find distinguished female politicians. The army and navy were officered by men and the exclusively male clergy had a stranglehold on teaching posts at the great universities. If women were to find an outlet for their abilities it would have to be in education, voluntary work, missionary activity, as hostesses or, in a small number of cases, as writers and artists, although even there a number found it wiser to publish under male *noms de plume*.

There were always women who proved more than capable of breaking through. Victorian society was, after all, presided over by a queen, and at the height of empire the mythmakers looked backwards to make comparison with another golden age in the reign of Elizabeth I. (Even Elizabeth, of course, inspired her troops gathered at Tilbury to resist Spanish invasion in 1588 by saying 'I know I have the body of a weak and feeble woman, but I have the heart and stomach of a king, and of a king of England too'.) The country has never lacked redoubtable women, from Boadicea and Hilda, Abbess of Whitby, to Florence Nightingale and Margaret Thatcher. It was women who helped to keep English culture alive after the catastrophe of the Norman invasion by marriage to the invaders and by patronizing writers identified with the old tradition. In the days when the English economy was built upon the wool trade, spinsters – spinners of wool – had a trade at the heart of the economy. And there were always women who threw off the sexual straitjacket they were expected to wear – Lady Caroline Lamb, Claire Clairmont and Lady Oxford, three of Byron's mistresses, are obvious examples.

Elizabeth Fry did more to better the lives of nineteenth-century prisoners than any man of her day. Octavia Hill's tireless and very practical campaigns to improve the housing conditions of the Victorian poor were imitated across Europe. Henrietta Barnett, the wife of an East End vicar, invented Hampstead Garden Suburb, steering through an act of Parliament to make it possible, then buying the land and building upon it. It led Asquith to call her 'the unofficial custodian of the children of the state'. We could go on. But the point about these women is that they were restricted to themes that could be seen as comparatively unthreatening extensions of their domestic lives. Florence Nightingale's mission to the hospitals of the Crimea came after an appeal from *The Times* correspondent at the front, 'Are none of the daughters of England, at this extreme hour of need, ready for such a work of mercy?' You can bet your last Penny Black that had Miss Nightingale been married to a conventional Victorian male, she would have been obliged to stay at home.

In general, that was where English men have expected their women to be. Respectable Society, with all its inhibitions, may have been a Victorian invention, but there is plenty of evidence that the division of the world into male and female spheres began much earlier. Certainly, by Hanoverian days English males in smart society were more comfortable in the company of their own sex than with women. César de Saussure, a French visitor, was baffled by the English habit of driving women from the table after dinner, which he could explain only because they 'generally prefer drinking and gambling to female company'.[14] He, by contrast, found English women friendly, tender-hearted and passionate, since 'They do not despise foreigners as the men do; they are not distant to them and sometimes will prefer them to their own countrymen.' The French visitor Joseph Fiévée, who hated just about everything about the English, was particularly incensed by the Englishman's rudeness towards women. He wrote in 1802 that

It's because they want to get down to drinking that Englishmen get the women to withdraw after dinner. Often, at eleven o'clock at night, they're still sat around the same table, while the women are yawning their heads off in some upstairs drawing-room. It's not uncommon for the master of the house to which the wife has invited guests, to leave their company and go off to the tavern to drink, chat and play to his heart's content with his friends.[15]

Men could get away with bad manners like that because of their assumption that women were incapable of holding worthwhile opinions on subjects outside the home. It implied a clear hierarchy: they left the table because the men were going to talk about matters that were above their heads, like politics, business or war. As Lord Chesterfield put it, 'women, especially, are to be talked to as below men and above children'.

There are two possible explanations of the fact that men talked in such terms. Either they really believed that women were second-class beings; or, uneasily aware of the injustice of denying women a full role in society, and aware too that it could not last, they were casting around for justifications. The stronger the challenge, the more vociferous the evangelism about how the family was the cornerstone of the safe and ordered society, and the wife and mother was the heart of the family. 'There can be no question but that the home is the woman's primary sphere of action', goes one early nineteenth-century sermon.[16] Elizabeth Sandford advised that 'There is something unfeminine in independence. It is contrary to Nature, and therefore it offends. A really sensible woman feels her dependence; she does what she can, but she is conscious of inferiority'.[17] We are talking here about the middle class, which came of age in Victorian England as the most important social group in the country. There grew up among the propagandists a view that working women were the mark of a 'barbarous society'. It followed that if a man was to maintain his position, the woman of the house could not be seen to go out to work. (One consequence of the need to preserve the appearance of prosperity on one income was that the husband and father figure was obliged to work longer and longer hours to earn the means to keep the family afloat, becoming in the process the distant, cold figure of caricature.)

It was because the assumption that men and women occupied quite separate worlds was so deeply ingrained that the Reform Acts of 1832 and 1867, which extended the franchise among men, did nothing at all to give the vote to women. The mind of man ran along practical, educated lines; the mind of woman was a mass of intuitions. It followed that the term 'educated woman' was an oxymoron: learning could necessarily be acquired only by displacing the instinctive reasoning that was the essence of womanhood. And at a practical level, if you taught women Latin and Greek, you clogged up valuable brain space that should have been occupied with the finer points of cooking and sewing and dealing with tradesmen. *Punch* had this portrait of the ideal little woman.

She looks attentively after the holes in her father's gloves. She is a clever adept at preparing gruel, white-wine whey, tapioca, chicken broth, beef tea, and the thousand little household delicacies of the sick room . . . She does not invent excuses for not reading to her father of an evening, nor does she skip any of the speeches . . . She knows nothing of crotchets [iconoclastic opinions], or 'Woman's Mission'. She studies housekeeping, is perfect in the common rules of arithmetic . . . She checks the weekly bills, and does not blush if she is seen in a butcher's shop on a Saturday.[18]

If men were producers and women merely consumers, if the home was a retreat from the world, the Angel in the House was invested with a scent of sanctity. By the middle of the nineteenth century, women were being seen as a mechanism for purifying industrial society. The *Quarterly Review* suggested the country 'make use of the engine God has placed in our hands . . . Pour into the corrupted stream the pure, healthy, disinfectant of English womanhood'.[19] Feminist interpretations of history have, not surprisingly, railed against the straitjacket into which women were forced by the idealized idea of womanhood that was imposed upon them. Mrs Rochester, who haunts Charlotte Brontë's *Jane Eyre*, is their metaphor. 'The madwoman in the attic' is the vehicle through which 'the female author enacts her own raging desires to escape male houses and male texts'.[20] Well, perhaps.

But it proved an astonishingly durable idea of femininity. The Celia Johnson character of *Brief Encounter* would certainly have recognized and respected it. In the 1930s Jan Struther's accounts of the simple joys of home life were hugely popular in *The Times* as 'Mrs Miniver' described the doings of her two boys and one girl, professional husband, nanny, parlourmaid, cook, and second home in Kent, a world troubled only by things like leaking pipes, sick pets and husbands who fell asleep under the newspaper after dinner. When Mrs Miniver was translated to the screen by Greer Garson, complete with Nazi plots and a husband doing his bit at Dunkirk, she was held to embody the pluck of the Englishwoman in wartime.

Churchill is said, improbably, to have believed that the film did more for the war effort than a flotilla of battleships.[21]

Any improvement in the status of women in England owes nothing much to the English upper classes, who so proudly boasted of being defenders of all that was best about their culture. If, as apologists for the heritage industry like to claim, the country house was the supreme cultural achievement of the English way of life, the role of the Englishwoman within it was clear enough. She was a maid or a cook. Or she administered the maids and cooks. When Hermann Muthesius was telling his German readers about the English house, he had to explain why they seemed to have so many more servants than was the case in his own country. Apart from the higher standards of physical comfort in English homes and the more specialized nature of English servants, there was the fact that 'the lady of the house merely presides over the household, without taking any active part in it. The lady of an English house never sets foot in the kitchen and the cook would not want her to do so. She sends for the servants when she is ready to give her orders'.[22] Mrs Beeton's bestseller, which first appeared in 1861 and was aimed at the rapidly growing middle class was, after all, called *Household Management*.

You can still find the grandchildren of Mrs Miniver. The antidote to the belief that England has really changed is to shop at Harvey Nichols during the working day, to lunch at Daphne's or Bibendum or just to glance at the faces smiling out from the photographs in 'Jennifer's Diary'. The magazine picture captions give the game away: once a woman has married, she not only loses her family name, the baptismal name goes, too. So, among the faces enjoying themselves at charity balls, elaborate bashes to celebrate daughters' 21sts, fashionable weddings and good-cause lunches, are Mrs Hugo Ford, Mrs Stephen Reeve-Tucker, Mrs David Hallam-Peel, and Lady Charles Spencer-Churchill. In one photograph, the then serving cabinet minister and Privy Councillor Virginia Bottomley becomes 'Mrs Peter Bottomley'. Doubtless, in this world, Margaret Thatcher, the most famous female politician in history, was 'Mrs Denis Thatcher'.

Perhaps they are no longer chattels, but all those healthy, well-fed faces belong to a world which Celia Johnson's character would also recognize at once. In the milieu from which the late Princess Diana came it is still scarcely considered worth educating women. She, a perfectly intelligent woman, after all, emerged from school with scarcely more than a certificate for the best-kept hamster. There is something about this attitude to education that is highly revealing. In 1930, the French writer Émile Cammaerts attempted to distil his twenty years' experience of life in England. He had noticed that English schools and colleges 'have played a far larger part in English life than any prominent educational institution has done in the life of other countries . . . they have succeeded in preserving and developing a certain type of character and a certain ideal of service, without which England would never have become what she is today'.[23] Cammaerts was an Anglophile and a more radical critique would interpret 'the ideal of service' which produced the Breed in much more jaundiced terms. Where the overall philosophy of education is concerned, it had serious implications for women. It made a firm connection between mind and body – *mens sana in corpore sano* – and its ideal was overwhelmingly masculine. In 1872, W. Turley explicitly linked maleness to the idea of national success. Writing in the journal the *Dark Blue* he thundered that 'a nation of effeminate enfeebled bookworms scarcely forms the most effective bulwark of the nation's liberties'.[24]

Women who dared to believe in education were either mocked or patronized, or both. The original 'Bluestockings' may have enjoyed the company of men such as Dr Johnson or Edmund Burke, but Sidney Smith advised them they should not flaunt their learning ('if the stocking be blue, the petticoat must be long'). Reading of these eighteenth-century pioneers is like watching a scattered flotilla of sailing boats on a stormy sea, desperately signalling to one another for comfort against the elements. Lady Mary Wortley Montagu wrote from Italy to a friend that 'to say truth, there is no part of the world where our sex is treated with so much contempt as in England'. Small wonder that while so many men were enthusiastically promoting themselves and their country as embodying the highest levels of civilization, many women, like Mary Wollstonecraft, that great enthusiast for the French Revolution, saw themselves not so much as English as part of a wider humanity.

The average middle- or upper-class Englishman had no such qualms. After all, the culture was a masculine culture. But Englishmen were determined to keep education to themselves. John Ruskin, whose idealization of women was so heartfelt that he is said to have been incapable of consummating his marriage because of the horrific discovery that his wife had pubic hair, thought that a woman only needed to know enough to 'sympathize in her husband's pleasure'.[25] In any case, women had smaller skulls than men, which meant smaller brains. And because they possessed only a finite amount of energy, the physical demands of menstruation, growing breasts and childbearing necessarily meant that there was less effort available for mental activity. There were even those who argued that since menstruation could be so incapacitating, education could tip women over into sterility. All in all, they would be well advised to steer clear of learning. Apart from anything else, educated women would take jobs away from men, which would force more of them to leave for the colonies, and so create more spinsters: ergo, women who had hopes of marriage should not demand better schooling.

It takes some believing, but it was not until 1869 that Emily Davies founded Girton as a Cambridge college for women, and when, in 1896, the university came to vote on whether women should be allowed to face examinations for degrees, *The Times* printed train timetables, to enable London-based graduates to travel to Cambridge to vote against the proposition. The university did not allow women full membership until 1948. Like the more generalized prejudice against 'intellectuals', this discrimination against women was worse in England than elsewhere: of the pioneers of women's right to practise medicine, Sophia Jex-Blake was only able to qualify by studying in Edinburgh, Elizabeth Garrett Anderson got her MD in Paris, Elizabeth Blackwell in the United States.

One remark is enough to sum it up. The institutions were made by and for men, even down to childhood. When the Girl Guides were set up as a counterpart to the Boy Scouts, a serial in their magazine, 'The Castlestone House Company', caught the tone perfectly. It is 1918 and the schoolgirls are talking about forming a Guide company. The sexual aspiration is explicit: '"I envy you awfully. Being a Guide is all very well, and quite nice, but nothing like being torpedoed and catching spies and all that."' Then one of them remarks sighingly of the Guides' uniform, '"Look at all the pockets," murmured Elsie, admiringly, "it's as good as being a boy."'[26]

In this environment, was it any wonder that the spiritual daughters of Mary Wollstonecraft became angry? In 1938, Virginia Woolf examined the idea of patriotism in *Three Guineas*, and decided that, as a woman, she had little reason to be grateful to 'her' country. Imagining a conversation between a brother and sister on the eve of mobilization, she decided that

She will find that she has no good reason to ask her brother to fight on her behalf to protect 'our' country. '"Our country",' she will say, 'throughout the greater part of its history has treated me as a slave, it has denied me education or any share in its possessions. "Our" country still ceases to be mine if I marry a foreigner. "Our" country denies me the means of protecting myself, forces me to pay others a very large sum annually to protect me, and is so little able, even so, to protect me that Air Raid precautions are written on the wall. Therefore, if you insist upon fighting to protect me, or "our" country, let it be understood soberly and rationally between us, that you are fighting to gratify a sex instinct which I cannot share; to procure benefits which I have not shared and probably will not share; but not to gratify my instincts, or to protect myself or my country. For,' the outsider will say, 'in fact, as a woman, I have no country.'[27]

The strict hierarchical division between the sexes was the consequence of the invention of the Ideal Englishman. As he would be honourable, decent, stoical and brave, so she would be stoical, motherly, submissive and chaste. It is astonishing how quickly the Respectable Society took root. Attitudes to the seventeenth-century writer Aphra Behn are a telling example. Behn, lauded by Virginia Woolf as the first woman to make a living from her pen, produced a series of plays and poems about bad marriages and their miserable consequences. She had to contend throughout her career with accusations (from male critics) of being obsessed with carnality – accusations they would never have levelled at a man: her works are mild compared to some of those of her contemporary, John Rochester. But the real challenge to Aphra Behn came after her death. In 1826, Sir Walter Scott sent a copy of her novel *Oroonoko*, the story of an African slave, to his great-aunt. The next time Scott saw his aunt, she returned the book, with the advice that he burn it. It was, she said, salacious. Even she recognized there was something curious about her actions. 'Is it not very odd,' she remarked, 'that I, an old woman of eighty and upwards, sitting alone, feel myself ashamed to read a book which, sixty years ago, I have heard read aloud for the amusement of large circles, consisting of the first and most creditable society in London?' Scott commented that 'This was, of course, owing to the gradual improvements of the national taste and decency.'[28]

Almost as quickly as Respectable Society took hold, it has crumbled away. Dr Acton, who had advised Victorian England that masturbation created 'peevish valetudinarians', recommended married couples not to have intercourse more than once every week or ten days. He remarked that 'The majority of women (happily for them) are not very much troubled with sexual feeling of any kind ... As a general rule, a modest woman seldom desires any sexual gratification for herself. She submits to her husband's embraces, but principally to gratify him; and, were it not for the desire of maternity, would far rather be relieved from his attentions'.[29] It is evidence of the hunger for more honest information that in 1918, only twenty years after the last edition of Dr Acton's book, Marie Stopes produced the first above-board sex manual, *Married Love*. Between March and December that year it went through five editions. By the mid-1920s it had sold half a million copies.

During the First World War, Women's Patrols had stalked the streets, on the lookout for fornicating soldiers and their girls. By the 1930s there was so much frottage going on in public parks that a visiting French schoolmistress was horrified. Odette Keun concluded that it was because Englishwomen were 'definitely sex-hungry' that the average Englishman was such a dull lover: he never needed to woo her into bed. 'English lovemaking is not an amusement but a function ... My real objection to the English male is that he will not give enough time, trouble or attention to the sexual act, and thereby makes it as flat, stale and deadly as a slab of one of his own cold suet puddings.'[30] (She has a point here – unlike the French, the English have never really considered seduction as an art form.)

As the twentieth century wore on, Respectable Society tumbled, such that all that is left are occasional caryatids, like the draped female figures that once supported the pediments of a long-gone Roman temple. The speed of change has been remarkable. Hippolyte Taine believed English married women were nearly always faithful, and it was only in 1918 that the number of divorces passed 1,000 a year, most of them between members of the comparatively small upper and upper-middle classes. Now, the country has the highest divorce rate in the European Union.[31] By the late 1990s, one quarter of unmarried women between 18 and 49 were cohabiting with men. The British had the highest rate of single-parent families in Europe. No one bats an eyelid that a pornographer, Paul Raymond, has become one of the country's richest men, rubbing shoulders with dukes and earls.

None of these trends is unique to England; family breakdowns, the growth of relationships unlicensed by the state, the tolerance of pornography are common to all western societies. Some of the reasons for the change are clear enough. Two massive wars, the second of which included the deliberate targeting of civilians, speeded the breakdown of hierarchical distinctions between men and women. The contribution of women to the war effort, in munitions factories, on the land and in the services made it increasingly hard to assert old-fashioned Mrs Miniver-like verities about the role of the Angel in the Home. The growing opportunities for female education, the advance of feminism and the assertion of equal rights for women all made it impossible for men to hang on to a belief in the old, masculine idea of Englishness. And the contraceptive pill released women from the fear of constant pregnancy.

Of course, the old stereotypes can give everyone a good laugh. It is a lot more fun to make things up than to try to figure out what's going on around you, which accounts for the phenomenal success of Bill Bryson's amiable 'non-fiction' about Britain. Visiting the country for the first time in 1973, he was struck by the contrast between British women's magazines and those back home in the American Midwest:

The articles in mother's and sister's magazines were always about sex and personal gratification. They had titles like 'Eat Your Way to Multiple Orgasms', 'Office Sex – How to Get It', 'Tahiti: The Hot New Place for Sex' and 'Those Shrinking Rainforests – Are They Any Good for Sex?' The British magazines addressed more modest aspirations. They had titles like 'Knit Your Own Twinset', 'Money-Saving Button Offer', 'Make This Super Knitted Soapsaver' and 'Summer's Here – It's Time for Mayonnaise!'[32]

If it was true then, it is long gone. The best-selling women's magazines are obsessed with sex, sexual problems, sexual health and sexual ethics.

The fact that the old model for the relationship between men and women has broken down so much more comprehensively in England than in many other parts of Europe argues that there was something specific to the English formula that didn't work in the late twentieth century. Perhaps the reason is that once the English had seen that the Empire, for which the models were invented, had failed, they found the prototypes irrelevant. Just as the Breed and the amateur were no longer serviceable as paragons for men, so the old archetypes that men had sought to impose on women were equally redundant. As the authority of the nation collapsed in the outside world, so, at home, did the authority of those who might have been expected to uphold the old moral certainties. It is noticeable that the two most public moralizers of the century, Cosmo Lang, the great Archbishop of Canterbury, and John Reith, the founder of the BBC, were not English, but Scots. What has emerged in place of the stiff upper lip of Trevor Howard and the trembling lower lip of Celia Johnson is the most effervescent youth culture in the world.

Alongside the exuberant music and fashion, the English have, it is said, the highest rate of teenage sexual activity in the industrialized world. The percentage of unmarried women who are sexually active by the age of nineteen is 86 per cent. In the United States, which has the second-highest rate, the figure is 75 per cent.[33] Fewer than 1 per cent of brides are virgins. The England which has emerged from the ruins of empire is one in which advancement is by ability rather than conformity or connections and one in which, although there is still a long road to travel, women have increasing parity with men in public life.

CHAPTER ELEVEN

OLD COUNTRY,
NEW CLOTHES

The English have a miraculous power of turning wine into water.

OSCAR WILDE

It is not merely that the roles of the English sexes have changed. So too has the land they live in. It is, like the rest of the world, dominated by brand names. The English wear baseball caps and jeans, eat versions of American, Asian or Italian food, drive cars made anywhere on the globe (even the grandest British car-maker, Rolls-Royce, is now owned by Germans), dance to international beats and play computer games designed in Seattle or Tokyo. In this new world neither geography nor history, religion nor politics exerts the influence it once did. And as external fashions have changed in the last half-century, so too have the internal certainties.

The Second World War, the time of *Brief Encounter* and *In Which We Serve*, was the last extended period when we could say with any confidence that the impression of England matched the reality. Even then, there were plenty of signs that the old certainties were crumbling. My father dated the country's decline from the occasion when he came home on leave from service on the North Atlantic convoys and heard hostesses boasting of the extra bits of meat they had bought on the black market to augment meagre food rations. A country in which otherwise 'respectable' figures felt no shame at bilking the rules was finished. The 'spiv' who could get you whatever you wanted, from nylons to bacon joints, was as authentically English as the self-denying Celia Johnson and Trevor Howard figures, whose restraint was a mark of their altruism.

Brief Encounter and *In Which We Serve* had both been written by Noël Coward, whose 'essential Englishness' had been acquired, like his accent and cigarette holder, on the journey from his birth as the son of a west London piano salesman to his friendship with England's royalty. Once peace had come, his idea of England would not last long. Within little more than a decade Coward was reduced to the indignity of railing against the 'kitchen sink' school of drama which had made his plays about middle-class life seem so brittle and dated. Citing the advice he claimed Churchill had given him that 'An Englishman has an inalienable right to live wherever he chooses', Coward fled the country for exile in Bermuda, Switzerland and Jamaica, rather than pay the taxes necessary to build the New Jerusalem.

The new stage sensation, *Look Back in Anger*, John Osborne's furious reaction against the fatuous place he found himself living in, was first produced in May 1956. It took as its premise that 'there aren't any good, brave causes left', and drove forwards on the bitterness of Jimmy Porter at the values of the 'Edwardian brigade' of his wife's posh family. As Osborne explained it in *Tribune*,

This is a letter of hate. It is for you, my countrymen, I mean those men of my country who have defiled it. The men with manic fingers, leading the feeble, betrayed body of my country to its death . . . I only hope it [his hate] will keep me going. I think it will. I think it may sustain me in the last few months. Till then, damn you, England. You're rotting now, and quite soon you'll disappear.[1]

Legions of writers have followed in Osborne's wake, feasting on the corpse of Edwardian England. So that even those who believed, in characteristically English fashion, that the attacks were going 'a bit too far', nonetheless felt that to live in England was to take part in a sort of wake. Certainly, the ruling class have signally failed to come up with a new design for the twenty-first century, which is why the English have found themselves walking backwards into the future, their eyes fixed on a point some time at the turn of the twentieth century. It is time to wonder whether this mourning for the past is justified.

We could start by considering what the English have given the world.

And here is the first problem. For the greatest legacy the English have bequeathed the rest of humanity is their language. When an Icelander meets a Peruvian, each reaches for his English. Even in the Second World War, when the foundations were being laid for the Axis pact between Germany, Japan and Italy, Yosuke Matsuoka was negotiating for the Emperor in English. It is the medium of technology, science, travel and international politics. Three quarters of the world's mail is written in English, four fifths of all data stored on computers is in English and the language is used by two thirds of the world's scientists. It is the Malay of the world, easy to learn, very easy to speak badly; a little learning will take you quite a long way, which is why an estimated one quarter of the entire world population can speak the language to some degree. By the late 1990s, the British Council was predicting that at the turn of the millennium 1 billion (thousand million) people would be learning English.[2]

Some of these students will become highly fluent, like the Dutch Secretary General of NATO, Dr Josef Luns, who once remarked that he preferred English because 'when I speak in my own language I feel as though I am vomiting'. But most want to learn the language as a means to an end. The compilers of the *Oxford English Dictionary* – the Bible of the English language – keep no records on where new words originate, but it is a safe bet that of the 3,000 or so new words which enter their database each year, only a minority have been minted in England; the rest come from America, Australia or the international language of computing and science. After all, of the 650 million or so people who speak English as a first or second language, perhaps 8 per cent are English.

The moment a Frenchman opens his mouth, he declares his identity. The French speak French. The English speak a language which belongs to no one. Professor Michael Dummett, Wykeham professor of Logic at Oxford, once stood in line to buy a railway ticket in Chicago and struck up a conversation with a fellow traveller. After a time, the man said, 'You must be from Europe.' 'Yes, from England,' said Dummett. To which the Spinoza beside him replied, 'You speak pretty good English.' Dummett was so astonished that he found himself blurting out that he *was* English. It was only later that he realized that for many Americans, 'English' is just the name of a language spoken in America, as 'Dutch' is the language spoken in Holland. The paradox of language is that it is at once precious and personal to the speaker and at the same time the property of everyone. What happens to a people if they cease to own their language?

When I visited the Oxford English Dictionary, the enquiry team were dealing with the latest query to drop on their desk from a member of the public trying to keep track of their language. The writer had been shocked to hear someone talking about a piece of technical equipment as 'the dog's bollocks'. What, the anxious letter-writer wanted to know, did it mean? And where on earth did the expression come from?

This is the sort of challenge lexicographers like. 'The dog's bollocks' does not appear in the magisterial 1933 edition of the *Oxford English Dictionary*, until recently the bible for defining the meaning of English words. Dog's-head ('a dog-faced baboon'), Dog's Nose ('a mixed liquor of beer and gin') and Dog-sleep ('feigned or pretended sleep') are all there, together with thirty-odd other words incorporating 'dog'. But no dog's bollocks.

In a vast open-plan office, notable for its astonishing quiet (in an hour and a half not a single telephone rings), the Oxford lexico-graphers try to keep track of how the language is changing. Desktop screens flash with messages from lookouts across the English-speaking world, bringing news of new coinings. An informant has contacted them to report what she thinks is the first sighting of the expression 'bad hair day'. It turns out to have been in a newspaper in Seattle. A correspondent in Cambridge, Massachusetts, has dis-covered a hitherto unknown early use of 'Maltese', predating anything in the dictionary. A subdued excitement follows.

Many English adults could define the dog's bollocks at once. If something is the DB, it is as good as it could be, the best of its kind, the Rolls-Royce of its type. 'Just the ticket', as they might have said thirty years ago. It is a mark of how fast the English language can change that it can take up a particular expression and assimilate it into common currency in months. Journalists, in particular, are forever inventing expressions, simply to see how long it is before others are using them as if they're a long-established part of the language. If you're lucky, it doesn't take more than a few weeks to invent a word and find it passing into everyday usage. When the lexicographer Jonathon Green compiled a list of everyday words invented between 1960 and 1990 he drew the line at 2,700, from AC/DC (bisexual), to zonked (intoxicated).[3] There is something Humpty-Dumptyish about the way the English language is used; words can mean whatever the user wants them to mean. The English seem not merely to have accepted the astonishing capacity for change of their language, but to exult in it. 'Languages only stop changing when they're dead,' says Patrick Hanks happily, in the great open-plan office of the Oxford English Dictionary, before turning back to his screen to examine the latest incoming message from a scout on the outer fringes of the English-speaking world.

One of the consequences of the growth of English as a medium for the world is that attempts at prescription have been more or less abandoned. The French, who have been the main losers in the contest to develop a world language, have reacted to the viral spread of English by a form of linguistic isolationism, attempting to ban the use of foreign words, specifying the proportion of music on radio stations that must be sung in French. The English laugh at them for it, not merely because they are the historic enemy and – in this war at least – they are on the losing side, but because they fail to understand that Canute-like attempts at proprietorship are doomed. The English language has no guardians, merely people like the Oxford Dictionary who record how it has changed. When a new edition of any dictionary of the English language appears, the question asked is not whether it safeguards old usages, but how many new words it acknowledges. The authors are willing to exult in the diversity of their language, from wherever it comes.

This easy-going attitude to their language is nothing new. The first dictionary of the English language was originally begun as an attempt to replicate what the *Académie Française* had done for French. The *Dictionnaire de l'Académie*, which had emerged in 1694, after fifty-five years of labour, was intended to provide the final word on the right and wrong uses of words. There had been proposals for a similar prescriptive approach to the English language, kicking around for years – Defoe had argued for an English Academy 'to encourage Polite Learning, to polish and refine the *English* tongue, and advance the so much neglected faculty of Correct Language'.[4] Jonathan Swift made a similar case in 1712 in his *Proposal for Correcting, Improving and Ascertaining the English Tongue*. Although Dr Samuel Johnson was beaten to the task of producing the first English dictionary in answer to the call (that honour went to the scientist, Benjamin Martin), his work remains the outstanding example of single-handed lexicography. It is to Johnson's credit that he saw the foolishness of trying to preserve the language in aspic. As he wrote in his Preface:

When we see men grow old and die at a certain time one after another, from century to century, we laugh at the elixir that promises to prolong life to a thousand years; and with equal justice may the lexicographer be derided, who being able to produce no example of a nation that has preserved their words and phrases from mutability, shall imagine that his dictionary can embalm his language, and secure it from corruption and decay ... The language most likely to continue long without alteration would be that of a nation raised a little, and but a little, above barbarity, secluded from strangers, and totally employed in procuring the conveniences of life.[5]

If Johnson had not saved the British from the idiocies of a prescriptive *Académie Anglaise*, someone else would have done. Verbal evolution is the mark of success, not failure. Curiously, it is America, the home of so many new coinings and usages, that provides the big market for historical dictionaries of the English language, because of the appetite for heritage. The English seem not merely to have adjusted to the fact that they no longer control their language, but positively to exult in its growth. It does not seem the behaviour of a people afraid of the future.

(The dog's bollocks, by the way, is an expression invented by printers to describe the sign:– in newspapers. It is authentically English.)

Like its language, the new England owes something and nothing to the past. The main change is that while the old England was built on templates for a model Englishman and -woman which were laid out centuries ago, the new England is vigorous, demotic, and highly inventive. And because the English cultural tradition was based upon individualism, the possibilities of the England that is emerging from the chrysalis of the last half-century or more are almost limitless.

The important changes are not switches of government, but shifts in the *Zeitgeist*. When the Labour party swept to power in May 1997, it proclaimed an ambition to 'rebrand' Britain: after reinventing itself as New Labour, with most of its ideological baggage discarded, now would come New Britain, a country which had shrugged off the succubus of its past. Within months, much of the media was dancing to their tune. 'RENEWED BRITANNIA' boasted *Time* magazine's cover story in October. 'After 50 years of struggling against what often seemed impossible odds, the United Kingdom is showing an unmistakable spring in its step', ran the copy.[6] Proof of the transformation came in profiles of successful film-makers, computer-games millionaires, fashion designers, performers and currency dealers. These were people, the magazine rightly suggested, who had ignored the inhibitions of belonging to an old country mired in class inhibition and social prejudice against wealth creation, and seized the opportunity to follow their commercial instincts. One of their main assets, though none mentioned it, was that they spoke the global language. Another was the accident of geography that placed their country in a position where it could do business with Asia in the morning and North America in the afternoon; a third, the long history of trading on which the Empire was built; a fourth, another consequence of empire, a network of connections across the world and a capacity for assimilating other cultures; a fifth the comparatively high levels of training and skill in the workforce; a sixth the attractive-ness of London as a base for foreign businesspeople to live because of English characteristics of lawfulness, business acumen and tolerance. We could go on. The point is that none of these was the consequence of a political decision by the new government.

The autumn following his election, Tony Blair played host to the heads of Commonwealth governments from around the world. Before they could hear his speech of welcome, they were obliged to sit in awkward silence through a video presentation celebrating the creative, commercial and scientific achievements of the new meritocratic Britain. With music from Oasis and the Spice Girls, pictures of dealing rooms, Formula One racing cars and pharmaceut-ical factories, the presentation battered relentlessly on the theme that Britain was now a young country. The Prime Minister's speech, when it came, repeated the message. 'The new Britain is a meritocracy where we break down barriers of class, religion, race and culture,' he said. The aim was that old Conservative goal of One Nation, 'for all the people, not a privileged few'.[7]

The silly slogan used for selling this new country was 'Cool Britannia', at which any truly cool person could only wince or shudder: when middle-aged politicians embrace youth culture they always get it wrong. The 'Britain' element was significant, though: no one talked of a Cool England. This was because the country was going through one of the phases in its history when an Englishman could be defined as someone who lived on an island in the North Sea governed by Scots. 'Britain' also has the advantage of being inclusive. You don't need to be a white Anglo-Saxon to be British. It seems that you can be Nigerian, Moslem, Jewish, Chinese, Bangladeshi, Indian or Sikh British, a great deal more easily than you can be English and any of those things. Precisely because 'Britain' is a political invention, it allows diversity.

The supreme embodiment of the idea of Britain is the country's royal family. The ambition of uniting the kingdom is spelled out in the lumbering list of titles of the heir to the throne: Charles is Prince of Wales, Duke of Cornwall, Duke of Rothesay, Earl of Carrick and Baron Renfrew, Lord of the Isles and Great Steward of Scotland. The institution of monarchy belongs to the world of red tunics and bearskins, the Union flag and the Gatling gun and Queen Elizabeth and Prince Philip are almost the last representatives of Respectable Society. How far the country they led had changed became bruisingly clear with the sudden death of Charles's former wife, Princess Diana, in 1997. Still subscribing to a code of behaviour which abhorred displays of emotion, monarch and consort were almost the only individuals who did not grieve her death in a sentimental way. Much of the rest of this nation of supposed stiff upper lips traipsed to the florist, bought bunches of flowers and then laid them as close as possible to any building with which this uniquely privileged young woman had been associated. Soon the gates of Kensington Palace,

Buckingham Palace, St James's Palace and the family home in Northamptonshire were all but submerged under a sea of petals and plastic. They lit candles in jam jars and left them as impromptu shrines. They hung cards and photos on roadside railings and trees in the parks, accompanied by scrawled messages. DIANA WE LOVE YOU and HEAVEN HAS A NEW ANGEL were among the most coherent. And then, when the funeral came, the public lined the route of the cortège for mile after mile, throwing flowers at the coffin and, most bizarrely of all, popping the flashbulbs of their cameras for a photo for the family album.

By no stretch of the imagination could this be called 'typical' behaviour from a nation whose impassivity in the face of emotion had been one of the elements of self-parody with which it was most at ease. George MacDonald Fraser, creator of the hugely successful series of *Flashman* historical romances, was appalled to see what C. S. Forester called 'lower deck sentimentality' having such an airing. Who knows how many he spoke for when he asked how the British cult of the hero had become the cult of the victim. 'Mr Blair felt proud. I felt ashamed,' he said. 'For grieving has become a positive virtue, and the response to tragedy, and especially to fatal crime, has become a ritual: the florists' shops must be stripped so that tributes can be strewn at the scene, there must be tears and harrowing interviews for the cameras.'[8]

Diana's death was tragic, as any sudden death in the prime of life is tragic. But was it any more tragic than that of any of the numberless thousands of young men and women whose short lives are commemorated on war memorials in every village and town in the land? Diana was beautiful, manipulative, compassionate, and had died enjoying the life of a rich nightclubber. Yet she had somehow become an underdog and you cannot exaggerate English sympathy for the underdog. This astonishingly favoured young woman had become a victim with whom the public could identify, because the House of Windsor ('the Germans' to the rat-pack of reporters) found itself in the position of one monarchy after another – out of touch with the people in whose name it purported to rule. What happened when she died was an outbreak of collective hysteria from a people who, through a prolonged period of peace, had got out of touch with the experience of sudden death. No one thought it odd that at her funeral Elton John should perform a reworking of the song he had originally composed as hero-worship to Marilyn Monroe, for she too was an icon for a secular age and in the end icons of that kind are interchangeable. The song sold five million copies in England. The mass of commemorative books, posters, T-shirts and crockery showed how thin was the pretence that the country was ruled by rationality and reserve.

The crowds that poured into the London parks to lay votive offerings at the impromptu shrines demonstrated how much and how little England had changed in the second half of the twentieth century. What was probably unchanged was the politeness and consideration of the crowd, who showed the sort of thoughtfulness I imagine you could have found in other large gatherings at any time this century. With the exception of the motorcycle outriders who accompanied the hearse, the police were unobtrusive. There was a quiet dignity everywhere. White Anglo-Saxons were in a strong majority, but a great variety of racial origins were represented. Women comfortably outnumbered men among the mourners. There were few enough of the rich and powerful represented; this was a genuine expression of popular emotion.

George MacDonald Fraser's objection to the public mourning underestimates that capacity of the English for sentimentality that Charles Dickens understood so well when he killed off Little Nell, or made Tiny Tim hobble forward to wish, 'Merry Christmas every one of us!' Had Diana died in the days when the dominant mores in England were set by the Breed and their compliant, domesticated wives, we should have seen a very different spectacle. But the English no longer live in such a country. The purpose for which the Breed was bred no longer exists. The freeing of English womanhood from its enforced restrictions has allowed something much more electric to emerge.

It is not that Diana was a mere victim. Her funeral assumed the dimensions it did because it became a pagan rite; Diana was a sort of goddess in a godless age. At one stage, when I began thinking about this book, I briefly thought of organizing it around ideas of the English hero and came across this description of how Admiral Nelson was treated by the London crowds in 1805, when he returned after chasing the French fleet across the Atlantic and through the West Indies: 'Wherever he appears he electrifies the cold English character,' wrote Lady Elizabeth Foster after watching him walking the streets, 'rapture and applause follow all his steps. Sometimes a poor woman asks to touch his coat. The very children learn to bless him as he passes, and doors and windows are crowded.'[9]

It could be a description of the adulation for Diana. Each had had their heads turned by the adoration heaped upon them (Nelson's famous signal 'England expects . . .' had originally read 'Nelson confides . . .'); each, for all their worshippers, had feet of clay. Each filled a need at a particular moment in their nation's history; Nelson, a martial hero for a martial age; Diana, the patron saint of a country preoccupied with its own failure. At the end, Nelson's coffin was carried into St Paul's for a four-hour state funeral, flanked by six admirals in full dress uniform. Diana's coffin was escorted to Westminster Abbey by civilian representatives of the charities with which she had been associated and the absolute minimum number of military pallbearers, for a funeral in which the trappings of formality had been reduced to the scantiest, amidst a congregation in which the focus of attention was on which film and pop stars were present. The difference between the two funerals shows how far imperial ideas of Englishness have ebbed away. What has come in their place is something altogether more personal. It is sometimes rather horrifying.

*

In the summer of 1998, soccer teams from around the world converged on France to compete for the Football World Cup. Despite some shambolic organization by the French authorities, the tournament was judged a great success, with untold millions sharing the excitement on live television. But there was, of course, 'the English problem'. the English problem is the hooligan problem. Its most tragic expression came at the Heysel stadium, in May 1985, when a major disturbance between Liverpool and Juventus fans left nearly forty Italians dead on the pitch. The challenge for the French and British police was, put crudely, to keep the hooligans from killing somebody else. That summer, they succeeded, although not before the world had been treated to scenes of drunken English youths throwing chairs, stones and anything else unlucky enough to incur their hostility. By contrast, Scottish fans were capable of drinking vast amounts and merely sleeping off the after-effects.

What is most shocking about the violence of English hooligans is its entirely casual nature. I recall one tiny incident after the opening game of the 1996 European football championship, between England and Switzerland. The English had put on a professionally indolent performance and the Swiss held them to a 1 – 1 draw, better than they had ever expected to do at Wembley in front of over 70,000 English fans. The Swiss, who included more women and children among their supporters than you would expect to find at an English ground, were jubilant. They were good-natured and, by the standards of loutishness common among English fans, quiet and totally unthreatening. Outside the stadium they sang and danced in the streets for hours afterwards. On one kerbside, about forty of them, men, women and children, had lined up to do a Mexican Wave. A young, shaven-headed Englishman on the other side of the street eyeballed them, ran across the road, shoved his face six inches from one of the young men in the crowd, and screamed 'Wanker!' at him. The Swiss looked baffled. The Englishman gesticulated, moving his hand up and down. 'You wanker!' he screamed again, drew back his fist, punched the man in the face and walked through the crowd. His walk was casual, cocky, slow enough to invite someone to try to retaliate for their friend's injury – he was now doubled up, with blood pouring from his nose. But none came, and the thug swaggered off down the pavement, doubtless eager to tell his friends that he'd 'done' one of the visiting fans.

This sort of viciousness may not be unique to the English, but no honest member of the English middle class would deny a fear of what the football mob may contain. In Turin in the late 1980s, the writer Bill Buford watched with horror as a group of bloated Manchester United football fans staggered off the aircraft that had brought them from England to watch their team play the Italian aces, Juventus. It was not even lunchtime, yet many were so drunk they could scarcely stand. The fans then colonized the town centre, sitting in their tattoos in sidewalk cafés singing 'Fuck the Pope' over and over again, occasionally getting up to piss in the street. And that was when they were being well behaved, and not attacking the 'fuckin' eyeties' with sticks, knives or bottles.

'Why do you English behave like this?' an Italian asked Buford. 'Is it because you are an island race? Is it because you don't feel European? Is it because you lost the Empire?'[10]

Buford was lost for an answer. The question arose from fear and genuine bafflement. Why *does* a minority of the English population think that the only way to have a good time is to get disgustingly drunk – and I mean *disgustingly* drunk, drunk to the point where the beer and the wine and the spirits have saturated their T-shirts and they are heaving their stomach up into the street – to shout obscenely and to pick a fight? Perhaps all the reasons suggested by the puzzled Italian played a part. Certainly, you don't expect to find plane-loads of Italians pouring into the centre of London and behaving in a similar fashion. The only honest answer that Buford could have given is that that is how part of the English population has always been. Far from being ashamed of their behaviour, they see fighting and drunkenness as part of their birthright. It is the way they proclaim their identity. A few years later, in Sardinia for the 1990 World Cup, Bill Buford watched as a mass of English football hooligans fought a pitched battle with the Italian police. Before he was clubbed senseless by furious policemen, he described a point at which the fans retreated in panic. But then

Someone shouted that we were all English. Why were we running? The English don't run ... And so it went on. Having fled in panic, some of the supporters would then remember that they were English and this was important, and they would remind the others that they too were English, and this was also important, and with renewed sense of national identity, they would come abruptly to a halt, turn around, and charge the Italian police.[11]

The problem is not exclusively English – Dutch and German fans have developed their own versions of the sickness in which puffy-faced young thugs proclaim their loyalty by kicking or stoning anyone who speaks a different language or wears different colours. But the truth is that the English gave the world soccer. They also gave it hooliganism.

There is nothing particularly new about the crudity and readiness to violence of English young people. In early Hanoverian times foreign visitors were as shocked by the behaviour of the mob as they were impressed by the civility of political culture. César de Saussure was so scandalized by the open drunkenness, the 'mighty swearing', the shirts-off wrestling (the sight of women taking part particularly shook him) and general licentiousness that he concluded that 'the lower populace is of brutal and insolent nature, and is very quarrelsome'.[12] To add a sense of superiority to this natural coarseness was very dangerous. By Victorian times the American writer Ralph Waldo Emerson had noted the way in which the general arrogance of the English towards foreigners expressed itself among many young people: 'There are multitudes of young rude English who have the self sufficiency and bluntness of their nation, and who, with their disdain for the rest of mankind, and with this indigestion and choler, have made the English traveller a proverb for uncomfortable and offensive manner.'[13]

Every time that English soccer fans rampage through a city centre, overturning the tables of sidewalk cafés, bloodying the noses of anyone unlucky enough to be in their way, the London press and politicians agonize about what it all means. They should save their breath. Thuggery is something the English do. 'The more blood they shed, the crueller and more ruthless they become ... They're fiery and furious, they quickly grow angry and take a long time to calm down', was Jean Froissart's (admittedly biased) thumbnail sketch of the character of the English troops which swept through fifteenth-century Normandy, burning and pillaging as they went. Four centuries later the Duke of Wellington remarked that his army was made up of 'the scum of the earth – the mere scum of the earth', and even though he did much to improve the rations and conditions, he could still lose control of it for days on end.

Football was a form of near-riot long before the rules were laid down, and if you were wise you kept well clear. The eighteenth-century French traveller who had been so uneasy about the crudity of the ordinary people of England made the mistake of walking into a game of football. 'They will break panes of glass and smash the windows of coaches', he wrote, 'and also knock you down without the slightest compunction; on the contrary, they will roar with laughter.'[14]

'Today's football violence would not have surprised those taking the waters in eighteenth-century Bath – a football match then was 'more like a battle than a game', is the way Ian Gilmour puts it in his history of street violence, *Riots, Risings and Revolution*.[15] The expression 'local derby' originated at this time, named after two parishes in the city where a game could last for days of free-for-all punch-ups. Once football became a spectator sport, violence took root in the crowd. Ever since the 1870s it has been played in England to an accompanying chorus of punches, kicks and obscenities: three authors who examined the records of the Football Association and back-issues of the *Leicestershire Daily Mercury* for the twenty years before the First World War discovered 254 cases of disorderliness among spectators. Even when the crowd merely threatened, it could be terrifying. An account in a gentleman's journal of 1903 shows how, even at the height of Edwardian England, the football crowd was already fearsome: 'Once at a famous North Country ground I saw and heard half of a crowd of 20,000 turn upon a poor referee who had done something distasteful ... The spiteful yells, the torrents of abuse, the fierce brandishing of sticks and fists ... made up a terrible picture of an English crowd.'[16]

The more you look back into English history, the more you are forced to the conclusion that alongside the civility and the deeply held convictions about individual rights, the English have a natural taste for disorder. Popular festivities could often – as on May Day 1517 in London – turn into physical attacks on supposed foreigners. A revel feast held at the village of Tockenham Wick, in September 1620, developed from the traditional cudgel-bashing in the street into a full-scale fight, when men from nearby Wootton Bassett arrived looking for trouble with the words 'Where are the middle sort of men in Tockenham?'. A historian who recently examined what happened there discovered numerous other punch-ups in the area, like the one in 1641 when villagers from Malmesbury, led by a man 'with a hobby-horse and bells on his legs' turned up at the Long Newnton revel looking for a fight, which ended with several local men seriously injured. ''Tis no revel unless there be some fightings' went the local saying.[17] But in the end, for all the apparent anarchy, certain rules applied: the violence seems to have a ritualistic element to it and the crowd understood and accepted the limits of what was permissible. As the century went on, some of the violence acquired a more political hue: rioting was the last recourse of poor people who discovered their rights being trampled upon by entrepreneurial aristocrats determined to appropriate common land that they had previously used for grazing their livestock.

And as people drifted towards the growing cities in search of work, they lost the old village constraints. The riots of June 1780 demonstrated to the ruling class how unstable things could become. The *casus belli* was a demand articulated by Lord George Gordon, as president of the Protestant Association, that Parliament reinstate the laws it had recently repealed, under which Roman Catholics were penalized for their religion, notably concerning the right to acquire or inherit property. Gordon was, to put it mildly, unpredictable. (He died while serving a five-year sentence for libel in Newgate gaol, by this time having become a Jew.) Faced with the howling mob he had taken to Westminster, Parliament prevaricated. The crowd then embarked on a spree of burning, rioting and looting that lasted for days. The homes of Catholics were destroyed, their churches were burned to the ground, Newgate prison emptied and a Catholic-owned distillery in Holborn sacked, with predictable consequences: they were said to be drinking gin from the gutter. Only on the third day was a strong force of militia deployed, by which time, some estimates claim that, in financial terms, more damage was done than Paris suffered during the French Revolution.

The Gordon Riots demonstrated how unstable big English cities could be. Crowds were prepared to become very violent in pursuit either of prejudice or, as Thomas Paine's *Rights of Man* and radical ideas from the French Revolution began to circulate, for the benefit of the disenfranchised. Once a riot had begun, it didn't much matter what had sparked it off; there was just a binge of destruction.

Here is Ian Gilmour's list of what happened in addition to the Gordon Riots:

In the eighteenth century, Englishmen (and Englishwomen) rioted against turnpikes, enclosures and high food prices, against Roman Catholics, the

Irish and the Dissenters, against the naturalisation of Jews, the impeachment of politicians, press gangs, 'crimp' houses [where men were seduced or entrapped into the navy or army] and the Militia Act, against theatre prices, foreign actors, pimps, bawdy houses, surgeons, French footmen and alehouse keepers, against the gibbets on the Edgware Road and public whippings, against the imprisonment of London's chief magistrates, against the Excise, against the Cider Tax and the Shops Tax, against workhouses and industrial employers, against the rumoured destruction of cathedral spires, even against a change in the calendar . . . There were riots at elections and after them, in prisons and outside them, in schools and colleges, at executions, at factories and workplaces, in the law courts at Westminster Hall, outside parliament and within the Palace of Westminster, at the office of the Bow Street magistrate, in theatres, in brothels, in a cathedral close, and in Pall Mall at the gates of St James's Palace.[18]

Although he goes on to argue that the violence was rarely mindless, and usually had a specific goal ('defensive aggression') it sounds an awesome list. Yet if we were to look back only at the last thirty years in England we could say that English mobs have rioted against the Poll Tax, against policing methods, inside and outside football grounds, on seaside promenades and in cinemas, against fascism and out of racial prejudice, against employment laws, against the Vietnam War, at collieries and in Whitehall, against long hair and against short hair, for the right to celebrate the summer solstice, against the exportation of live animals and the importation of new technology, for union recognition, for the right to drive stolen cars, because gangs enjoy fighting, because they ran up against another gang of football supporters, and so on. Food riots, commonplace in the eighteenth century, have disappeared, but a continuous thread links the eighteenth-century attacks on cotton mills, through the 'Captain Swing' resistance to machinery and cheap labour in the 1830s, to the protests against Rupert Murdoch's introduction of new printing methods at Wapping in the 1980s. The list puts into perspective the horror and disdain affected by the English when they look across the Channel and see the way in which mass disobedience, open flouting of the law and civil insurrection are condoned by feeble French governments unwilling to take on protesters. The difference between the two cultures is that while mass protests are an accepted, expected part of the political process in France, in England, street insurrection is less often to do with politics and more to do with an innate readiness to trade punches. An after-dark visit to half the market towns across the country will show how 'a bit of a punch-up' between drunken young men and women is as much part of a good Saturday as a kebab or a curry. ''Tis no revel unless there be some fightings.'

The English passion for alcohol has something to do with it, of course. In how many other major European cities does the traveller leave the rail station, as they do at Manchester or Liverpool, to take a taxi in which the driver is caged off from his passengers for his own safety and a notice warns that 'sickness due to alcohol will incur a £20 surcharge'?

It has been like this for centuries. The story goes that before the Battle of Hastings, while the Normans spent the night in prayer, King Harold's men sat up drinking. Medieval proverbs confirm the picture of a half-sozzled nation: 'The Auvergner sings, the Breton writes, the Englishman drinks', goes one. 'The Norman sings, the German guzzles, the Englishman boozes',[19] is another. William of Malmesbury (c.1095–1143), in his *Chronicle of the Kings of England*, observes that at the time of the Norman Conquest, 'drinking in particular was a universal practice, in which occupation they passed entire nights as well as days . . . They were accustomed to eat until they became surfeited and drink till they were sick'.[20] When King John went to visit the King of France at Fontainebleau, in July 1201, he was given the run of the palace. After he had gone, the anonymous historian who wrote the *Chronique Français des Rois de France* observed that 'The king of France and his people had a good laugh among themselves about the way the people of the English king had drunk all the bad wines, and left all the good ones'.[21] In 1362 the Archbishop of Canterbury was complaining that, given the slightest opportunity, the English would binge themselves stupid, because on holy days 'the tavern is rather worshipped than the church, gluttony and drunkness is more abundant than tears and prayers, men are busied rather with wantonness and contumely than with the leisure of contemplation'.[22]

Left to itself, you sometimes feel, the whole country would be permanently drunk every weekend. In the early eighteenth century there was such an abundance of cheap gin and other liquor available that it seemed society might implode: in 1742, a population one tenth the size of today's downed 19 million gallons of industrial-strength gin – ten times as much as is drunk today. G. K. Chesterton's affectionate, unthreatening creature, 'the rolling English drunkard [who] made the rolling English road',[23] is the congenial expression of the phenomenon. Other times, the English were gloomy, brutish drunks. Dostoevsky's depiction of a London pub is vivid: 'Everyone is drunk, but drunk joylessly, gloomily and heavily, and everyone is strangely silent. Only curses and bloody brawls occasionally break that suspicious and oppressively sad silence ... Everyone is in a hurry to drink himself into insensibility ... wives in no way lag behind their husbands and all get drunk together, while children crawl and run about among them.'[24]

In February 1915, Lloyd George, then Chancellor of the Exchequer, told the people of Bangor that 'Drink is doing us more damage in the war than all the German submarines put together.'[25] A deputation of shipbuilders who came to beg the government to introduce prohibition to improve production was told that 'We are fighting Germany, Austria and drink; and, as far as I can see, the greatest of these three deadly foes is drink.'[26]

The British government's attempts to tackle the problem, by severely limiting the opening hours of pubs and restricting the sale of alcohol for drinking at home, among other measures, had the result they wanted. Convictions for drunkenness fell, and the restraint seemed to last for two or three generations. In the 1930s, Mass Observation claimed that many men in Bolton pubs drank half-pints. The privations of the Second World War accustomed another tranche of young men and women to take their drink moderately, and it was not really until the 1970s that increased prosperity and the collapse of parental authority allowed many of the English to revert to their ancestral patterns of behaviour. By the 1990s, the next generation was combining hedonistic drinking with widespread drug use.

Because the English do not consume significantly more alcohol than other European peoples, this booziness must be something to do with the *way* in which they drink. George Steiner once told me, 'You'd never find Sartre in an English café for two reasons. A: No Sartre. B: No café.' He is right. The collapse of British imperial power produced no explosion of creative thought to match that of Vienna in the dying days of the Habsburg Empire – Freud, Brahms, Mahler and Klimt and the rest – and one of the reasons may perhaps be to do with the lack of a café society. Marxism was a café phenomenon until it gained power. From Lisbon to Leningrad you can go into a café, order a glass of wine or while away hours with a single coffee. In cafés, the generations and sexes mix, time matters less. Pubs, by contrast, are male, adult, alcoholic and somehow more urgent. You do not go to pubs to engage in solitary activities like reading the newspaper (common enough in European cafés), nor to stretch the mind in a quiet game of chess. The pub is for drinking.

At first sight, this readiness to booze and fight is hard to reconcile with the reputation of the English for restraint. What was D. H. Lawrence on about when he said that 'I don't like England very much, but the English *do* seem a rather lovable people. They have such a lot of gentleness'[27]? What could George Orwell have been thinking of when he wrote that 'The gentleness of the English civilization is perhaps its most marked characteristic. You notice it the moment you set foot on English soil. It is a land where bus conductors are good-tempered and policemen carry no revolvers. In no country inhabited by white men is it easier to shove people off the pavement'[28]?

The point, I think, is that all these things are relative. The vast majority of English people do *not* spend their time getting drunk, fighting and throwing up. Even that comparatively small number who do, tend to stick to Friday and Saturday nights. At a day-to-day level, English society retains a remarkable basic civility. Just try counting how many 'please' and 'thank yous' are involved in buying a newspaper, or register the number of occasions on which someone apologizes for bumping into you on the train. Unlike some other sophisticated societies, where police forces developed as a way of enforcing the will of the state, most of English society is not frightened by the police. The pattern of crime follows a general preference for non-violence, too: in England and Wales, robberies account for about 1 per cent of recorded crime, while burglaries run at 24 per cent.[29] In the United States, while burglaries still outnumber robberies, the proportion of robberies in the crime total is four times higher.[30] It is hard to resist the conclusion that the English prefer sneaky crimes to anything involving confrontation and violence. Most revealing of all are the figures for the most serious crime of all. While the number of murders has steadily increased since World War Two, England still has a quite astonishingly low rate of killings. For all the sensationalist newspaper headlines, you stand less chance of being murdered in England than in most other industrialized societies. The murder rate for England and Wales is below that for Japan, less than half the rate for France or Germany, one eighth of the rate for Scotland or Italy and twenty-six times lower than the rate for the United States.[31] It is hard to resist the conclusion that for all the readiness of some of the English to drink and fight, deep down most have quite a considerable respect for one another.

What has happened is that as Respectable Society has evaporated, a tolerance has developed for older, less gentrified ways. The strict codes of manners and dress and etiquette seem, from this perspective, to have been developed by the English to protect themselves from themselves. England enters the third millennium not in a dark suit but in an exuberant variety of guises, owing everything and nothing to the past.

Take the English obsession with betting. For over 250 years, between the late sixteenth and early nineteenth centuries, the government was happy to acquiesce in the taste for gambling by organizing state lotteries, the proceeds helping to fund, among other things, the wars against Napoleon and the building of the British Museum. But with national self-confidence came growing sensitivity: there was plenty of evidence that the lotteries had bad social effects,[32] and Lord Liverpool's government decreed that they must be abolished. It did not kill the taste for gambling, though, and other forms of betting rapidly took root: you could bet on the outcome of human contests like foot-racing, prize-fighting or wrestling, or on cock-fighting, bull-baiting, dog-fighting or horse-racing. Such was the appetite that there were even bets laid on races between men with wooden legs. Small wonder that in Lancashire gambling was known as the poor man's Stock Exchange.[33] By the 1890s coupon gambling on the results of football matches was a regular weekly activity in many homes. Within sixty years, the new football pools, which invited gamblers to predict the outcome of soccer matches, had become the biggest privately owned gambling operation in the world.

The attitude of authority towards this phenomenon was typically hypocritical: a state-sanctioned lottery would have involved the government in endorsing what some were now calling 'the vice of the twentieth century' – as alcohol had been the vice of previous eras. But it was quite happy to profit as much as it could, by levying taxes on the football-pools companies and the bookies. Finally, in 1994, a Conservative party government ('the party of the family' and of 'sound money') succumbed to the lure of easy income and established another state lottery. With twice-weekly draws televised by the BBC in a blitz of vulgarity and half-truths about the social good done by gambling, it rapidly became the biggest lottery in the world. Over two thirds of the adult population regularly bought tickets, and 95 per cent had done so at some time or other. There was ample anecdotal evidence that the ready availability of scratch-cards had contributed to gambling addiction, but everyone preferred to look the other way. It was a telling sign that the Respectable Society was dead and buried.

There are plenty of other examples we could examine, from changing sexual attitudes to the fact that in 1998 a serving Foreign Secretary, the country's supreme ambassador, could, with scarcely a murmur of disapproval, conduct an affair, divorce his wife and cohabit with his secretary in his official residence. But perhaps it is attitudes to food that show how far the country has travelled.

In 1949, Raymond Postgate, a radical journalist, classicist and social historian, grew so cross with English tolerance of bad eating that he proposed a Society for the Prevention of Cruelty to Food. He chose as his target the sauce bottles found on the tables of every restaurant:

They were provided on the assumption that you would want to hide completely the taste of what you would be offered. Sodden, sour, slimy, sloppy, stale or saccharined – one of these six things (or all) it certainly would be, whether it was fish, flesh, vegetable or sweet. It would also be overcooked; it might be reheated. If the place was English, it would be called a teashop or caffy; if foreign it would be called a restaurant or caffy. In the second case it would be dirtier, but the food *might* have some taste.[34]

There was a reason English food was so awful: the English were not bothered enough about how it tasted to demand it be any better. When John Cleese was taken out for a meal by his parents in the 1950s, the priorities were clear-cut. His father had worked in India, Hong Kong and Canton. Yet for all the breadth of vision that the

Empire gave that generation, they retained the very clearest sense of themselves. 'You'd think it might have opened their palates,' he told me. 'But they were completely uninterested in food. My parents used to choose a restaurant not because of the food on offer but because the plates were hot.'

The style of restaurants patronized by this middle class reflected their approach to life. They were dark, wood-beamed, furnished with a lot of leather. They were masculine places. There was a right piece of cutlery for each stage of the meal, and a right and wrong way to use it. You drank soup out of the side of the spoon by sitting with a straight back and tilting the spoon on to your lower lip; you did not insert the spoon into your mouth. And, although the language changed from one social class to another, you showed your satisfaction at the end of the meal by words to the effect of 'delightful meal. I'm quite full': satisfaction was a matter of quantity. If you were offered second helpings you accepted with an apology for enjoying the food: 'I really shouldn't, you know, but perhaps a little.'

And yet there was always plenty to celebrate about English food. Historically, English cooking, for the privileged few, at least, could have held its own with any in Europe. Richard II is said to have employed 2,000 cooks to manage his entertaining. Edward III's son, the Duke of Clarence, threw a banquet for 10,000 with thirty courses, while Henry V celebrated his coronation by having the conduit of Palace Yard run with claret. No creature was too great or small to escape the dinner plate. Cattle, pigs, sheep, goats, deer and boar are unremarkable enough (although not – as frequently happened at medieval banquets – in the same meal). But then there were the fowl: chickens, swans, peacocks – often served in their feathers – pheasants, partridges, pigeons, larks, mallard, geese, wood-cock, thrushes, curlews, snipe, quail, bitterns, to say nothing of cygnets, herons and finches. There were fish, from salmon and herring to tench and eels, shellfish from crabs to whelks, all finished off with custards and purées, curds, fritters, cakes and tarts.

Even in the midst of the food rationing which accompanied the Second World War, George Orwell was able to produce a list of delicacies that were nearly unobtainable abroad. He included kippers, Yorkshire pudding, Devonshire cream, muffins and crumpets, Christmas pudding, treacle tart and apple dumplings, potatoes roasted under the joint, minted new potatoes, bread, horseradish, mint and apple sauce, numerous pickles, Oxford marmalade, marrow jam and bramble jelly, Stilton and Wensleydale cheeses and Cox's orange pippins.[35] We could all add to it. But the English failed to see food as an art form. The word 'restaurant' is French and the reason menus appear in French is that the English language never developed the vocabulary to describe cooking properly. The commanding heights of English *cuisine* have been occupied by French *chefs*.

The ideal Englishman and -woman had not, in the immortal words, been put on earth to enjoy themselves. Throughout English history the élite has told the rest of the country that too much interest in food is somehow immoral. The seventeenth-century Puritans, with their firm belief that plain food was God's food, cast a long shadow. Once the Industrial Revolution had drawn workers into the towns, knowledge of country cooking died. Certainly it ranked very low in the priorities of empire-builders. 'Roast beef and mutton are all they have which is good', said the German poet Heinrich Heine after a visit early in the nineteenth century. 'Heaven keep every Christian from their gravies ... And heaven guard everyone from their naïve vegetables, which, boiled away in water, are brought to the table just as God made them.'[36]

Among the metropolitan élite it has become fashionable to claim that everything has changed since then and that the English have lost their indifference to food. London, it was being confidently asserted, is the gastronomic capital of the world, food the new rock-'n'-roll. We shall see. While it is true that the country now has an abundance of first-class restaurants, they tend to be concentrated in London and a handful of cities outside, and to be high-price. If you want to eat well in Birmingham or Manchester, you are best advised to head for Chinatown or the Bangladeshi district.

It would be hard to exaggerate the benefit for English cooking of the arrival of a sizeable immigrant community. Although most English people still seem to cite fish and chips as the quintessential English food, the number of fish-and-chip shops in Britain has almost halved: at one time there were 15,000 of them, a figure which has now fallen to 8,500. Testament to the astonishing rise in popularity of food from other cultures is that there are as many Chinese and other oriental restaurants in Britain, and a further 7,300 Indian food outlets. John Koon, the man who invented the Chinese takeaway, built his fortune and career on the discovery that while the English might not know what beansprouts were, they could tell the difference between the letters A and B. His Cathay Restaurant, near Piccadilly Circus, would never have taken off had he not found a way of making the exotic mundane through Set Menus. As Chinese food gained in popularity after World War Two, he was invited to open a kitchen in Billy Butlin's holiday camps, then catering to the British taste for holidays *en masse*. Here, he solved the problem of resistance to funny foreign food by inventing the revolting combination of chicken chop suey and chips. Customers loved it.

The point is not that the general standard of food in England is now superb; it is not. For the majority of people, eating out is to consume fat-filled fast food, and to eat in, to be a victim of something prepackaged in industrial quantities in a factory somewhere. But *attitudes* to food have changed. Every decade serves up a new confection of television chefs who can expect to get very rich from their cookery courses. The kitchen, rather than the drawing room, sitting room or parlour, has become the centre of the house and you are no longer thought degenerate if you confess a liking for good food. It is part of a wholesale broader change.

The patterns from which the model Englishman and Englishwoman were to be cut have been torn up. In their place is something else, as yet not fully formed. The old hierarchies are finished, and as they crumbled, we have seen energy unleashed in fashion and music. Who can explain why England produced many of the world's greatest bands, while France thought Johnny Halliday was cool? Perhaps it was something to do with the unendurable tedium of the English suburbs or the miserably changeable weather. But the super-abundance of street tribes, mods and rockers, punks, technos and travellers, indie-kids and raggamuffins, and further tribes within tribes, based on different tastes and looks and views, all express a basic belief in the liberty of the individual. Style is no longer homogeneous and it no longer takes its tone from the top: the reason British designers are so sought-after by the fashion industry is that they belong to the same creative culture as those who drive the thriving music scene.

It used to be said of the great Sussex and England batsman Ranjitsinghji (the first man to make 3,000 runs in a season), that he was the person who 'put India on the map for the ordinary Englishman'. But he belonged to a small and very privileged class who, in their speech and manners *were* Englishmen. The arrival of substantial numbers of immigrants from other cultures has forced the English to break out of their complacency, to re-examine themselves, and to recognize and exult in diversity. They may not yet have entirely shaken off a sense that their country lost its way. They have not entirely lost their suspicion of 'abroad', either. How could they, for it is the fruit of millennia of island life? Every schoolchild on an exchange visit to France, Germany or Holland has grandparents, great-grandparents, great-great-grandparents whose only experience of the Continent was as a place their country sent them to fight. Over 1 million of them never returned.

But they live in a country that, for all its Lilliputian political spats, is firmly based in a tradition of personal liberty, that still believes in fair play, that is tolerant, easy-going and slow to anger. They live in a culture where the supposition is that the individual may do as he or she likes, providing it is not banned by law, instead of the reverse, which is true of much of the rest of the world: in Germany there are even laws about when you may beat your carpets or wash your car. They live in a civilization where words matter, that gives them some of the most vigorous theatre in the world, more newspapers and a higher overall standard of television than anywhere else in the world. They have a capital city with a greater variety of entertainment on offer than any other city in the world. They have some of the finest domestic and church architecture on earth. They remain a highly inventive, entrepreneurial people. They have the finest choral music and the greatest diversity of musical performance in Europe. They have some of the loveliest countryside in the world, not an acre of it untouched by the care of previous generations. They have, in Oxford, Cambridge and many other institutions in London, Manchester and elsewhere, some of the finest minds and intellectual traditions of the world.

And yet they remain convinced they're finished. That is their charm.

William and Valerie Plowden are moving out of the house their family has occupied for the last 800 years. It is a squat, half-timbered manor house squirrelled away in the blue remembered hills of A. E. Housman's *A Shropshire Lad*. There is no sign to Plowden Hall, there are no open days, no pots of National Trust jam on sale, no teas served by sturdy ladies in tweed skirts. On the drive, immature, tailless pheasants scuttle out of the way as you pass. In the drowsy fields, sheep and cattle wander aimlessly. A gardener is clipping the edges of the lawn outside the big house. Hidden away from the rest of the world, the loudest sound is the slicing of his shears. No cars, no trains, no aircraft.

The Plowden family have been 'seated' here at least since the twelfth century, when one of their ancestors fought at the Crusader siege of Acre. It is only twenty miles or so to Ironbridge and the valley where, 200 years ago, industrial iron-smelting was discovered and the world's first cast-iron bridge built, held together by the dovetail and mortise-and-tenon joints of earlier technology. The carnival has moved on from there, too, and the Severn valley, once black with the smoke of foundries, has fallen back to turbid sleepiness. The Plowden family have seen it all, over the years. And still they are here, the Plowden family, living at Plowden Hall, in the village of Plowden, in a land of quiet contentment.

Theirs is not a particularly heroic story. There was a Plowden who became a prominent lawyer under Elizabeth I, another who commanded the Second Foot Guards at the battle of the Boyne, one who made a small fortune with the East India Company, another who died at school from 'eating a surfeit of cherries', an admiral lost in action on the North Atlantic convoys, but no Prime Ministers or philosophers. Their life revolves around farming, half-a-dozen black labradors, hunting, shooting and fishing. It is not the sort of life that brings your name to the attention of editors of *Who's Who*: public service is restricted to sitting on the bench of magistrates and occasionally turning out as High Sheriff when the Queen visits the county. For the rest, it is *Farmers Weekly*, *Horse and Hound* and the *Shooting Times*.

The received wisdom about this type of English family is that they have been consigned to history, destroyed by the First World War, death duties, taxation, Lloyd's and congenital incompetence at handling their affairs. The image is of Evelyn Waugh's Brideshead, ancestral piles abandoned by families unable to meet the demands of modern life. Like all images, it is partly true. But among those who have survived, it is utterly wrong. William Plowden was twenty, on army service, when his father died, leaving him Plowden Hall. There seemed little chance of hanging on to the family home and he began trying to find a tenant who would rent the Hall. But no one was prepared to take it on. So he resigned his commission, went to Oxford, 'discovered my brain wouldn't function', and took himself off to the Royal Agricultural College at Cirencester. When he took on the estate, he had 450 acres 'in hand'. Within a few years, he was running 2,000 acres. Now, the estate employs a manager, twelve people on the farm, another five in the woods, a full-time mason, a carpenter, gamekeeper, odd-job man and gardener.

Plowden and his wife are moving out of the ancestral home for a farm on the estate, so that their son can move in. Assuming William Plowden lives another seven years, Plowden Hall will pass to another generation of Plowdens, free of tax. He hands on a thriving business that gives the lie to the claim that time is up for all these old families who embody a traditional idea of Englishness.

These families were the core of rural English society, unemotional, practical, professedly 'non-political' but deeply conservative, quiet, kindly, unintellectual. Ask him what he thinks of the state of England now and you get terse answers about standards slipping: 'We built six affordable houses in the village for people on low incomes. Five out of the six are occupied by couples who aren't married.' But it is when you see his car that you realize what really bothers him. He has been down to the local printers and had his own stickers printed in Day-Glo orange. They read

SOD THE EU

HOME RULE FOR BRITAIN

'Sooner or later,' he says, 'the Common Market is going to collapse. I don't see how you can run a country with two systems of law – our own national law and then all these laws from people in Brussels which override our laws. The sooner it ends, the better.' In the rolling hills of Shropshire, the heart of England still beats. It is driving around with a sticker in the back window telling the rest of Europe to sod off.

You can see his point. What are the badges of nationality? The English lost control of their language long ago. And if the European single currency, the Euro, is a success, the British pound, symbol of nation and empire, will be consigned to history. The question that then arises is what the English would have that they could feel was uniquely their own. In their everyday lives, the English metropolitan élite now has more in common with Parisians or New Yorkers than it does with rural or suburban England. And so many of the other outward signals of Englishness, from clothing to language, are now universal property.

Dr David Starkey once ended a lamentation bemoaning the lack of celebrations for St George's Day saying that 'England itself has ceased to be a mere country and become a place of the mind . . . England, indeed, has become a sort of vile antithesis of a nation; we are similar to our neighbours and differ from each other.'[37] There will doubtless be more jeremiads in similar vein. They are of a piece with the obsession with decline that has poisoned the country's idea of itself since the war. But all nations are places of the mind: the idea of a country is what informs its laws, its politics and its art. When French politicians talk about 'La France' they do not mean what they see around them but an idea of the national destiny. What is America without the American Dream? It is true that you cannot spend fifty years listening to people anatomize your decline and not be affected by it. Yet, for all claims that the country is 'finished', the attitudes of mind that made the English culture what it is – individualism, pragmatism, love of words and, above all, that glorious, fundamental cussedness – are unchanged.

The England that the rest of the world knows is the England of the British Empire. Like a pair of newly-weds in a sabotaged car, every people sets off into the future clattering behind it the tin-cans of its history. But to most of the English, their history is just that, history. The contrast is with Scotland or Ireland, where every self-respecting adult considers themselves to belong to an unbroken tradition stretching back to the wearing of woad: oppressed peoples remember their history. One-time oppressors forget it. The English now have nothing in common with the tradition they see celebrated in the red-white-and-blue. Look at the Last Night of the Proms. How many of those joyous, nerdish faces belting out 'Land of Hope and Glory' believe a word of it? 'Wider still and wider shall thy bounds be set'? Come on.

The rebels of the 1960s will soon be grandparents, their gestures of protest quietly accommodated, their places taken by wave after wave of other anarchistic inventors. The norms of the 1940s are dead and buried and they have not been replaced by new norms. No one has seen a stiff upper lip for years. Shorn of any sense of clear national purpose, each post-war generation has turned out more self-obsessed and selfish than the last. There is no longer even any consensus on questions like dress, let alone any prescriptive rules.

Yet Starkey's complaint may actually point to a strength in the English. Might it not be that individuality, firmly rooted in a sense of individual rights, is preferable to the conformity that occurred when the great boys' schools were turning out thousands of as-near-as-possible-identical young men to run an empire that no longer exists? Once such a master-class existed, everyone else knew their place in the pecking order. The stage Englishman had his elements of nobility, but to an extent, it was built on hypocrisy. The new generation are refining their own identity, an identity based not on the past but on their own needs. In a world of accelerating communications, shrinking distances, global products and ever-larger trading blocks, the most vital sense of national identity is the individual awareness of the country of the mind.

The English are simultaneously rediscovering the past that was buried when 'Britain' was created, and inventing a new future. The red-white-and-blue is no longer relevant and they are returning to the green of England. The new nationalism is less likely to be based on flags and anthems. It is modest, individualistic, ironic, solipsistic, concerned as much with cities and regions as with counties and countries. It is based on values that are so deeply embedded in the culture as to be almost unconscious. In an age of decaying nation states it might be the nationalism of the future.

ACKNOWLEDGEMENTS

This book began life in conversations some time before the Boer War with Susan Watt. Susan was then my editor at Michael Joseph, and it is to her that I owe my biggest editorial debt. After she moved on, Tom Weldon had loads of helpful suggestions and saw the book through production. My other big debt is to my family, who have had to put up with this cuckoo for the last few years, with scarcely a murmur of complaint.

In the course of research I interviewed over 200 people, and where I have quoted from interviews in the text, it is, I think, obvious. Most conversations were valuable more for the ideas they provoked than anything else. It seems unfair to single out individuals from among the large number who helped, but I should like to thank in particular Raymond Blanc, James Landale, John Cleese, Ian Jack, John and Penny Mortimer, Sir Roy Strong, Dr Nick Tate, Ian Smith, Helen McManners, John Simpson and Patrick Hanks at the Oxford University Press, Hugh Massingberd for the generous use of his contacts book, Dr George Steiner, George Walden, Lord Dahrendorf, Prof. Michael Dummett, David Willetts MP, Jim Gray, Mary-Anne Sieghart, Canon Donald Gray, the Rt Revd Richard Harries, Patrick Wright, the Revd Donald Gray, Melvyn Bragg, the Revd David Edwards, Prof. David Starkey, John Gillingham, West de Wend Fenton, William Plowden, Roderick Gradidge, Christopher Driver, Simon Raven, Dr Keith Thompson, Sir John Smith, Edmund Staunton, Margot Lawrence, Shani d'Cruze, Roger Bolton, Ivo Dawnay, Henry Porter, David Twistan-

Davies, Paul Boateng MP, Paul Hardacre and Ewan McCallum at the Met Office, Elsie Owusu, James Blitz, Prof. John Burrow, Stephen Haseler, Bernie Grant MP, Mark Fisher MP, Michael Wharton, Sebastian Faulks, C. H. Sisson, Jessica Rees, Edward Faulks, Julian Turton, Andrew Roberts, Dr Trevor Bennett, Prof. Anthony King, Sir Denys Lasdun, Gavin Stamp, Richard North, John Armit, Andrew Mitchell, Ned Dawney, Robert Hewison, Lord Runcie, John Fowles, Georgia Langton, Richard Curtis, Peter Collison, the Revd Donald Reeves, Timothy Garton Ash, Prof. Richard Hoggart, Prof. Bernard Crick, Ruthie and Richard Rogers, Blanche Blackwell, the Duke and Duchess of Devonshire, Roy Faiers, Sir Bob Horton, Tony Knox, John Eliot Gardiner, Jacqueline Gough (Hartlepool Borough Council), the Commonwealth War Graves Commission, the Charities Aid Foundation, the Royal Horticultural Society, Blenheim Palace, and Suffolk Record Office.

I could not have managed the book without the enthusiastic research help at one time or another of Ade Thomas and Hettie Judah. I am grateful, too, to Julian Holloway and Dr Jon Lawrence of Liverpool University, who read the finished manuscript and spotted at least some of the blemishes. Those which remain are all my own work.

NOTES

CHAPTER ONE *The Land of Lost Content*

1. Geoffrey Gorer: *Exploring English Character*, p. 303.
2. In 1995, the most recent figures available, 174,000 marriages in England and Wales ended in divorce (source: Office of National Statistics). In September 1997, women made up 46.3% of the workforce: the comparable figure in 1947 was 30%.
3. London Research Centre: *Education in London: Key Facts, 1997*, p. 18.
4. George Orwell: 'The Moon under Water', in the *Evening Standard*, 9 February 1946.
5. George Orwell: *The Lion and the Unicorn*, p. 48.
6. W. C. Sellar and R. J. Yeatman: *1066, And All That*, p. 25.
7. Ibid., p. 123.
8. A. S. Byatt: 'What It Means to Be English', in *The Times*, 6 April 1998.
9. Stephen Haseler: *The English Tribe*, pp. 3–4.
10. Clive Aslet: *Anyone For England?*.
11. Ibid., p. 22.
12. 'English – and not very proud of it', *Times Educational Supplement*, 23 May 1997.
13. Alan Bennett: *The Old Country*, p. 58.
14. John Fowles: *On Being English But Not British*, p. 71.

CHAPTER TWO *Funny Foreigners*

1. Quoted in Peter Collett: *Foreign Bodies*, p. 119.
2. Quoted in Christopher Hibbert: *The Grand Tour*, p. 47.
3. Quoted ibid., p. 10.
4. Robert Graves: *Goodbye to All That*, p. 240.
5. George Orwell: *The Lion and the Unicorn*, p. 28.
6. *Présentation du Marché Britannique*, Maison de France, London, p. 12.
7. William Shakespeare: *Richard II*, II. i.
8. Elias Canetti: *Crowds and Power*, p. 171.
9. *Hansard*, vol. xciii, cols 1574–5 (13 May 1901).
10. *The Cambridge History of British Foreign Policy*, Vol. III, pp. 9–10.
11. Quoted in Nicholas Harman: *Dunkirk, the Necessary Myth*, p. 1.
12. See Robert Gibson: *Best of Enemies*, p. 231.
13. Andrea Trevisano: *A Relation, or rather a true account of the Islands of England*, pp. 20–1.
14. Reprinted in William Benchley Rye: *England as seen by foreigners in the reign of Elizabeth and James the First*, p. 7.
15. Quoted ibid., p. 70.
16. Ibid., p. 186.
17. John Milton: *The Doctrine and Discipline of Divorce*.
18. George Orwell: 'Boys' Weeklies', in *Horizon*, March 1940.
19. Gerald Newman: *The Rise of English Nationalism*, p. 63.
20. Quoted in Christopher Hibbert: *Nelson*, p. 43.
21. Byam Martin: *Polynesian Journal*, p. 53.
22. Quoted in Alistair Horne: *Macmillan*, Vol. I, p. 160.
23. Winston S. Churchill: *The Second World War*, Vol. III, p. 384.
24. In 1994, Britain recorded 14,269,128 transatlantic arrivals and departures, Germany 6,566,159, France 4,980,929 and the Netherlands 3,307,112 (*Eurostat*).

CHAPTER THREE *The English Empire*

1. Letter from R. Brown, April 1998.
2. Charles Dilke: *Greater Britain*, quoted in Richard Faber: *High Road to England*, p. 86.

3. Quoted in John Gillingham: 'The Beginnings of English Imperialism', in *Journal of Historical Sociology*, Vol. 5, No. 4, December 1992, p. 394.

4. *Gesta Stephani*, quoted ibid., p. 396.

5. Ibid., p. 397.

6. Ibid., p. 397.

7. Richard of Hexham: *De Gestis Regis Stephani*, p. 152, quoted in John Gillingham: 'Foundations of a Disunited Kingdom', in *Uniting the Kingdom* (ed. Alexander Grant and Keith Stringer).

8. Quoted in Gillingham, op. cit. (1), p. 399.

9. A. A. Gill: 'Smile – You're on Cameo Camera', in the *Sunday Times*, 28 September 1997.

10. The complaint was unsuccessful, because comments in the press were outside the remit of the Commission for Racial Equality.

11. See Kenneth O. Morgan: *Rebirth of a Nation: Wales 1880–1980*, p. 20.

12. Quoted in Linda Colley: *Britons*, p. 13.

13. James Boswell: *Life of Johnson*, Vol. I, p. 425, 6 July 1763.

14. Richard Faber: *High Road to England*, p. 132.

15. Presidential address to the National Literary Society, 25 November 1892, quoted in R. F. Foster: *Paddy and Mr Punch*, p. 270.

16. Alan Cochrane: 'Flower of Thatcherism', in the *Spectator*, 2 March 1996.

17. Quoted in Foster, op. cit., p. 184.

18. Irving Welsh: *Trainspotting*, p. 78.

19. W. B. Yeats: *The Celtic Twilight*, p. 22.

20. Prof. C. S. Coon: *The Races of Europe*, p. 395.

21. Nikolaus Pevsner: *The Englishness of English Art*, p. 197.

22. George Orwell: *The English*, p. 8.

23. Daniel Defoe: *The True-Born Englishman*, 1701.

CHAPTER FOUR *'True Born Englishmen' and Other Lies*

1. Claudio Veliz: 'A World Made in England', in *Quadrant*, March 1983, p. 8.

2. Luigi Barzini: *The Impossible Europeans*, p. 35.

3. G. W. Steevens: *With Kitchener to Khartoum*, p. 300, quoted in John Ellis: *The Social History of the Machine Gun*, p. 86.

4. Henry Labouchere, the splendid radical MP, former Mexican circus artist and journalist, replied to Kipling's exhortation with

> Pile on the Brown man's burden!
> And, if ye rouse his hate,
> Meet his old-fashioned reasons
> With Maxims – up to date,
> With shells and Dum-Dum bullets
> A hundred times make plain
> The Brown man's loss must never
> Imply the White man's gain.

5. D. O. Sypniewski: *Impressions of England*, pp. 33, 38.
6. Quoted in Richard Faber: *The Vision and the Need*. p. 64.
7. Ibid.
8. See Ronald Hyam: *Empire and Sexuality*, p. 95.
9. Quoted ibid., p. 172.
10. Quoted ibid., p. 89.
11. Lord Crewe's Circular on Concubinage, Enclosure 'A'. See Ronald Hyam: 'Concubinage and Colonial Service', in *Journal of Imperial and Commonwealth History*, XIV, 1986, pp. 170–86.
12. Dr Barot: *Guide Practique de l'Européen dans l'Afrique Occidentale*, quoted in John Hargreaves: *France and West Africa, An Anthology of Historical Documents*, pp. 206–9.
13. Quoted in Ian Gilmour: *Inside Right*, p. 87.
14. James McAuley: 'My New Guinea', *Selected Prose 1959–74*, p. 172.
15. 'Peter Simple', *Daily Telegraph*, Friday 18 July 1997, p. 26.
16. Sir Arthur Bryant, *Illustrated London News*, 27 March 1963.
17. Enoch Powell, speech, 20 April 1968.
18. Ceri Peach: *Ethnicity in the 1991 Census, Vol. 2, the Ethnic Minority Populations of Great Britain*, p. 14.
19. The biggest obstacle you might expect would be an elementary test based on something like how you celebrate Christmas: a tree on 24 and 25 December is good enough to show that you don't belong to the eastern Orthodox church.

20. 'You've Made Us Feel So Welcome', in the *Daily Telegraph*, 17 January 1998.

CHAPTER FIVE *We Happy Few*

1. Editorial, *This England*, Vol. 1, no. 1.
2. Ibid., Vol. 1, no. 3.
3. Ibid., Summer 1997.
4. Stephen Garnett: 'The Battle for the Real Counties of Britain', ibid.
5. Angus Calder: *The Myth of the Blitz*, p. 196.
6. Lord Ismay: *Memoirs*, pp. 179–80.
7. John Keegan: *The Second World War*, pp. 93–4.
8. Peter Haining: *Spitfire Summer*, p. 82.
9. Ibid.
10. *Daily Express*, 14 August 1940.
11. Linda Colley: *Britons*, p. 29.
12. John Foxe: *The Book of Martyrs, containing an account of the sufferings and death of the Protestants in the reign of Queen Mary the first*, pp. 723–4.
13. Owen Chadwick: *The Reformation*, p. 128.

CHAPTER SIX *The Parish of the Senses*

1. 'So tender a care hath He alwaies had of that England, as of a new Israel', John Lyly: *Euphues*, an astonishingly tedious book quoted in Hans Kohn: *The Genesis and Character of English Nationalism*, p. 73.
2. Henry Fielding: *Tom Jones*, Book III, Chap. 3.
3. Quoted in Paul Fussell: *The Great War and Modern Memory*, p. 118.
4. T. S. Eliot, 'Lancelot Andrewes', in *Essays on Style and Content*, p. 14.
5. Robert Runcie, 'Lecture on the 1400th Anniversary of the Mission of St Augustine to Canterbury', 27 February 1997.
6. Like many of Melbourne's *bons mots* (e.g. 'While I cannot be a pillar of the church, I must be regarded as a buttress, because I support it from the outside' or his question after cabinet discussions on Corn Law reform 'Now, is it to lower the price of corn, or isn't it? It is not much matter which we say, but mind, we must all say *the same*') the remark is attributed. G. W. E. Russell, *Collections and Recollections*, Chap. 6.

7. The talk is reprinted in *The Spirit of England*, Allen & Unwin, 1942, pp. 74–9.

8. See Margot Lawrence, 'Tudor English Today', in *English Today*, October 1986.

9. A survey of 360 priests ordained in 1990 revealed that one quarter considered themselves 'not well informed' about the Book of Common Prayer, while only 16 said that their worship at theological college had been mainly taken from the BCP. *Daily Telegraph*, 21 February 1996.

10. D. W. Brogan: *The English People*, p. 39.

11. Fyodor Dostoevsky: *Summer Impressions*, p. 68.

12. David Hare: *Racing Demon*, p. 3.

13. Ibid., p. 51.

14. Andrew Graham-Dixon: *A History of British Art*, pp. 22–3.

15. Quoted in *The Identity of English Music: The Reception of Elgar 1898–1935*, Jeremy Crump, in *Englishness: Politics and Culture*, eds. Robert Colls and Philip Dodd.

16. Raymond Seitz: *Over Here*, p. 15.

17. *Johnsonian Miscellanies*, Vol. ii, p. 15.

18. Nikolaus Pevsner: *The Englishness of English Art*, p. 39.

19. Tyndale was executed before he could finish the job, but by then had rendered into English the whole of the New Testament, all of the Old Testament as far as the second book of Chronicles, the Book of Jonah and various other passages. Ninety per cent of Tyndale's work in the New Testament and about 80 per cent of his Old Testament translation survived into the twentieth century. On 6 October 1536 he was strangled to death for heresy, his body burned at the stake.

20. J. Foxe: *Actes and Monuments*, ed. J. Pratt (1877), V, p. 527.

21. An abundance of other English versions of the Bible had followed Tyndale's original, many affectionately identified by their misprints – the Place-maker's Bible ('Blessed are the place-makers'), the Wicked Bible, in which the seventh commandment lost its 'not' and became 'Thou shalt commit adultery', the Murderers' Bible (a misprint for 'murmurers'), the Breeches Bible (Adam and Eve made themselves trousers), the Bug Bible ('thou shalt not nede to be afrayed for eny bugges by night'), the Standing Fishes Bible (instead of 'fishers' standing

on the river bank), the Vinegar Bible (instead of the 'Parable of the Vineyard').

22. Thomas Wilcox: 'An Admonition to Parliament', from *Puritan Manifestos*, ed. Frere and Douglas, p. 15.

23. W. H. G. Armytage: *Heavens Below*, p. 260.

24. John Milton: *Defence of the people of England, Concerning their right to call to account kings and magistrates and after due consideration to depose and put them to death*.

25. 4 September 1654, in *The Speeches of Oliver Cromwell*, Everyman Library, p. 28.

CHAPTER SEVEN *Home Alone*

1. Elias Canetti: *Crowds and Power*, p. 172.

2. Alexander Kinglake: *Eothen*, pp. 200–202.

3. Max O'Rell: *John Bull and his Island*, p. 18.

4. Michael Lewis: 'Oh, not to be in England', in the *Spectator*, 23 May 1992.

5. Hermann Muthesius: *The English House*, p. xv.

6. Ibid.

7. Ibid., p. 8.

8. Ibid., p. 9.

9. Ralph Waldo Emerson: 'English Traits', in *Collected Works*, Vol. V, pp. 59–60.

10. George Santayana: *Soliloquies in England*, p. 14.

11. Samuel Johnson: *The Idler*, No. 11.

12. Bill Bryson: *Notes from a Small Island*, p. 278.

13. Johnson, op. cit.

14. Prof. C. G. Collier, letter, 29 October 1996.

15. André Maurois: *Three Letters on the English*, pp. 261–2.

16. Odette Keun: *I Discover the English*, p. 151.

17. Quoted in Vincent Cronin: *Napoleon*, p. 48.

18. Jean Duhamel: *The Fifty Days: Napoleon in England*, p. 61.

19. Ibid., p. 69.

20. Quoted in Beram Saklatvala: *The Origins of the English People*, p. 99.

21. Alan Macfarlane: *The Origins of English Individualism*.

22. Quoted in Jonathan Sumption: *The Hundred Years War*, pp. 67–8.

23. Carl Philip Moritz: *Journeys of a German in England in 1782*, p. 56.

24. Alexis de Tocqueville: *Journeys to England and Ireland*, p. 88.

25. Ibid., p. 81.

26. *The Times*, 14 September 1883.

CHAPTER EIGHT *There Always Was an England*

1. Dave Hill: *Out for the Count*, p. 37.

2. John Major, speech to the Conservative Group for Europe, 22 April 1993.

3. Stanley Baldwin, speech to the Annual Dinner of the Royal Society of St George, 6 May 1924. It all sounded so mellifluously plausible when Baldwin spoke like this that *Punch* once ran a cartoon suggesting that the only surviving genuine Englishman was alive and well and living at Bewdley, Worcestershire, Baldwin's birthplace.

4. Raymond Williams: *The Country and the City*, pp. 281–2.

5. According to Paul Fussell in *The Great War and Modern Memory*, the anthology 'presides over the Great War ... there were few of any rank who had not been assured that the greatest of modern literatures was English and who did not feel an appropriate pleasure in that assurance'.

6. Arthur Quiller-Couch: *Studies in Literature*, pp. 300–301.

7. H. J. Massingham: *Chiltern Country*, p. 27.

8. Philip Gibbs: *England Speaks*, pp. 3–4.

9. C. Henry Warren: *England is a Village*, p. ix.

10. Virginia Woolf: *Between the Acts*, p. 42. It was Steve Ellis's *The English Eliot* that put me on to this idea of what he calls the 'metonymic strategy', in which the village becomes a model for all English life.

11. Colin Watson: *Snobbery With Violence*, pp. 169–70.

12. Quoted in Patrick Wright: *On Living in an Old Country*, pp. 83–4.

13. John Betjeman: *Coming Home*, BBC Home Service, 25 February 1943, reprinted in the *Listener*, 11 March 1943, 'Oh to be in England ...'

14. Vicomte de Chateaubriand: *Mémoires d'Outre-tombe*, 1848–50, quoted in Robert Gibson, *Best of Enemies*, p. 179.

15. Émile Cammaerts: *Discoveries in England*, p. 92.

16. Evelyn Waugh: *Brideshead Revisited* (1959 edn), preface, p. 8.

17. Asa Briggs: *Victorian Cities*, p. 57.

18. H. G. Wells: *Experiment in Autobiography*, Vol. 1, p. 277.

19. Charles Dickens: *Hard Times*, Chap 5.

20. Richard Jefferies: *The Gamekeeper at Home*, p. 1.

21. Edward Thomas: *The South Country*, p. 1.

22. Fyodor Dostoevsky: *Summer Impressions*, p. 61.

23. Quoted in H. Rider Haggard: *A Farmer's Year*, p. 466. The lessons of Gibbon's *Decline and Fall of the Roman Empire* hung over the century. In 'The Discovery of Rural England' (in *Englishness, Politics and Culture, 1880–1920*), Alun Howkins claims that this remark together with similar comments from Lord Milner in 1911 were symptomatic of a conscious attempt to invent an idea of England based on Good Queen Bess, maypoles and Merrie England.

24. Thomas de Quincey: *The English Mail Coach*, p. 74 (1913 edn).

25. H. V. Morton: *What I Saw in the Slums*, pp. 37–9.

26. D. H. Lawrence: *Nottingham and the Mining Country*.

27. Quoted in Patrick Wright: *The Village That Died for England*, p. 150.

28. Arthur Bryant: *Protestant Island*, p. 39. For the full hatchet-job on Bryant, see Andrew Roberts's *Eminent Churchillians*, Chap. 6.

29. Countryside Survey, 1990, Dept of Environment.

30. William Morris: *The Lesser Arts, Collected Works*, Vol. XXII, p. 17.

31. Interview, 'Waterland', in the *Guardian*, 15 April 1997.

32. Emanuel Swedenborg, *A Treatise Concerning Heaven and Hell*, p. 81.

CHAPTER NINE *The Ideal Englishman*

1. Quoted in Richard Usborne: *Clubland Heroes*, p. 155.

2. Quoted in Nicolas Soames and Duncan Steen: *The Essential Englishman*, p. 23.

3. Quoted in Steven Marcus: *The Other Victorians*, p. 19.

4. Quoted in Alex Comfort: *The Anxiety Makers*, p. 47.

5. Quoted in Ronald Hyam: *Empire and Sexuality*, p. 13.

6. Ford Madox Ford (Ford Hermann Hueffer): *The Spirit of the People*, pp. 147–8.

7. Quoted in Christopher Hitchens: 'Young Men and War', in *Vanity Fair*, February 1997, p. 21.

8. Roger Wilmut (ed.): *The Complete Beyond the Fringe*, p. 74.
9. John Arbuthnot: *The History of John Bull*, p. 50.
10. Ibid., p. 9.
11. Quoted in Roger Longrigg: *The English Squire and His Sport*, p. 46.
12. Quoted ibid., p. 111.
13. Hippolyte Taine: *Notes on England*, p. 105.
14. Quoted in Hans Kohn: 'The Genesis and Character of English Nationalism', *Journal of the History of Ideas*, p. 78.
15. Victor Hugo: *William Shakespeare*, quoted in Robert Gibson: *Best of Enemies*, p. 215.
16. Ralph Waldo Emerson: 'English Traits', in *Collected Works*, Vol. V, p. 46.
17. Simon Schama: *Citizens*, p. 859.
18. Gudin de la Brunellerie, quoted in Gibson: op. cit., p. 104.
19. T. S. Eliot: *Notes Towards the Definition of Culture*, p. 30.
20. Vera Brittain: *England's Hour*, p. 115.
21. Vita Sackville-West: 'Outdoor Life', in *The Character of England*, p. 410.
22. *Dictionary of National Biography*, 1931–1940, p. 651.
23. Osbert Sitwell: *Great Morning!*, p. 199.
24. Quoted in Paul Fussell: *The Great War and Modern Memory*, p. 26.
25. Peter Parker: *The Old Lie*, pp. 213-14.
26. C. B. Fry: *Life Worth Living*, p. 373.
27. Simon Raven: *The English Gentleman*, p. 9.
28. Ibid., p. 95.
29. Robert Winder: *Hell for Leather*, p. 28.
30. Tony Mason: *Sport in Britain*, p. 126.

CHAPTER TEN *Meet the Wife*

1. Thomas Hughes: *Tom Brown's Schooldays*, p. 80.
2. Paul Ferris: *Sex and the British*, p. 260.
3. Quoted in Lawrence Stone: *The Family, Sex and Marriage*, p. 279.
4. Ian Gibson: *The English Vice*, p. 13.
5. Kingsley Amis: *Take a Girl Like You*, p. 14.
6. Quoted in Robert Gibson: *Best of Enemies*, p. 227.
7. Michael Ryan: *Doings in London*, pp. 92–3.

8. Fyodor Dostoevsky: *Summer Impressions*, p. 66.

9. Hippolyte Taine: *Notes on England*, p. 31.

10. Ibid., pp. 98–9.

11. Quoted in R. Chambers: *The Book of Days*, Vol. 1, pp. 487–8.

12. Quoted in William Benchley Rye: *England as seen by foreigners in the reign of Elizabeth and James the First*, pp. 72–3.

13. Quoted in 'George Smith and the *DNB*', in the *Times Literary Supplement*, 24 December 1971, 1593–5.

14. César de Saussure: *A Foreign View of England in the Reigns of George I and George II*, p. 206.

15. Joseph Fiévée: *Lettres sur L'Angleterre*, quoted in Gibson, op. cit., p. 158.

16. 'A Mother's Sermon for her Children', Kirkby Lonsdale 1829, quoted in Deborah Valenze: *Prophetic Sons and Daughters*, p. 278.

17. Elizabeth Sandford: *Woman in Her Social and Domestic Character*, quoted in Walter Besant: *Fifty Years Ago*, p. 119.

18. *Punch*, 14 (1848), p. 230.

19. Quoted in Joan Burstyn: *Victorian Education and the Ideal of Womanhood*, p. 31.

20. Sandra M. Gilbert and Susan Gubar: *The Madwoman in the Attic*, p. 85.

21. Alison Light: *Forever England*, p. 113.

22. Hermann Muthesius: *The English House*, p. 70.

23. Émile Cammaerts: *Discoveries in England*, p. 133.

24. Quoted in J. A. Mangan: *Athleticism in the Victorian and Edwardian Public School*, p. 189.

25. John Ruskin had suggested to his young wife Effie that they would not consummate their marriage until she was twenty-five. In the last year of their marriage he confessed to her that he had imagined women to be different from the sight that had met his eyes on their wedding night. Quite what it was that led to his disgust is unknown. The idea that it was the traumatic discovery that Effie had pubic hair, which convinced him that she was some sort of freak of nature, comes from Mary Lutyens.

26. Quoted in Jane Mackay and Pat Thane: 'The Englishwoman', in *Englishness: Politics and Culture 1880–1920*, ed. Robert Colls and Philip Dodd, p. 222.

27. Virginia Woolf: *Three Guineas*, pp. 165–6.
28. John Gibson Lockhart: *Memoirs of the Life of Sir Walter Scott*, pp. 596–7.
29. Quoted in Alex Comfort: *The Anxiety Makers*, pp. 52–3.
30. Odette Keun: *I Discover the English*, p. 188.
31. In 1995, there were 170,000 divorces in Great Britain, an average in England (where the divorce rate is higher than in Wales, Scotland or Northern Ireland) of 13.4 per 1,000 of the population. (*Britain 1998*, HMSO, pp. 34–5).
32. Bill Bryson: *Notes from a Small Island*, pp. 21–2.
33. Glenda Cooper: 'British teenagers lead the world in their sexual activity – why?', in the *Independent*, 16 May 1998.

CHAPTER ELEVEN *Old Country, New Clothes*

1. *Tribune*, 18 August 1961.
2. 'English Language Teaching: Frequently asked questions', British Council website, *http://www.britcoun.org./engfaqs.htm*. See also Godfrey Howard: *The Good English Guide*, p. vii.
3. Jonathon Green: *Neologisms: New Words Since 1960*.
4. Daniel Defoe: 'Essay Upon Projects', 1697.
5. Samuel Johnson: *Dictionary of the English Language*, Preface.
6. *Time*, 27 October 1997.
7. *The Times*, 25 October 1997.
8. George MacDonald Fraser: 'The Hero and the Heroine Now and in the Future', speech to the *National Review* annual seminar, reprinted in the *Daily Telegraph*, 3 January 1998.
9. Quoted in Christopher Hibbert: *Nelson*, p. 340.
10. Bill Buford: *Among the Thugs*, p. 52.
11. Ibid., p. 296.
12. César de Saussure: *A Foreign View of England in the Reigns of George I and George II*, p. 180.
13. Ralph Waldo Emerson: 'English Traits', in *Collected Works*, Vol. V, p. 74.
14. de Saussure: op. cit., p. 295.
15. Ian Gilmour: *Riots, Risings and Revolution*, p. 5.

16. H. F. Abell, quoted in Dunning et al.: *The Roots of Football Hooliganism*, p. 44. The same book contains the statistics (p. 50).

17. David Underdown: *Revel, Riot and Rebellion*.

18. Gilmour: op. cit., p. 16.

19. Quoted in Robert Gibson: *Best of Enemies*, p. 36.

20. Quoted in Andrew Barr: *Drink, An Informal Social History*, p. 25.

21. *Chronique Français des Rois de France*, by an Anonymous of Béthune, in *Receuil des Histoires des Galles et de France*, Vol. 24, pt 2, p. 760. I am indebted to John Gillingham for this tale.

22. Quoted in Derek Wilson: *The People and the Book: The Revolutionary Impact of the English Bible*, p. 11.

23. G. K. Chesterton: *The Rolling English Road*.

24. Fyodor Dostoevsky: *Summer Impressions*, p. 61.

25. Quoted in Barr, op. cit., p. 301.

26. Ibid.

27. D. H. Lawrence, letter to Ernest Collings, 22 July 1913, in *The Letters of D. H. Lawrence*.

28. George Orwell: *The Lion and the Unicorn*, p. 17.

29. Source: *Criminal Statistics, England and Wales, 1994*, Cmd 3010, London, HMSO, November 1995.

30. Source: *Sourcebook of Criminal Justice Statistics, 1995*, Office of Justice Programs, US Department of Justice.

31. You have to handle comparative murder statistics very carefully because different police forces assess crimes differently. But the victimization rate for males in England and Wales is so far below other countries as to be beyond statistical error. The rate for the United States is 15.9, for Italy it is 4.8, for Scotland 4.7, for Norway 2.2, for Sweden 1.7, for France 1.5, for Germany 1.4, for Ireland 0.8, and for Japan 0.7. For England and Wales, the figure is 0.6. See Elliott Leyton, *Men of Blood*, p. 22.

32. 'Idleness, dissipation and poverty are increased, the most sacred and confidential trusts are betrayed, domestic comfort is destroyed, madness often created, crimes, subjecting the perpetrators of them to the punishment of death, are committed, and even suicide itself is produced,' said the report of a parliamentary investigation in

1808 (Cmd 182, p. 12). Quoted in Mark Clapson: *A Bit of a Flutter*.

33. Clapson, op. cit.
34. *Leader* magazine, 23 April 1949.
35. George Orwell, *Evening Standard*, 15 December 1946.
36. Quoted in Philippa Pullar: *Consuming Passions*, p. 190.
37. David Starkey: 'The Death of England', in *The Times*, 20 April 1996.

BIBLIOGRAPHY

There is a vast number of books published on England and the English. The bibliography lists all the books mentioned in the text and some others which may be of interest to anyone wanting to explore the subject further.

ACKROYD, PETER: *Blake*, London, Sinclair-Stevenson, 1995.

ACTON, WILLIAM: *The Functions and Disorders of the Reproductive Organs in Youth, in Adult Age and in Advanced Life*, London, John Churchill, 1857.

ADICKES, SANDRA: *The Social Quest: The Expanded Vision of Four Women Travellers in the Era of the French Revolution*, Peter Lang, New York, 1991.

ALLISON, LINCOLN: *The Condition of England*, London, Junction Books, 1981.

AMIS, KINGSLEY: *Take A Girl Like You*, London, Gollancz, 1960.

ARBUTHNOT, JOHN: *The History of John Bull*, Oxford, OUP, 1976.

ARMYTAGE, W. H. G.: *Heavens Below: Utopian Experiments in England 1560– 1960*, London, Routledge & Kegan Paul, 1961.

ARNOLD, MATTHEW: *The Study of Celtic Literature*, London, Smith Elder, 1867.

ASLET, CLIVE: *Anyone For England?*, London, Little Brown, 1997.

BALDICK, CHRIS: *The Social Mission of English Criticism, 1848–1932*, Oxford, Clarendon Press, 1983.

BALDWIN, STANLEY: *On England*, London, Hodder & Stoughton, 1926.

BALLASTER, ROS: *Seductive Forms: Women's Amatory Fiction from 1684–1740*, Oxford, Clarendon Press, 1992.

BARKER, ERNEST: *National Character*, London, Methuen, 1927.

BARKER, ERNEST (ed.): *The Character of England*, Oxford, Clarendon Press, 1947.

BARNETT, CORRELLI: *The Collapse of British Power*, London, Eyre Methuen, 1972.

BARR, ANDREW: *Drink, An Informal Social History*, London, Bantam Press, 1995.

BARZINI, LUIGI: *The Impossible Europeans*, London, Weidenfeld & Nicolson, 1993.

BEERBOHM, MAX: *Mainly on the Air*, London, Heinemann, 1946.

BENNETT, ALAN: *The Old Country*, London, Faber & Faber, 1978.

BENNETT, ALAN: *Writing Home*, London, Faber & Faber, 1994.

BESANT, WALTER: *Fifty Years Ago*, New York, 1899.

BETJEMAN, JOHN: *Coming Home*, London, Methuen, 1997.

BICKNELL, E. J.: *A Theological Introduction to the Thirty-Nine Articles of the Church of England*, London, Longman Green, 1932.

BINDOFF, S. T.: *Tudor England*, London, Penguin, 1950.

BLUNDEN, EDMUND: *Votive Tablets*, London, Cobden-Sanderson, 1931.

BLYTHE, RONALD: *Divine Landscapes*, London, Viking, 1986.

BONE, JAMES: 'The Tendencies of Modern Art', in *Edinburgh Review*, Vol. 217, 1913.

BRACEWELL, MICHAEL: *England is Mine*, London, Harper Collins, 1997.

BREARS, Peter, et al.: *A Taste of History: 10,000 Years of Food in Britain*, London, English Heritage, 1993.

BRIDGET, T. E., Revd.: *Our Lady's Dowry*, London, Burns & Oates, 1875.

BRIGGS, ASA: *Victorian Cities*, London, Oldhams Press, 1963.

BRITTAIN, VERA: *England's Hour*, London, Macmillan, 1941.

BROGAN, D. W.: *The English People*, London, Hamish Hamilton, 1943.

BRYANT, ARTHUR: *Spirit of England*, London, Collins, 1982.

BRYSON, BILL: *Mother Tongue: The English Language*, London, Hamish Hamilton, 1990.

BRYSON, BILL: *Notes from a Small Island*, London, Doubleday, 1995.

BUCHAN, JOHN: *Memory Hold-the-Door*, London, Hodder & Stoughton, 1940.

BUFORD, BILL: *Among the Thugs*, London, Secker & Warburg, 1991.

BURKE, JOHN: *The English Inn*, London, Batsford, 1981.

BURSTYN, JOAN N.: *Victorian Education and the Ideal of Womanhood*, New Jersey, Barnes & Noble, 1980.

BURT, RICHARD, and ARCHER, JOHN MICHAEL (eds): *Enclosure Acts: Sexuality, Property and Culture in Early Modern England*, Ithaca, NY, Cornell University Press, 1994.

BYAM MARTIN, CAPT. HENRY: *The Polynesian Journal*, Australian National University Press, 1981.

CALDER, ANGUS: *The Myth of the Blitz*, London, Jonathan Cape, 1991.

CAMERON, KENNETH: *English Place Names*, London, Batsford, 1996.

CAMMAERTS, ÉMILE: *Discoveries in England*, London, Routledge & Sons, 1930.

CAMPBELL, BEATRIX: *Goliath: Britain's Dangerous Places*, London, Methuen, 1993.

CANETTI, ELIAS: *Crowds and Power*, London, Gollancz, 1962.

CAPEK, KAREL: *Letters from England*, London, Geoffrey Bles, 1925.

'A Cavalry Officer': *The Whole Art of Dress, or The Road to Elegance and Fashion, Being a Treatise Upon That Essential and Much Cultivated Requisite of the Present Day*, London, 1830.

CHADWICK, OWEN: *The Reformation*, London, Penguin, 1964.

CHAUDHURI, NIRAD C.: *A Passage to England*, London, Macmillan, 1959.

CHESTERTON, G. K.: *The Bodley Head G. K. Chesterton* (ed. P. J. Kavanagh), London, Bodley Head, 1985.

CHURCHILL, WINSTON S.: *A History of the English-Speaking Peoples*, London, Cassell, 1953.

CHURCHILL, WINSTON S.: *The Second World War*, London, Cassell, 1948.

CLAPSON, MARK: *A Bit of a Flutter: Popular Gambling and English Society*, Manchester, Manchester University Press, 1992.

CLARKE, PETER: *Hope and Glory: Britain 1900–1990*, London, Allen Lane, Penguin, 1996.

COHN, ELLEN G.: 'Weather and Crime', in *British Journal of Criminology*, Vol. 30, No. 1, Winter 1990.

COLLETT, PETER: *Foreign Bodies: A Guide to European Mannerisms*, London, Simon & Schuster, 1993.

COLLEY, LINDA: *Britons*, London, Yale University Press, 1992.

COLLISON, PETER, and KENNEDY, JOHN: 'Urban Life and the English', in *Town and Country Planning*, December 1989.

COLLS, ROBERT, and DODD, PHILIP (eds): *Englishness: Politics and Culture, 1880–1920*, London, Croom Helm, 1986.

COMFORT, ALEX: *The Anxiety Makers*, London, Nelson, 1967.

COON, C. S.: *The Races of Europe*, New York, Macmillan, 1939.

CRISP, QUENTIN: *The Naked Civil Servant*, London, Jonathan Cape, 1968.

CRITCHFIELD, ROBERT: *Among the British*, London, Hamish Hamilton, 1990.

CRONIN, VINCENT: *Napoleon*, London, Collins, 1971.

CUMMINS, JOHN: *Francis Drake*, London, Weidenfeld & Nicolson, 1995.

DEIGHTON, LEN: *Battle of Britain*, London, Jonathan Cape, 1980.

DE LA NOY, MICHAEL: *The Church of England*, London, Simon & Schuster, 1993.

DE MARLY, DIANA: *Fashion For Men, An Illustrated History*, London, Batsford, 1985.

DE SAUSSURE, CÉSAR: *A Foreign View of England in the Reigns of George I and George II*, London, John Murray, 1902.

DE TOCQUEVILLE, ALEXIS: *Journeys to England and Ireland*, London, Faber & Faber, 1958.

DICKENS, CHARLES: *Hard Times*, Leipzig, 1854.

DOSTOEVSKY, FYODOR: *Summer Impressions* (trans. Philippe Julian), London, John Calder, 1955.

DOYLE, BRIAN: *English and Englishness*, London, Routledge, 1989.

DRIVER, CHRISTOPHER: *The British at Table*, London, Chatto & Windus, 1983.

DRUMMOND, J. C., and WILBRAHAM, ANNE: *The Englishman's Food*, London, Jonathan Cape, 1939.

DUFF, CHARLES: *England and the English*, London, Boardman, 1954.

DUFFY, EAMON: *Stripping the Altars: Traditional Religion in England 1400–1580*, London, Yale University Press, 1992.

DUFFY, MAUREEN: *The Passionate Shepherdess: Aphra Behn 1640–89*, London, Jonathan Cape, 1977.

DUHAMEL, JEAN: *The Fifty Days: Napoleon in England*, London, Hart-Davis, 1969.

DUNNING, ERIC, MURPHY, PATRICK, and WILLIAMS, JOHN: *The Roots of Football Hooliganism, An Historical and Sociological Study*, London, Routledge, 1989.

EASTON, SUSAN, et al.: *Disorder and Discipline: Popular Culture from 1550 to the Present*, Aldershot, Temple Smith, 1988.

ELIOT, T. S.: *Essays on Style and Content*, London, Faber & Faber, 1928.

ELIOT, T. S.: *Notes Towards the Definition of Culture*, London, Faber & Faber, 1949.

ELLIS, JOHN: *The Social History of the Machine Gun*, London, Croom Helm, 1976.

ELLIS, STEVE: *The English Eliot*, London, Routledge, 1991.

ELTON, GEOFFREY: *The English*, Oxford, Blackwell, 1992.

EMERSON, RALPH WALDO: *Collected Works*, Vol. V, 'English Traits', Cambridge, Mass., Harvard University Press, 1966.

ENGELS, F.: *The Condition of the Working Class in England* (trans. Henderson and Chaloner), Oxford, Basil Blackwell, 1971.

FABER, RICHARD: *The Vision and the Need: Late Victorian Imperialist Aims*, London, Faber & Faber, 1966.

FABER, RICHARD: *High Road to England*, London, Faber & Faber, 1985.

FERRIS, PAUL: *Sex and the British*, London, Michael Joseph, 1993.

FISHER, A. L.: *Napoleon*, Oxford, OUP, 1967.

FORD, FORD MADOX: *The Spirit of the People*, London, Alston Rivers, 1907.

FORTESCUE, J. W.: *A History of the British Army*, London, Macmillan, 1920.

FOSTER, R. F.: *Paddy and Mr Punch: Connections in Irish and English History*, Harmondsworth, Allen Lane, 1993.

FRANKS, OLIVER: 'Anglo-American Relations and the Special Relationship, 1947–52', lecture, University of Texas, 1990.

FRENCH, RICHARD VALPY: *Nineteen Centuries of Drink*, London, Longman, 1884.

FRIEDMAN, OSCAR MICHAEL: *Origins of the British Israelites: the lost tribes*, Mellen Research University Press, 1993.

FRYER, PETER: *Mrs Grundy: Studies in English Prudery*, London, Dobson, 1963.

FUSSELL, G. E. and K. R.: *The English Countrywoman*, London, Andrew Melrose, 1953.

FUSSELL, G. E. and K. R.: *The English Countryman*, London, Andrew Melrose, 1955.

FUSSELL, PAUL: *The Great War and Modern Memory*, Oxford, OUP, 1975.

GARTON ASH, TIMOTHY: *The File*, London, Harper Collins, 1997.

GATRELL, V. A. C.: *The Hanging Tree: Execution and the English People 1770–1868*, Oxford, OUP, 1994.

GEIJER, ERIK GUSTAF: *Impressions of England 1809–10*, London, Jonathan Cape.

GIBBS, PHILIP: *England Speaks*, London, Heinemann, 1935.

GIBSON, IAN: *The English Vice: Beating, Sex and Shame in Victorian England and After*, London, Duckworth, 1978.

GIBSON, ROBERT: *Best of Enemies: Anglo-French Relations Since the Norman Conquest*, London, Sinclair-Stevenson, 1995.

GIBSON LOCKHART, JOHN: *Memoirs of the Life of Sir Walter Scott*, London, A & C Black, 1912.

GILBERT, SANDRA M., and GUBAR, SUSAN: *The Madwoman in the Attic: The Woman Writer and the Nineteenth Century Literary Imagination*, New Haven, Yale University Press, 1979.

GILLIATT, PENELOPE: *To Wit: In Celebration of Comedy*, London, Weidenfeld & Nicolson, 1990.

GILMOUR, IAN: *Riots, Risings and Revolution: Governance in Eighteenth-century England*, London, Pimlico, 1993.

GORER, GEOFFREY: *Exploring English Character*, London, Cresset Press, 1955.

GRAHAM-DIXON, ANDREW: *A History of British Art*, London, BBC Books, 1996.

GRANT, ALEXANDER, and STRINGER, KEITH (eds): *Uniting the Kingdom?*, London, Routledge, 1995.

GRANT, ROLAND (ed.): *The Prose of Edward Thomas*, London, Falcon Press, 1948.

GRAVES, ROBERT: *Goodbye to All That*, London, Penguin edn, 1960.

GREEN, JONATHON: *Chasing the Sun: Dictionary-Makers and the Dictionaries They Made*, London, Jonathan Cape, 1996.

GREEN, JONATHON: *Neologisms: New Words Since 1960*, London, Bloomsbury, 1991.

GREEN, J. R.: *A Short History of the English People*, New York, Colonial Press, 1884.

HAGGARD, H. RIDER: *A Farmer's Year*, London, Longman, 1899.

HAINING, PETER: *The Spitfire Summer: A People's Eye-view of the Battle of Britain*, London, W. H. Allen, 1990.

HALLER, WILLIAM: *Foxe's Book of Martyrs and the Elect Nation*, London, Jonathan Cape, 1967.

HARE, DAVID: *Racing Demon*, London, Faber & Faber, 1990.

HARE, DAVID: *Asking Around*, London, Faber & Faber, 1993.

HARGREAVES, JOHN D.: *France and West Africa, An Anthology of Historical Documents*, London, Macmillan, 1969.

HARMAN, NICHOLAS: *Dunkirk, The Necessary Myth*, London, Hodder & Stoughton, 1980.

HARRIS, JOSE: *Private Lives, Public Spirit: Britain 1870–1914*, Oxford, OUP, 1993.

HASELER, STEPHEN: *The English Tribe*, London, Macmillan, 1996.

HASTE, CATE: *Rules of Desire*, London, Chatto & Windus, 1992.

HAZLITT, WILLIAM: 'Merry England', *New Monthly Magazine*, 1825.

HEINE, HEINRICH: *English Fragments*, Edinburgh, R. Grant & Son, 1880.

HENNESSY, PETER, and ANSTEY, CAROLINE: *Moneybags and Brains: The Anglo-American Special Relationship*, Glasgow, Strathclyde University, 1990.

HEWISON, ROBERT: *Culture and Consensus*, London, Methuen, 1995.

HIBBERT, CHRISTOPHER: *The English, A Social History 1066–1945*, London, Harper Collins, 1987.

HIBBERT, CHRISTOPHER: *The Grand Tour*, London, Weidenfeld & Nicolson, 1969.

HIBBERT, CHRISTOPHER: *Nelson, A Personal History*, London, Viking, 1994.

HIBBERT, CHRISTOPHER: *No Ordinary Place: Radley College and the Public School System*, London, John Murray, 1997.

HOBSBAWM, ERIC, and RANGER, TERENCE (eds): *The Invention of Tradition*, Cambridge, CUP, 1983.

HOGGART, RICHARD: *The Uses of Literacy*, London, Chatto & Windus, 1957.

HORNE, ALISTAIR: *Macmillan*, London, Macmillan, 1988.

HOWARD, GODFREY: *The Good English Guide*, London, Macmillan, 1993.

HOWARTH, PATRICK: *Play Up and Play the Game*, London, Eyre Methuen, 1973.

HUIZINGA, J. H.: *Confessions of a European in England*, London, Heinemann, 1958.

HUTTON, RONALD: *The Rise and Fall of Merrie England*, Oxford, OUP, 1992.

HYAM, RONALD: 'Concubinage and Colonial Service: The Crewe Circular (1909)', *Journal of Imperial and Commonwealth History*, XIV, 1986, pp. 170–86.

HYAM, RONALD: *Empire and Sexuality*, Manchester, Manchester University Press, 1990.

INGE, W. R.: *England*, London, Ernest Benn, 1926.

INGRAMS, RICHARD: *England, An Anthology*, London, Collins, 1990.

ISMAY, LORD: *Memoirs*, London, Heinemann, 1960.

JENKINS, DANIEL: *The British, Their Identity and Their Religion*, London, SCM Press, 1975.

KAZANTZAKIS, NIKOS: *England*, London, Simon and Schuster, 1965.

KEATES, JONATHAN: *Purcell*, London, Chatto & Windus, 1995.

KEEGAN, JOHN: *The Second World War*, London, Hutchinson, 1989.

KENNER, HUGH: *The Sinking Island: The Modern English Writers*, London, Barrie & Jenkin, 1988.

KEUN, ODETTE: *I Discover the English*, London, Bodley Head, 1934.

KEYNES, JOHN MAYNARD: *The Economic Consequences of the Peace*, London, Macmillan, 1919.

KINGLAKE, ALEXANDER: *Eothen, or Traces of Travel Brought Back From the East*, London, 1844.

KITSON CLARK, G.: *The English Inheritance*, London, SCM Press, 1950.

KOHN, HANS: 'The Genesis and Character of English Nationalism', *Journal of the History of Ideas*, January 1940, Vol. 1, No. 1, pp. 69–94.

LAWRENCE, D. H.: *The Letters of D. H. Lawrence*, Cambridge, CUP, 1981.

LEES-MILNE, JAMES: *Ancestral Voices*, London, Chatto & Windus, 1975.

LEES-MILNE, JAMES: *Prophesying Peace*, London, Chatto & Windus, 1977.

LEMOINNE, JOHN: *Wellington From a French Point of View*, London, J. W. Parker & Sons, 1852.

LEYTON, ELLIOTT: *Men of Blood – Murder in Modern England*, London, Constable, 1995.

LIGHT, ALISON: *Forever England: Feminity, Literature and Conservatism Between the Wars*, London, Routledge, 1991.

LONGFORD, ELIZABETH: *The Years of the Sword*, London, Weidenfeld & Nicolson, 1969.

LONGRIGG, ROGER: *The English Squire and His Sport*, London, Michael Joseph, 1977.

LUCAS, JOHN: *England and Englishness*, London, Hogarth Press, 1990.

MACAULAY, RICHARD BABINGTON: *Lord Macaulay's Essays*, London, Popular Edition, 1906.

McCRUM, ROBERT, CRAN, WILLIAM, and MACNEIL, ROBERT: *The Story of English*, London, Faber & Faber, 1992.

MACFARLANE, ALAN: *The Origins of English Individualism*, Oxford, Basil Blackwell, 1970.

McKIBBIN, ROSS: *Classes and Culture: England 1918–1951*, Oxford, OUP, 1998.

MALMGREEN, GAIL (ed.): *Religion in the Lives of English Women 1760–1930*, London, Croom Helm, 1986.

MANDELL, RICHARD D.: *Sport, A Cultural History*, New York, Columbia University Press, 1984.

MANGAN, J. A.: *Athleticism in the Victorian and Edwardian Public School*, Cambridge, CUP, 1981.

MARCUS, STEVEN: *The Other Victorians*, London, Weidenfeld & Nicolson, 1966.

MARTIN, C., and PARKER, GEOFFREY: *The Spanish Armada*, London, Hamish Hamilton, 1988.

MARX, KARL, and ENGELS, FRIEDRICH: *Selected Correspondence*, Moscow, Foreign Languages Publishing House, 1950.

MASON, MICHAEL: *The Making of Victorian Sexuality*, Oxford, OUP, 1994.

MASON, TONY: *Sport in Britain, A Social History*, Cambridge, CUP, 1989.

MASSINGHAM, H. J.: *Chiltern Country*, London, Batsford, 1940.

MASTERMAN, CHARLES F. G.: *The Condition of England*, London, Methuen, 1909.

MASTERMAN, CHARLES F. G.: *England After the War*, London, Hodder & Stoughton, 1922.

MAUDE, ANGUS, and POWELL, ENOCH: *Biography of a Nation*, London, Phoenix House, 1955.

MIDDLEMASS, KEITH, and BARNES, JOHN: *Baldwin*, London, Weidenfeld & Nicolson, 1969.

MIKES, GEORGE: *English Humour for Beginners*, London, André Deutsch, 1980.

MINOGUE, KENNETH: *Nationalism*, London, Batsford, 1967.

MODOOD, TARIQ: *Not Easy Being British: Colour, Culture and Citizenship*, Stoke on Trent, Trentham, 1992.

MORGAN, KENNETH O.: *Rebirth of a Nation, Wales 1880–1980*, Oxford, OUP, 1981.

MORITZ, CARL PHILIP: *Journeys of a German in England in 1782*, London, 1795.

MORLEY, SHERIDAN: *Tales from the Hollywood Raj*, London, Weidenfeld & Nicolson, 1983.

MORTON, H. V.: *In Search of England*, London, Methuen, 1927.

MORTON, H. V.: *What I Saw in the Slums*, London, Labour Party, 1933.

MOTION, ANDREW: *The Poetry of Edward Thomas*, London, Routledge, 1980.

MUIR, FRANK: *The Oxford Book of Humorous Prose: From William Caxton to P. G. Wodehouse: A Conducted Tour*, Oxford, OUP, 1992.

MUTHESIUS, HERMANN: *The English House*, London, Crosby Lockwood Staples, 1979.

MYERS, SYLVIA HAVESTARCK: *The Bluestocking Circle: Women, Friendship and the Life of the Mind in Eighteenth Century England*, Oxford, OUP, 1990.

NEWMAN, GERALD: *The Rise of English Nationalism, 1740–1830*, London, Weidenfeld & Nicolson, 1987.

O'RELL, MAX: *John Bull and his Island*, London, Leadenhalle Presse, 1883.

ORWELL, GEORGE: *The Lion and the Unicorn*, London, Penguin, 1941.

ORWELL, GEORGE: *The English People*, London, Collins, 1947.

ORWELL, GEORGE: *Collected Essays, Letters and Journalism*, Sonia Orwell and Ian Angus (eds), London, Secker & Warburg, 1968.

PARKER, PETER: *The Old Lie: The Great War and the Public School Ethos*, London, Constable, 1987.

PARTRIDGE, FRANCES: *A Pacifist's War*, London, Hogarth Press, 1978.

PEACH, CERI (ed.): *Ethnicity in the 1991 Census: The Ethnic Minority Populations of Great Britain*, London, HMSO, 1996.

PEVSNER, NIKOLAUS: *The Englishness of English Art*, London, Architectural Press, 1956.

PIPER, DAVID: *The English Face*, London, Thames & Hudson, 1957.

PIRIE, PETER: *The English Musical Renaissance*, London, Gollancz, 1979.

POLHEMUS, TED: *Streetstyle: From Sidewalk to Catwalk*, London, Thames & Hudson, 1995.

'PONT': *The British Character*, London, Collins, 1951.

PRIESTLEY, J. B.: *The English*, London, Heinemann, 1973.

PRIESTLEY, J. B.: *English Journey*, London, Mandarin, 1994.

PRIESTLEY, J. B. et al.: *The English Spirit*, London, Allen & Unwin, 1942.

PULLAR, PHILIPPA: *Consuming Passions: A History of English Food and Appetite*, London, Hamish Hamilton, 1970.

QUILLER-COUCH, SIR ARTHUR: *Studies in Literature*, Cambridge, CUP, 1918.

RALEIGH, SIR WALTER: *Shakespeare's England*, Oxford, Clarendon Press, 1916.

RAPHAEL, SAMUEL: *Patriotism: The Making and Unmaking of British Identity*, London, Routledge, 1987.

RHEES, ERNEST (ed.): *The Old Country: A Book of Love and Praise of England*, London, Dent, 1917.

RIBEIRO, AILEEN, and CUMMING, VALERIE: *The Visual History of Costume*, London, Batsford, 1989.

ROBERTS, ANDREW: *Eminent Churchillians*, London, Weidenfeld & Nicolson, 1994.

RODGER, N. A. M.: *The Safeguard of the Sea*, London, Harper Collins, 1997.

ROWSE, A. L.: *The English Spirit*, London, Macmillan, 1946.

RYE, WILLIAM BENCHLEY: *England as seen by foreigners in the reign of Elizabeth and James the First*, London, John Russell Smith, 1865.

SACKVILLE–WEST, VITA: 'Outdoor Life', in *The Character of England* (ed. Ernest Barker), Oxford, Clarendon Press, 1947.

ST GEORGE, ANDREW: *The Descent of Manners*, London, Chatto & Windus, 1993.

SAKLATVALA, BERAM: *The Origins of the English People*, Newton Abbot, David & Charles, 1969.

SANTAYANA, GEORGE: *Soliloquies in England*, London, Constable, 1922.

SCHAMA, SIMON: *Citizens: A Chronicle of the French Revolution*, London, Viking, 1989.

SELLAR, W. C., and YEATMAN, R. J.: *1066, And All That*, London, Methuen, 1930.

SHEPPARD, FRANCIS: *London 1808–1870: The Infernal Wen*, London, Secker & Warburg, 1971.

SHOWALTER, ELAINE: *The Female Malady: Women, Madness and Culture 1830–1980*, London, Virago, 1987.

SHUKER, ROY: *Understanding Popular Music*, London, Routledge, 1994.

SISSON, C. H.: *Is There a Church of England?* Manchester, Carcanet, 1993.

SITWELL, OSBERT: *Great Morning!*, Boston, 1947.

SMITH, ANTHONY D.: *National Identity*, London, Penguin, 1991.

SMITH, GODFREY: *How It Was In the War*, London, Pavilion, 1989.

SMITH, SIR THOMAS: *De Republica Anglorum: The maner of Governement or policie of the Realme of England*, 1583, reprinted Scolar Press, Aldershot, 1970.

SOAMES, NICOLAS, and STEEN, DUNCAN: *The Essential Englishman*, London, Cassell, 1989.

SPENDER, STEPHEN: *Love-Hate Relationships: A Study of Anglo-American Sensibilities*, London, Hamish Hamilton, 1974.

STEEVENS, G. W.: *With Kitchener to Khartoum*, London, Blackwood & Sons, 1898.

STRONG, ROY: *Lost Treasures of Britain*, London, Penguin, 1990.

SUMPTION, JONATHAN: *The Hundred Years War*, London, Faber, 1990.

SWEDENBORG, EMANUEL: *A Treatise Concerning Heaven and Hell and the wonderful things therein, as heard and seen by the author*, London, James Phillips, 1778.

SYPNIEWSKI, D. O.: *Impressions of England*, London, 1843.

TAINE, HIPPOLYTE: *Notes on England*, London, Thames & Hudson, 1957.

TAYLOR, A. J. P.: *English History 1914–1945*, Oxford, OUP, 1965.

THATCHER, MARGARET: *The Downing Street Years*, London, Harper Collins, 1993.

THOMAS, EDWARD: *The South Country*, London, Dent, 1909.

THOMPSON, MARGOT: *Thomas Cranmer, Portrait of an Englishman*, Manchester, Prayer Book Society, 1995.

TILBURY, ANN: *The Battle of Britain*, London, Macdonald, 1981.

TURNER, E. S.: *All Heaven in a Rage*, London, Michael Joseph, 1964.

UNDERDOWN, DAVID: *Revel, Riot and Rebellion: Popular Politics and Culture in England 1603–1660*, Oxford, Clarendon Press, 1987.

USBORNE, RICHARD: *Clubland Heroes*, London, Constable, 1953.

VALENZE, DEBORAH: *Prophetic Sons and Daughters: Female Preaching and Popular Religion in Industrial England*, Princeton, Princeton University Press, 1985.

VANSITTART, PETER: *In Memory of England: A Novelist's View of History*, London, John Murray, 1998.

VELIZ, CLAUDIO: 'A World Made in England', in *Quadrant*, Sydney, March 1983.

VELIZ, CLAUDIO: 'A World Made in English', *Conversazione*, La Trobe University, 1989.

WARREN, C. HENRY: *England is a Village*, London, Eyre & Spottiswoode, 1940.

WATERS, MICHAEL: *The Garden in Victorian Literature*, Aldershot, Scolar Press, 1988.

WATSON, COLIN: *Snobbery With Violence: English Crime Stories and their Audience*, London, Eyre Methuen, 1979.

WEITZ, JOHN: *Hitler's Diplomat: Joachim Von Ribbentrop*, London, Weidenfeld & Nicolson, 1992.

WELLS, H. G.: *Experiment in Autobiography*, London, Gollancz/Cresset Press, 1934.

WELSH, IRVING: *Trainspotting*, London, Secker & Warburg, 1993.

WIENER, MARTIN: *English Culture and the Decline of the Industrial Spirit 1850–1980*, Cambridge, CUP, 1981.

WILKINSON, ALAN: *The Church of England and the First World War*, London, SPCK, 1978.

WILLIAMS, RAYMOND: *The Country and the City*, London, Chatto & Windus, 1973.

WILMUT, ROGER (ed.): *The Complete Beyond the Fringe*, London, Methuen, 1987.

WILSON, DEREK: *The People and the Book: The Revolutionary Impact of the English Bible 1381–1611*, London, Barrie & Jenkins, 1976.

WILSON, FRANCESCA M.: *Strange Island: Britain Through Foreign Eyes*, London, Longman Green, 1955.

WINDER, ROBERT: *Hell for Leather: A Modern Cricket Journey*, London, Gollancz, 1996.

WOODHAM-SMITH, CECIL: *The Reason Why*, London, Constable, 1953.

WOOLF, VIRGINIA: *Between the Acts*, London, Hogarth Press, 1941.

WOOLF, VIRGINIA: *Three Guineas*, London, Hogarth Press, 1938.

WRIGHT, PATRICK: *On Living in an Old Country*, London, Verso, 1985.

WRIGHT, PATRICK: *A Journey Through Ruins*, London, Paladin, 1992.

YEATS, W. B.: *The Celtic Twilight*, London, A. H. Bullen, 1902.

YOUNG, G. M.: *Victorian England, Portrait of an Age*, Oxford, OUP, 1936.

INDEX

PENGUIN CELEBRATIONS

COLLECT ALL THIRTY-SIX

1. REGENERATION Pat Barker
2. THE SECRET HISTORY Donna Tartt
3. WHAT A CARVE UP! Jonathan Coe
4. CONGO JOURNEY Redmond O'Hanlon
5. A CERTAIN JUSTICE P. D. James
6. JANE AUSTEN Claire Tomalin
7. THE CHIMNEY SWEEPER'S BOY Barbara Vine
8. THE BEACH Alex Garland
9. THE ENGLISH Jeremy Paxman
10. WHITE TEETH Zadie Smith
11. THE CONSOLATIONS OF PHILOSOPHY Alain de Botton
12. ENGLISH PASSENGERS Matthew Kneale
13. HOW TO BE GOOD Nick Hornby
14. THE SHADOW OF THE SUN Ryszard Kapuściński
15. FAST FOOD NATION Eric Schlosser
16. ANY HUMAN HEART William Boyd
17. THE IMPRESSIONIST Hari Kunzru
18. DARK STAR SAFARI Paul Theroux
19. EVERYTHING IS ILLUMINATED Jonathan Safran Foer
20. NOTES ON A SCANDAL Zoë Heller
21. EMPIRE Niall Ferguson
22. HEGEMONY OR SURVIVAL Noam Chomsky
23. THE FABRIC OF THE COSMOS Brian Greene
24. THE OTHER SIDE OF THE STORY Marian Keyes
25. LEONARDO DA VINCI Charles Nicholl
26. THE WORLD ACCORDING TO CLARKSON Jeremy Clarkson
27. LETTER FROM AMERICA Alistair Cooke
28. HOW I LIVE NOW Meg Rosoff
29. RUMPOLE AND THE PENGE BUNGALOW MURDERS John Mortimer
30. ADRIAN MOLE AND THE WEAPONS OF MASS DESTRUCTION Sue Townsend
31. BLINK Malcolm Gladwell
32. A SHORT HISTORY OF TRACTORS IN UKRAINIAN Marina Lewycka
33. FREAKONOMICS Steven D. Levitt and Stephen J. Dubner
34. THE ACCIDENTAL Ali Smith
35. THE CLASSICAL WORLD Robin Lane Fox
36. THE REVENGE OF GAIA James Lovelock

WHAT'S NOT TO CELEBRATE?